DETROIT...
Why the Circus Left Town

Evelyn,

DETROIT...
Why the Circus Left Town

A Definitive Memoir

ROBERT RILEY

another 60 70 game :!

Bt Riley

RR :

First Edition
2015

Printed in the United States of America.

ISBN-13: 978-1502479808
ISBN-10:150247980X

Cover photograph: © istock.com/Bim

Cover design and author's photograph:
Main Street Design, San Diego

"Her voice was ever soft,
Gentle and low, an excellent thing in woman."

King Lear
Act V, Scene iii

To my Susan.

Co-founder, exemplar and standard-bearer for our niche of the Riley family.
Over the years, producer of five children,
coordinator of twelve family moves
and welcomed participant and observer
of each child's marriage
and subsequent child rearing.

The resulting 18 Riley members have aggregated
approximately 225,000 man-days.
If one does the math, these 18 people have generated
153 unique 1-on-1 familial relationships.

The result: To the best of my knowledge, never has there been one day or one
night of estrangement between any of the participants.

Remarkable!

But not surprising if one considers the capacity for loving
and the personal stature of the guru.

We have been blessed.

Acknowledgements

Dr. Alan Blinder who, in exasperation at a Princeton financial seminar, blurted out a rhetorical question: "G. M. just stopped trading! Can anyone tell me what the hell happened?" Thereby goading me to write this narrative.

The early readers and encouragers: Ralph Frederick, lifelong friend and best man, and Terry Lehr, longtime friend and, with his wife, Mary, expeditors for all the Riley family.

Before I get too far, the wonderful education I received in the Detroit School System from underpaid, devoted teachers who challenged, encouraged and individualized. They taught not only the subject matter but how to think and become observant citizens. Circa 1954: "Doesn't it seem that mediocrity is becoming a premium in American society?" (Still a good question, from a teacher who lived in a Frank Lloyd Wright house.)

Publishing insiders, such as the distinguished automotive observer Dr. David Cole, the author Jo Coudert and many others advising that the Bennett Cerf and the Nelson Doubleday types have either retired or have washed out of the business, rendering it a grim one, perhaps even as grim as the car business. Oh, and yes, even the most eloquent Motown voice will require an inordinate amount of editing to become generally coherent.

Later on, Bernard Mendillo edited, recommended the publishing scenario, consolidated the proof corrections and coordinated with the book company. Also helpful were proofers Beth Magann, Susan Riley and Jennifer Ottinger. Of particular help was Beverly Wilk, so generous with her encouragement and professional expertise, yet still niggardly at the bridge table.

Thanks to the proprietress of Main Street Design for the bodacious cover, the author's photo and, by the way, for preparing 17,059 dinners.

CONTENTS

DETROIT ...
Why the Circus Left Town

AUTHOR'S NOTE

You would probably agree that David Brooks is one of the more astute observers and commentators regarding changes in America's social and political outlooks. In a recent *New York Times* op-ed piece he noted that those having been reared in the "least attractive places to live" expressed an almost inordinate loyalty and attachment to those areas as compared to those who were bought up in more desirable areas.

Guilty!

I love Detroit.

But this story isn't *about* Detroit. Rather, this story is immersed in and influenced by Detroit: its culture, the mindset of its industrial operatives and its idiosyncrasies. I was born and raised in middle-class Detroit, went to its schools and was inculcated into a set of values to which you will be exposed.

In somewhat the same manner, like most Americans, I love cars—not particularly from the standpoint of design or features, but from the ease and comfort provided in getting to the place of one's personal choosing.

But this story isn't *about* cars.

What I really, really loved was being immersed in the *business* of making American cars, starting at a time almost 60 years ago when the American automotive industry basked in almost universal admiration.

Simultaneously lurking, however, were various influences, public and private, that sensed that they were being "stiff-armed" by the industry, when they felt that their own sensible ideas should be embraced and embodied.

The "real" story here is the saga of how these six or seven new outside influences affected the American automotive industry. It generally follows a timeline of events, describing those events, the players, their purported motivations and the subsequent brittle and temporary equilibrium that ensued.

It's hard to imagine how any American is pleased with the current overall outcome, particularly from an economic standpoint. As the old saying went, "when the industry catches cold, Chrysler catches pneumonia." A new mega-saying might be, "When the American automotive industry catches pneumonia, Detroit crashes."

Let's follow the treadmill of the industry and its Detroit host to their current status and attempt to find them a re-emergence to a sustainable position of respect and prosperity.

PREFACE

How did I come to believe that by writing this book I might contribute something useful to the American conscience?

A confluence of events put me over the top!

First and most important, there was the fifty-year decline of the U.S. automotive companies—GM, Chrysler and Ford—as well as the decline of the many suppliers that provided these companies with engineering expertise and the resultant components. Here we're talking about American jobs, big time!

Second, the phenomenon of inertia with key American institutions—government, fuel providers, unions, component suppliers and the domestic industry itself—that were capable of solving the seemingly intractable problems, but instead sat on their hands, whining that they were politically, financially and emotionally (whatever) incapable of acting alone toward a sustainable automotive industry.

It appears that every institution and every person, particularly in the political sphere, puts their own survival above all other considerations.

"Why don't some of the other institutions get with it?" they moan.

To which I'd respond: Why don't we consider getting together to establish plausible parameters for a sustainable automotive industry, creating an optimal system of vehicles, fuel, highways, labor force, rules of operation and oversight—the kind of project that America used when it put together the most innovative and colossal economy in the history of the world?

Third, our reliance on petroleum-based products has given the entire world economic hiccups and political pneumonia over the last forty years—not to mention the looming ecological disaster created partly by the exhausts of transportation equipment and systemic effluents created by their modes of manufacture.

What could be a better time for an explanation of how the automotive business got into its recent predicament?

This is the time and that's why I'm writing this book.

Why would I be the appropriate person to do that? As sales manager for several of the largest component suppliers, I was out and about the industry during the period when it started its slide, consequently enduring some of the frustrations and simultaneously witnessing how these events played out with various characters and executives at "the big three" and other vehicle manufacturers. A lot of other Motown mavens either were too busy running a large operation to get around much or didn't seem to have the broader perspective.

I did seem to have the knack of looking objectively at situations and their resolutions that, in quite a few cases, turned out less than rational. Having such a perspective usually led to the consternation of my superiors and associates.

Perhaps I had this view because I lacked a deep attraction to the vehicles and their features, finding the business part more interesting. I was involved with product lines that exposed me to at least half the drops of the water torture of the past fifty years.

Where do we, as a country, go from here? It is dicey for any one person to say they know the exact path to an idyllic future of any industry, particularly one that affects so many people's lives; nonetheless, I am more than willing to give you my hip-shot suggestion after wading through quite a bit of expert opinion. I've always found it helpful for someone to step forward with a "first shot" plausible solution when a recognized problem needs to be solved.

Not everyone feels comfortable leading with their chin, particularly some of those quiet thinkers. Oh, well—Mrs. Riley was never accused of raising only smart kids.

My ending proposal, perhaps when modified for technical reasons, might actually be very close to a genuine solution. If not, those "quiet thinkers" might, at least, be stimulated to come forth with tweaks or plausible alternatives. We need to start a dialogue.

If nothing else, I hope I am able to convince you that the solution lies with "big picture" thinking rather than the "boutique" offerings that are presented by the backyard inventors and so interestingly bantered about the talk shows and Internet blogs.

Otherwise, the totality of the automotive industry might best be sold in the Christmas edition of the Neiman Marcus catalog.

The purpose of this book is to provide the readers enough information about the industry so that they may understand the events and draw their own conclusions about the past. And, perhaps even more importantly, it is to enable them to formulate ideas as to how the industry should be structured and organized in the future.

CHAPTER ONE
Introduction

"GM stopped trading!"

Those were the first words uttered by distinguished Princeton economist Alan Blinder at a special seminar on November 7, 2008.

"I heard it on my radio driving in. It's the 58th thing I've recently heard that I never thought I would hear in my lifetime. I shudder to think of what number 59 might bring!"

I was shocked but not surprised. Resembling a slowly administered torture, ten or twelve events over the past fifty years, including those self-inflicted, had eroded the Detroit automobile-makers' competitive position, limited their options and generated unremitting cost pressures.

Although a few years younger than I and brought up in the Eastern United States, Dr. Blinder's youthful impression of the automakers, at least from the standpoint of stability, was somewhat like mine. GM, for instance, represented fully 1 percent of the Gross National Product; produced cars that captured 50 percent of the market; employed thousands of executives, many of them brilliant in their field and exemplary citizens; and, perhaps most important of all, employed many hundreds of thousands without any particular skills and paid them a wage that, with only a modicum of prudence, could put their children through college. It seemed that a kid could always get a summer job to help pay for school or that a faithful employee could always find an apprentice toehold for a niece or nephew—leading to a productive, full-time job. People would wink and call it "Generous Motors." How could a company of this stature, which was held with the rest of the U.S. automotive industry in the world's highest esteem, become a shell of its former self, called to Washington for derision and degradation?

During grad school in the 1960s, a noted professor of finance from Michigan State University walked us through GM's financial statements. This was a guy who not only knew all the tricks, but he knew where to find the doves. He knew all the appropriate ratios, fastidiously read all of the footnotes, checked to see if options might be diluting the stock, walked us

11

through the "hoax" of a stock dividend and could deduce whether the company was keeping up with technology by analyzing their capital and product-development spending as compared to competitors. His analysis had more detail than anyone could remember, so much so that it was difficult to keep up with notes. Upon completion, he held the GM annual report and 10-K above his head and made a gesture as if he were a chef having just finished his finest coq au vin. Some of that analysis might have helped us avoid the currently difficult financial situation. I understand there are still guys around like him, but I just learned a new profundity: "It is difficult to teach a man something when his personal well-being depends upon his not knowing."

In the Sixties, the products of Motown convinced the public that two cars per family was the norm, permitting them to live in places with a little more elbow room.[1] With lots of vacant countryside, America had the luxury of creating sprawling suburbs, with many of the jobs, particularly the white-collar ones, following that trek. By the Sixties, the industry was annually building about 8.5 million cars per year and 1 million trucks.

As American families of those days tended to have more children, and with cars being used for recreation and vacationing as well as commuting, cars and light trucks tended to be commodious, particularly as compared to those from the soon-to-be competitors from Europe and Asia. By all standards, gasoline was inexpensive and most middle-class kids, with great anticipation, secured their operator's license at the minimum age of sixteen.

If we were "pitching" this book as a TV special on HBO, I think we would go about it thusly: "A narrative story of the post WWII American automobile industry, 1946-2014, a la *Zelig* or *Forrest Gump* (in that the protagonist is at least peripherally connected to all the real players), embodying the guileless 'Motown speak,' a la Lido Iacocca, with a touch of cynical witticisms, a la P. J. O'Rourke or Jean Shepherd." (Did you notice how smoothly a Detroit native worked in the sophisticated European idioms?)

I'd also pitch that, toward the end, it presents a solution that sets up an environment for stability for the industry (particularly for the U.S. guys). This solution would simultaneously enable us to leapfrog any Kyoto obligation and cause many Middle Eastern countries to reconsider how they

---

[1] To the drastic detriment of the downtown areas in a substantial number of American cities, including my favorite.

will price their oil and fund public budgets. Beyond that, such a solution would permit us to use otherwise useless fuel, and, perhaps best of all, it would also agitate and aggravate both Jane Fonda and Dick Cheney.

What I hope to present is a reasonably objective but non-technical narrative of one participant's observations and perspective of the (primarily U.S.) post-WWII automotive business and the events and people that have brought us to the current crisis.

Why me? Well, I grew up and was educated in the geometric center of the corporate offices of the (then) four largest automotive companies (the furthest of which was five miles away, even closer than the erstwhile Alaskan governor emeritus was to Russia); I attended undergraduate engineering school at General Motors Institute in Flint and took post-grad MBA courses at the Michigan State program, brought to Motown suburbs primarily for the automotive guys.

Later in my career I would run into former associates or acquaintances and, in certainly more than a half dozen cases, the conversation would go something like this: "Oh hi, Rile. You're certainly looking—er—healthy. I was thinking of you the other day. I was with a group of friends talking about 'XXX' and I remember you expounding on that subject years ago. I hope you didn't know but, at the time, it sounded to me like gobbledygook. [I knew.] When exposed to that same subject after a lapse of several years, it dawned on me that you must have had some unusual insight or you were ahead of the curve. In the midst of that group conversation, I espoused the gist of your observations to a unanimity of nodding heads."

Now, such belated acknowledgment of insight tends to reinforce one's sense of having contributed helpful information. On the other hand, perhaps it's only the phenomenon of "an infinite number of monkeys—"

I will generally follow a timeline, taking breathers for an occasional excursion to present an insider's sniff of the business—for example, Who speaks Motown and who doesn't? I will discuss in some detail what events of the last fifty years impacted the industry, both favorably and unfavorably, what seemed to motivate the actors and what are the factors that bring us to the current situation. I will attempt to honestly discuss some fact-based details about the industry that I think are contrary to public understanding or supposition (in short "debunk'), and I will maintain that some of such purported misinformation was and continues to be purposefully cultivated. I will attempt to propose direction for a final solution for equilibrium in the

13

industry that may have by-products that will solve several other domestic and international problems. (What a modest guy!)

Lastly, I hope that the presentation will be perceived by readers as factual enough and rational enough (thereby absolving the author of having been immersed in a suspect universe). I also hope that readers can generate their own conclusions, most hopefully gleaning enough realism from this exercise so that their own perspective of the industry will emerge in some unpredictable and wonderfully insightful manner. Allegorically speaking, the narrative will intellectually welcome readers into the stable, demonstrate how the shovel can be manipulated and let them find their own damn pony.

Perhaps the reader is beginning to question his judgment that he has just plunked down good money to be exposed to this sort of stuff. As one of our favorite Chrysler purchasing agents used to say, "I think I've just been kissed."

CHAPTER TWO
Sunny Detroit—1937-1945

Is it good? Is it ill?
Am I Blessed? Am I cursed?
Is it honey on my tongue, or brine?
            [Fate, as sung by Alfred Drake, from the musical *Kismet, 1953.]*

Let me set the tone by writing about my memories as a child.

My earliest recollection was Dr. Nolting's delightedly exaggerated reaction to my latest exploit, while he sat at the foot of my bed. I was lying in the southwest corner of the boy's bedroom of our Elmira Avenue home (NW Detroit) and the blessed pediatrician was making a house call, just as he did two or three times a year when any of us had the mumps, the chicken pox or some other childhood disease. It was 1938 and I don't recall the particular malaise that prompted his visit, but I do remember the exploit. I was responding to mother's prompting, "Whistle for Dr. Nolting."

Now it was very possible that Dr. Nolting had never before heard a small child whistle nor had he probably heard one do a Bronx cheer or a disgusting underarm noise. Our family, especially mother, encouraged us to exploit even the most trivial of talents.

At any rate, these few paragraphs are about the timing and the memories.

I remember the sunny day one summer when the inclination was not to waste nap time by falling asleep. I went downstairs, intending to tell grandpa Riley that I was going out to play instead of napping. He was preoccupied with the paper—no need to disturb him. I went out to play with Ronnie Gray, five doors down the street. I finished up playing in a couple of hours and went home to "fess up." Grandpa was still preoccupied. I went upstairs and made noises as if waking from nap.

"Hi, Grandpa."

No harm, no foul. I was three.

15

I remember that we were with Dad at the city airport watching planes take off and land when we heard the news about World War II.

I remember going to the A&P with Mother two or three times a week (no frozen food yet) and regularly getting a single lamb chop for little Bobby's lunch.

I remember the doughnut machine at Kresge's where the dough was fed in one end and floated for three long passes in a river of hot oil, turning itself in the middle of the second straightaway and automatically being ejected at the end into a wire basket.

I remember the 'fraidy-cat kid from across Wyoming Street who was spooked by a cat on the way to first day of kindergarten (Ralph was later my best man), but I can even better remember the taste of the bottle caps that we were *compelled* to lick—from our one-cent daily bottle of milk.

Even with the bad economic times and the war, I remember our neighborhood (I was then less than ten years old) as being sunny, tree-lined and generally pleasant, much like any urban residential area with forty-foot lots and three-bedroom homes. At that time, the milkmen and the icemen were not yet totally motorized. Many had horses that self-actualized by keeping pace with the vendor, actually minimizing his steps as compared to those who were motorized. Several neighbors down near the railroad tracks kept chickens. There were also walking vendors such as a knife or scissors sharpener or a photographer with an appropriately sized pony.

Father, a generous man but a lifetime financial conservative, had a successful uncle, Clyde Craine, who hired and mentored him. He benevolently encouraged Father to acquire those habits and skills that were then undervalued and which in the future would enrich his and his family's life. This gave him the means to acquire a north-woods hunting and fishing cabin, as well as a membership in a businessmen's golf club; useful assets for an industrial salesperson.

During the war, I remember being able to ride in a "Duck" amphibious vehicle when father bought $25 war bonds (for $18.75) at a war-support rally and I remember buying a weekly savings stamp at school for 18 cents.

From a retrospective point-of-view, two situations stand out. The first was the universal and publicly voiced hatred for the war enemies, from both a cultural and visceral standpoint. There were popular songs about looking forward to being united with loved ones and longing for things returning to normal—such as "Bluebirds over the white cliffs of Dover." But there were also ones gleefully defiant of the enemy, "The Fuhrer says we are the master race; we (Bronx cheer), (Bronx cheer), right in the Fuhrer's face." Instilled in even the littlest citizens was the idea, along with graphic depictions, that the Japanese were "yellow, buck-toothed, slanty-eyed, bow-legged, rapacious" whatevers.

Let's get the memory thing out in the open and done. At least the family seems to use me for a touchstone on family events.

Q. "When did Aunt Bea die?"

A. "Just before Christmas 1946 and nine days after she took me to see *Pinocchio.*"

Q. "What about the aforementioned Uncle Clyde?"

A. "Don't you remember? We had to delay the once-in-a-lifetime western driving trip for a week in 1952; incidentally you must remember that Bud Shultz died just a few days before Uncle Clyde."

Q. "Who blew third trombone for Kenton in 1953?"

A. "Keith Moon."

Q. "Who won the PGA that same year?"

A. "Wally Burkemo; don't you remember, he beat Felice Torza at Birmingham (Michigan) Country Club. I happened to be there."

So? Am I blessed or am I cursed? Once I got over the notion early in life that no one person can be totally Christ-like, two current thoughts caused me to come down on the "blessed" side: (1) at least I haven't been sleepwalking through life, although one wouldn't know it from my accumulated accomplishments or possessions (except for family!), and (2) it helps me justify writing this without having to do a hell of a lot of research, otherwise a book with this spectrum of material would take about as much time to research as the time it took me to get from whistling for Dr. Nolting to the present.

Let's get to the subject, Motown business!

I lived through my pre-college years in the geographic center of the corporate homes of the (then) Big Four and began to notice the finer things to be gotten for one's motoring pleasure.

[See map, next page.]

1. HOME - 8635 ELMIRA
2. GM HEADQUARTERS
3. FORD HEADQUARTERS
4. CHRYSLER HEADQUARTERS
5. NASH-KELVINATOR HEADQUARTERS (AMC)
6. PARKER GRADE SCHOOL
7. MACKENZIE HIGH SCHOOL
8. GENERAL MOTORS INSTITUTE
9. AMERICAN METAL PRODUCTS (LSI)
10. LIVERNOIS AVE.
11. BAKER'S KEYBOARD LOUNGE

Also, Nash-Kelvinator was only a few hundred yards further out Plymouth Road from my Ward Memorial Church. I remember at a very young age that I wanted our next car to be either a convertible or a Chrysler model where the headlights "blinked" closed. I remember family friend Wendell Mouw had a 1939 Lincoln Zephyr that changed radio stations via a button on the floor. Cool! Fifty years later, my daughter Julie had borrowed "the Trout," my father's battered hand-me-down Skylark that I used as a "station" car and that displayed a Trout Unlimited sticker. Technically disadvantaged, Julie drove for many miles frantically trying to get the headlights to dim. Neither she nor any of her friends ever dreamed there ever was anything like a foot button to change any functional feature of a vehicle.

I will admit, however, although I always appreciated nice cars with nice features and earned an engineer's degree from General Motors Institute (GMI), that I seemed to gravitate toward the automobile business itself. I never did tinker with cars or dream of new styles or features, but I later came to realize (or perhaps rationalize) that although I could understand and explain most technical elements in most situations, there was a benefit to not getting sidetracked during key business deliberations or negotiations by an emotional attachment to the subject product, its relationship to the vehicle, its history or its internal workings.

Henceforth, you'll be able to decide for yourself.

Later, I hope to do for you an equivalent rationalization regarding learning and using languages during international negotiations.

CHAPTER THREE
POST WWII

As the war ended in August, 1945, Americans realized that the depression had also ended, an occurrence somewhat obscured by the hardships of the war. There was pent-up technology and pent-up consumer demand just waiting to be exploited.

The last cars built were a few 1942 models, as total automobile production abruptly ended when the war started at the end of 1941. Detroit played "Arsenal of Democracy" for five years, in a manner that is marveled at to this day. Unfortunately, the justifiable pride engendered by these accomplishments didn't concurrently engender a gracious humility. Rather, it evolved into a ferocious struggle to see which company could get up and running to recapture automotive market share after the war, such share that was then believed would only grow over time.

I've been privileged to see a few big-picture Detroit guys at work.

Here's a fanciful example that recaptures the mood as I remember it.

"Okay, big-shot GM guy, you've got to make 50,000 fighter planes over the next three years. As the government, we'll see that you get whatever you need in the way of equipment and supplies. What do you need first?"

Then comes 105 seconds of silence. Blank expression on Mr. Big Shot's face. He's thinking.

"First, we'll need 325 steamrollers," he finally says.

"What! Steamrollers? How do you come to that conclusion?"

"Order the steamrollers while I tell you. To make 17,000 fighters a year will take 3 assembly lines, 3 shifts, which I think we can fit into Willow Run. That's mostly labor so we don't need any long lead equipment. The engines can be made in the nearby warehouse. I think we can modify the GMC engine and move the lines, although we may have to buy some; that should be no problem. Fabrication can go where we now keep inventory. Electricity? Should be okay. Let's see, I understand there are about 5,300 direct man hours per plane, so if we plan for that for six days a week, we'll need X people per shift plus about .8 indirect for assembly and .5 indirect for fabrication and machining. That means all together we'll need about Y thousand total people per shift. Holy crap, no way can the roads handle this many vehicles for employees and some of the incoming material. (The rest arrive by train, and the finished planes go out via the runway.) So, we'll need three lanes, two ways, 12-miles long, to handle traffic. Since one steamroller in a day and a half can lay a furlong and a half—we need 325 steamrollers!"

Notice that Mr. Big Shot has, before your eyes, performed a "critical path" analysis that will be refined in time. They'll probably really need 297 steamrollers. This is the "Motown" type of guy who doesn't stand around waiting for direction, particularly from New York or Washington. He doesn't want input from accountants, lawyers or tax accountants. He seldom thinks about his "bedside manner" to the general public, and he is only marginally polite when non-connected "car buffs" want to share a feature or idea they long thought should be incorporated in the industry.

Accordingly, I will reluctantly agree that there has been a noticeable "swagger" or arrogance in the Motown crowd, which in turn has tended to cause "sophisticated" (or non-automotive) executives to "talk down" or lecture to what they think of as the "unwashed" Detroit executive. In particular situations, this can have dire consequences when that "sophisticate" is the new executive of a supplier and that "unwashed" is a major customer. Exaggerating the problem is the perceived notion that the Detroit tin benders shouldn't be trusted in running three of the five biggest U.S. companies (remember, GM itself represents 1 percent of GNP) and making decisions that have implications for the overall economy.

At war's end, the U.S. automobile fleet must have averaged about eight years of age and it took some time for the automakers to gear back up. The first government intervention in the automotive industry that I recall occurred during this period. The demand for new cars was so great and the supply so low that the real monetary value of any car became greater than sticker price. Accordingly, the government made it illegal for dealers to sell a new car for more than sticker, a seemingly well meaning policy. One of father's fellow club members was soon indicted for selling new Buicks to one of the "homeless" (although the word hadn't been invented yet), buying it back for about $50 more and selling it for several hundred more than that. Of course, there was no practical way of controlling the price of "used" cars.

Another story with a moral was told many times by my father about a prominent Ford dealer (no need to name names here, even now) who was so successful and self-satisfied that when the war started he was dumfounded and panicked. He had no plans, no fallback, no cash flow! A friend suggested that he would try, through channels, to access some screw machines that could be put on the showroom floor to make tank or airplane parts for the duration. That effort succeeded. As the war ended, the friend gleefully announced that his son had made it through the war, was being discharged and that he dreamed of having a spanking new gift car in the driveway upon his return.

"What's he got to trade in?" asked the dealer.

"He doesn't, of course, have any trade-in. As I told you he's been overseas in the war!"

"Sorry," said the dealer, "we've got a policy that we're only selling new cars to people with good trade-ins."

Of course the dealer himself had unilaterally established the "policy."

Undoubtedly, my father kept telling the story in the hope of having this guy ostracized from good company.

Here I was, less than ten years old, and already I'd learned a couple of things: first, that the government sometimes intervenes in ways it believes are for the greater good, and that these interventions sometimes have unintended consequences; and, secondly, that the automaker's conduit to the customer, in at least some instances, is somewhat less than honorable.

Lastly, I must have subliminally learned that on special occasions breaking a real law isn't all that repugnant, while occasionally some actions made within the law are so repugnant that steps must be taken by citizens to restore a semblance of equity. (Probably, the subliminal morphed into cognizance only when demonstrated by Mr. Puzo many years later.)

The resolution of the cases above were that the guy who was fudging on the "used car" deals got only a slap on the wrist, e.g., only one onion per Gibson for three months, whereas the auto dealer who stiffed his machine procurer was ousted from some of his business and social circles.

And these were the retail guys! I'd heard rumors that the resale guys, the used-car dealers, were maybe even a notch below. In that automobile-centric area where I lived was Livernois Avenue, acknowledged as the world's largest concentration of used-car dealers, the nearest one being about two miles from home. This avenue later earned my respect as having, at its northernmost Detroit edge, Baker's Keyboard Lounge, showcase of many of the great small-group jazz musicians over a period of more than thirty years.

The next post-war national concern was the expansionist policies and apparent independence of our former ally, the USSR, which had developed its own atomic bomb and was thought of as a threat to world peace. All Americans were tested for blood type and given a plastic "dog tag" designating the type that was to be administered when the bomb hit. Although I had pieces of my blue "O-negative" tag until about thirty years ago, they're now gone, so please make note of that if I am found lying bleeding at a book signing: O-*negative*. As a "service" boy at school, at age ten, I was stationed about twenty feet inside the enclosed musty equipment-access tunnel during air-raid evacuation drills to alert people not to bump their head as the ceiling suddenly lowered. The only one to consistently hit her head was our gangly principal, Miss Dougherty, who seemed to ignore my warnings. To supplement our air-raid exercises there were informational films dealing with the power of A-bombs and the conditions under which one might not totally succumb. We learned that it was possible to survive if one was five miles or further from ground zero, which we assumed to be downtown Detroit, coincidental with the notice of a sign on Wyoming Street, half a block from home, that said, "Detroit—7 1/2 miles." What a relief! We'd probably only suffer first- and second-degree burns.

There was a frenzy to build houses. This was happening faster than the building of schools to accommodate the children living therein; consequently, kids from the new outskirts of Detroit proper were being bussed back towards us. Although we all thought our public-school education more than adequate, during the late 1940s, I recall that all classrooms at Parker School contained five rows of nine permanent desks. We always had a couple of kids sitting at side tables, indicating class sizes of 47 to 50, something unheard of today. Also unique was the variety of classes beyond the academic subjects, such as vocal and instrumental music, shop (home economics for girls), auditorium and art. These were provided to help students discover their aptitudes and how they might be applied in the real world.

Outside of school, I learned to play baseball; I learned to play cards with Grandpa Reichheld; I caddied for my father. My skills as a clarinetist led me to the Detroit Boys Police Band at age eleven, eventually becoming concertmaster at age thirteen. Mother told friends that we practiced on Tuesday nights at the "Knudson" church on East 7 Mile Road, the start of automotive lexicon and personalities being integrated with everyday living.

With two or three gigs a month, we got to know our way around town: the parks, the veterans' hospitals, colleges; and we met a lot of people: doctors, nurses, the police commissioner and even the mayor (Cobo). I auditioned for the Ted Mack radio talent show, when it came to Detroit, only to realize a nightmare with a dry reed and an overzealous accompanist. No matter, the boys' band was scheduled to play for the show anyway. Oops! Not if the unions had anything to say about it. (They did, my first such experience). I auditioned for Leonard Smith, renowned cornetist and leader of the Detroit Concert Band, only to muff the "essay." To this day, when I visit Detroit I love to ask professional "boosters" specific questions about certain areas of the city—if only to perniciously admonish them, "I moved away from here more than 25 years ago, and yet I seem to know more about the town than you do!"

The automobile was again gaining favor—as was TV—with the emerging consumer society. At the first auto show, I recall seeing the "Automotive Parade of Progress," consisting of a large flat panorama depicting a rural neighborhood morphing into a citified pleasant community through a series of revolving panels demonstrating how car and truck utilization would advance the state of gracious living.[2] The layout must have been saved from the 1939 New York World's Fair. Very complicated and interesting although we didn't get to see the whole show. I later deduced that when unexpectedly encountering particularly interesting entertainments, mother was fearful that a money collector would shortly arrive, which she just hated! Mostly, I remember the top-of-the-line Cadillac which sold for $5,000. (Someday, maybe).

We visited the Ford museums that, to this day, continue to house the finest automobile collections. When we visited Dr. Nolting's successor in the Fisher building, we often took the pedestrian underground tunnel to the GM building, where the ground floor had a representative GM car line-up, probably one or two "concept" cars, the Fisher Body Craftsman Guild miniature-car design winner, and the soap-box-derby winner. To me, the most fascinating thing was a machine, glassed in the wall and only about 18-inches

---

[2] I think that we can agree that this concept was a general "buy" on the part of Americans. It was also to a lesser extent a "buy" on the part of the Chinese 50 years later.

square. It ejected steel ball bearings[3] onto a round steel pillar, beveled at a certain angle; then they bounced across and through the hole in a rapidly non-axially revolving bearing race. Finally, they bounced on another pillar and back up into the second hole. The speed was such that there were always two or three bearings in view, and you just knew that if you watched long enough there was bound to be chaos.

Ford finally and with much fanfare introduced its first "notchback"[4] in 1949. Father made a purchase of which we were very proud, except for the fact that the doors hardly sealed at all, creating havoc when traveling on the dusty roads on the way to the cabin. We tried wadding newspaper into the cracks to no avail.

I remember when one of Father's best trout-fishing buddies, Ed Shaw, a Chevrolet manufacturing executive, took early retirement from the company. He was rewarded with a Chevy dealership in L.A. and came back raving, "You've never seen anything like California! You can drive for twenty miles and you're still in the same city. There are very few tall buildings. There is no need for busses or trolley cars."

It later occurred to me that he was participating in the development of the largest metropolis designed after the advent of the automobile. Probably his dealership became pretty valuable also.

Although we couldn't at the time foresee the third- and fourth-order events that would lay claim to most "Center City" demises, things certainly looked good from a future Detroit standpoint.

---

[3] Must have been a submission for New Departure, GM's bearing division.

[4] Heretofore, all Fords had "rounded" backs like the Volkswagen Beetle.

CHAPTER FOUR
Continued Prosperity—1951-1955

On to high school. Now I could test what talents I had against a much larger field. The student "crunch" was still existent and the facility utilized a hybrid or split shift—eleven periods from 8:00 A.M. to 4:30 P.M. More than compensating for the general crowded conditions was the teaching talent that was thrown at us. There were three levels for most offered classes, in addition to special help. We had eight gym and team coaches for boys, several of which were renown for their specialty and who plied their trade on a three-level department (pool, gym, indoor track) in addition to the outdoor fields. We had an eight-person music department, including separate band and orchestra leaders and two full-time accompanists, one of whom was affiliated with the Detroit symphony. I've still got the "scrolled" pictures depicting the two- or three-hundred simultaneous performers at the Christmas and Spring concerts. High school was exhilarating. I participated in band (concertmaster), orchestra, play cast, track, cross country, politics (12B class president), all the while recognizing the nubility of female classmates. No need to take technical classes other than math and sciences to become an automotive engineer; that would be provided later. In fact, as a kicker I was a drama summer-school scholarship attendee two summers at Cranbrook Institute.

I discovered with some dismay that I wasn't a "natural" golfer, but I was allowed to play with Father and my more sophisticated contemporaries at Father's club. The lack of such natural skill was somewhat assuaged and appreciation of the classic game engendered by exposure to my father's best friend, Chuck Kocsis, an outstanding amateur Walker Cup player and club member. There were also three visits by the PGA tour at the club during the 1950s, where my hero became Lloyd Mangrum, a great golfer and cool personification of a riverboat gambler who I recognized in the locker room as the spokesperson in *Life Magazine* for Camels.

I had a golfing friend named Hugh who kept talking about family, particularly about his father who complained about him having hit new golf balls into the "lake" at home. I concluded this was the most flagrant act of entitlement I had theretofore encountered. For several years I couldn't place the guy's father, recognizing of course that his "grandfather" was a long established and distinguished member of the club. I finally realized that my golfing buddy was the child of a second marriage of a GM executive, a not uncommon occurrence given the dedication required of such executives during and after the war, combined with the risk of non-parallel personal growth of the original spouses. Hugh had been born when his father was in his sixties; no wonder I had been carrying a misperception of his actual parentage.

The auto industry wasn't waiting for my presence to insinuate itself on the American psyche: Cars were becoming spiffier than ever, with hardtops (no center pillar); there was the Corvette, later the Thunderbird; new entries Kaiser and Fraser with their Polynesian motifs; Nash with its contortioning seat "bed." And there were altered stylish or sporty images for Dodge, Pontiac, Buick and Mercury, not even considering George Romney's Metropolitan and Ramblers, all contributing to record-busting sales records in the mid-1950s.[5] GM's former chairman, "Engine Charlie" Wilson, was making his "What's good for General Motors—" comments as Eisenhower's Secretary of Defense without, as I recall, much flack from the press, the UAW, the public or either political party.

I knew my life was going to be enriched when I drove away from home, solo for the first time in November, 1954, on my way to be made up for our first performance of *Angel in a Pawnshop*.[6] I think about 250 million Americans have had the same sensation in the interim. My high-school sweetheart's father suggested that I be available to have lunch with one of his contemporaries, Ed Cole, newly appointed chief engineer of Chevrolet and "a really nifty guy." (Author's note: He certainly was!)

In the spring of 1955 we were scheduled to take the entrance exam for GMI engineering college with the knowledge that it was designed to cull many of the applicants who were deliberately without any knowledge of how

---

[5] Crosley, like Kool cigarettes, embodied *almost exactly* the right characteristics to prosper, e.g. smallness and mentholness, respectively, but both were just enough askew so as never to hit the big time.

[6] As "Duke," the raspy talking black jazz clarinetist.

to prepare. It turned out to be a hodgepodge of "story book" mathematical problems, IQ problems and various other logic-oriented problems over what one imagined were four or five standardized tests of the day, all in different format with, naturally, some duplication. I was learning that GM didn't do things the usual way; they did it the GM way. After taking the test and being generally satisfied with my efforts, it dawned on me that "cream was not of greater density than milk," as they would goad you to believe in written form; we know it rises to the top, as seen in visual form, thereby exhibiting its lack of density. Holy crap! I've gotten the same three wrong answers on three separate tests! Might I be doomed to a life as a musician as a result of the sludge I used to have to lick off bottle tops a dozen years earlier?

While otherwise going about the business of graduation, it took about six weeks to get a missive about the test. In terse language it gave the results: B. Shouldn't they give some idea of how that will wind up in the pecking order? Uh, oh, I thought, being an A student in high school only put me 17th in a class of about 500. One could extrapolate that in a very competitive situation that even being in the top 5 percent might not cut it. I called the administrator who cavalierly offered, "Congratulations, everyone knows that B gets one admitted. In fact, this year we're probably going to admit all of our B/C results."

Sometimes GM's conveyance of information isn't on my own wavelength.

I wound up my adolescence full of optimism, ready to attend GMI, ready to spend a lifetime of prosperity in the automotive business. I left for Flint Michigan, with $35 I had earned caddying at Forest Lake Country Club in October, 1955.

Incidentally, Detroiters were proud that J.L. Hudson Co. (Detroit's flagship department store) had in 1954 opened its second store in the near northwest suburbs that was the "anchor" for one of the first suburban malls, Hudson's Northland. It was really convenient and clean. There were stores of many types there. Generally, you could walk from one to the other under cover, at the same time getting fresh air. Of course, they couldn't be expected to have the same extensive inventory and experienced sales clerks as the downtown store, but in the event you needed something special, as I did with my girlfriend's bunny coat from the cover of *Seventeen Magazine*, you could always go to the downtown store to find a broader product range. (Note:

Hudson's downtown was dynamited in the late 1990s, accidentally taking down part of the Detroit People Mover in the process.)

In the days of the U.S. occupation of Japan after the war, General McArthur had encouraged U.S. industrial companies to come to Japan to help with restoration and gain a toehold in Asia. For the most part, he was greeted with silence. Check that. I took the lack of response to mean that the companies expressed their disinterest in getting into the fields of cupie dolls, inexpensive costume jewelry or animated tin toys. Obviously unbeknownst to me at the time, the international department of my future employer, Bendix, was executing a technical-assistance agreement for the manufacture of automobile brakes. This brought about the general disdain of Bendix U.S. oriented operatives who were frantically converting back to domestic production and surmised that the international department was setting up titular licensees so as to substantiate their continued international joy riding.

CHAPTER FIVE
Fun Over

After being thought of as perhaps overly "nerdy"[7] in high school, it dawned on me that such a demeanor might actually serve me well in GM engineering school. How little did I know! Compared to the rest of my classmates, I seemed like Jack Kerouac.

The school was a "cooperative" one. One was admitted through a "sponsor" division where one worked (in the manner of an apprentice) for four weeks, six times each year, and spent two semesters (four weeks for three times each) at the Institute. School schedules averaged about thirty class hours a week, including labs, and were designed to require about an equivalent amount of homework.[8] The "orientation" class not only encouraged diligence and hard work it also suggested that most people couldn't do all of the homework and so we were urged to learn triage and prioritization.

They also gave hints on how to "game" the system. For multiple-choice quizzes, we were to insist that the instructor state whether he subtracted wrong answers from right answers. If not, we were told to insist that he give two-minutes' notice so that we could randomly check answers to all questions we hadn't yet reached. We were told to never change an answer unless it was contradicted by a subsequent question. And, when you're not pressed for time, we were told to look out the window, refresh our countenance and dig in again.

The hours at my sponsor, Fisher Body Central, General Motors Technical Center (ca. 1954), were 7:30 A.M. to 4:12 P.M. Pay was $2.01 per

---

[7] Modern idiom, can't seem to recall what the equivalent was in the Fifties, bookish, square, unhep?

[8] I observed that while perhaps two or three guys could do previous class homework at greetings of next class, netting no homework after classes, many dozens never, ever caught up.

hour, with time-and-a-half for overtime. Not too great a schedule to hit the nightspots (although I did learn the trick of shaving before going to bed). Mother rightfully stated that she had gotten breakfast for eighteen years and accordingly shouldn't have to continue to do so, particularly at six in the morning. For a while I tried cold cereal, but that was a depressing eating scene in the winter darkness. I soon learned that M&Ms and chocolate milk, devoured at my enormous horizontal drafting table at Fisher, provided an excellent and soothing segue to a substantial lunch at 11:30 in the cafeteria. When I really needed a kick in the morning, I substituted Coke for the chocolate milk and was very proud of the fact that I was replicating the behavior of John O'Hara's heroes.

One got to know one's classmates. One classmate in particular was sponsored by Pontiac and I inquired as to his working hours when not in Flint.

"We start at 6:30 A.M. Wouldn't you know it, right in the middle of the day!" (He was rural if you hadn't already guessed.)

I got off to a good start academically, at the same time realizing that some of the material was review for those who hadn't had as good of a high-school background. Still, the pace was really quick. I will admit I was impressed when GM insisted on the re-opening of a snow-swept Flint Bishop Airport and provided the plane so that students from Connecticut and New York could get home for the holidays.

I joined a fraternity. I got my first car, a 1956 black Chevrolet convertible—former executive car from GM, 3,000 miles, excellent care, debugged—for $1,920. Six cylinders with 145 horsepower.

"Who would ever buy a car with a pukey 145 horsepower?" my classmates asked.

Didn't bother me at all as it had all the visible features of a convertible and an added feature that with the top down, the windshield washers, when actuated, would hit the passenger exactly in the kisser with both spigots. Although a generally passive and accommodating soul, it did let me distract anyone who was getting sassy in the passenger seat. Thereafter I was an okay student, becoming a reasonably diligent, although not outstanding, scholar. During the preparation of my final thesis, my school advisor offered, "I'm going to hold your feet to the fire on correct English, particularly on technical English. Some of the niches I've been exposed to within the company, and particularly your own sponsor, use their own vernacular, sounding like gibberish to the average educated person."

My overall recollection of the four years at GMI was one of mild drudgery and sleep deprivation, thereby gleaning the ability to sleep through all but the most violent of events.

I won't go into detail here, but at this time you should know that I had an older brother, Bill, who died of brain cancer while I was a sophomore. One of the finest brain surgeons (and one of my favorite heroes) along with the newly introduced cobalt radiation treatments at the University of Michigan gave Bill nine months of hope and quality living; he thereafter struggled and finally succumbed after a year.

The rest of my school years seem somewhat petty looking back now on it. I dated, but no one in particular, as my high-school sweetheart had become a stewardess for Capitol Airlines. I performed in *Witness for the Prosecution* for the Flint Community Players and, although that was fun and a time out of the rut, it further aggravated the sleep deprivation.

The Western Open was being held at the golf club and I became a minor official, interfacing with the players by collecting scores as they finished sixteen holes. Arnold Palmer had recently won the National Amateur at the Country Club of Detroit and was playing at the very start of his pro career. "Champagne" Tony Lema was of even higher personal stature than his fabled reputation. (He was beloved by the press corps for "buying" after being runner-up at Augusta in the Masters.) Doug Sanders' swing, as advertised, could almost be accomplished in a phone booth, although he won his first tournament ($5,000) in spite of the bleeding calluses on his hands. It hadn't dawned on me that on the last day, many of the competitive players were interested and entitled to know who in the preceding field was leading and by what score. Dow Finsterwald in the last group expressed surprise at the leader and requested that I seek out more info and keep him up to date.

"I think from the crowd reaction, he must have only parred seventeen," I offered.

Fifteen minutes later, Finsterwald sought me out on the tee at eighteen to find out that Sanders had birdied eighteen, allowing Finsterwald only second place even if he birdied the hole. Rarified stuff for a golf fanatic of twenty.

Two fraternity brothers and I visited Cuba a year and a half before Castro took over. We drove to Key West[9] and took the ferry. Although Castro was a known commodity, he was then lurking with his supporters in the hills and more closely covered by magazines as an idealistic rebel rather than by hard-news sources. To our surprise, Cuban customs confiscated our then popular "suntan" trousers, suggesting that we probably didn't want to be confused in Havana with a Castro operative, as Batista's guys were tending to shoot first and water board later. These were returned upon our exit.

Havana in 1957 made Las Vegas seem like Fred Rogers' neighborhood. Although it took some physical effort and considerable questioning of our masculinity, we were able to fend off the ladies of the evening and their representatives. Otherwise, there were about three or four elaborate nightclub/casinos with twenty-piece orchestras playing until 4:00 A.M., featuring elaborate entertainment with showgirls, horses and other acts. The streets were sunny and live Latin music was constantly within earshot. Beaches were accessible by bus. One of the guys bought an authentic conga drum, eighteen inches in diameter and three-feet tall—a constant irritant for those trying to sleep in the back seat on the way home.

All in all, this was the "exotic vacation on the cheap" that we had envisioned, but we did get a sense of the unrest of the ordinary citizens—such as taxi drivers and bartenders—and the corruption of the existing system.

My folks had moved to the northernmost limits of Bloomfield Township about the time I graduated from high school, partly because of their own increasing prosperity and partly because of their desire for more elbow room, as was a general trend of the 1950s. As a result, though, for me there was no neighborhood to return to, no congregation where I would meet other college-oriented kids at holidays or summer vacations. When I was a junior in college it dawned on me that my brother Dan had spent three years at the recently opened Bloomfield Hills High School and may have met over such years there a nubile female or two that might like to go out with a somewhat nerdy but presentable GM tech guy (for appearance then, think Pete Sampras; in recent years, think Jeff Garner or Charlie Weiss). Upon a brief meeting with the neighbor senior girl, Dan and she came up with three names, one of which was that of a daughter of a GM vice president.

---

[9] 36 hours on the road then, now considerably less. Thanks, Ike!

At the fraternity in Flint, there was a mantra particularly useful to those guys who didn't live anywhere near Flint (Indianapolis and Dayton were typical) and who were subject to prey by Flint girls thinking of grabbing a more luxurious life. That mantra was: "Don't get involved until you meet the mother. You're getting a free look 30 to 40 years into the future!" At the time, my work assignment was called "pilot," the activity that debugged tooling in a simulated factory setting and attempted to make the first or "pilot" bodies for the 1959 model GM cars. There were about three elements that made this thankfully short-term assignment particularly undesirable: (1) the factory was an otherwise abandoned one of early 1900s vintage, in the grittiest part of industrial Detroit; (2) the shift was 3:30 P.M. to 11:15 P.M.; and (3) the only tannery in town (think pungent) was catty-corner to us on Beaubien and Hastings. To this day, however, I feel that during this experience I learned to work under the most distracting of conditions, a characteristic that helped me work when overseas or en route.

At any rate, I called the VP's daughter; she sounded somewhat interested but would be away for three weeks. I called the next girl (all of a sudden, an embarrassment of riches) who knew and liked my brother and seemed very nice on the phone. We made a date to play tennis at 10:00 A.M. on a day in the near future, July 2, 1958. Well, the home was elegant and the "mantra" problem was diligently defused as the "mother" answered the door (think Nancy Reagan). Susan was even more elegant than the house or the mother and I haven't had a date with another woman in the interceding fifty-odd years. She beat me silly at tennis that day, on top of everything else being able to "toss" the ball up from the ground to her hand reflexively by squeezing it between her racquet and either foot (really, really intimidating, but no matter, I forgot about that thirty years ago). At any rate, I suggested that we quit after about half an hour and go swimming or something. Although we had regular dates on weekends, I later understood that her parents had some concern about my weekday schedule and where it might be leading. (Harry Shoptall?) Susan seemed to understand. She assured them that if my current situation didn't work out, "He could become a professional musician." (As I recall, not assuaging to the prospective parents-in-law.)

However, there was an open issue at that time: Susan, having Swedish ancestry, was untraditionally Catholic; me, being of Irish ancestry (at least in name) was untraditionally Protestant. Before getting too involved I was obligated to take "Catholic lessons." Ironically, our "parish" priest in Flint was one Father James Kavanaugh, who you may recall as an extremely attractive, intellectual and forward-looking priest, later becoming famous for leaving the priesthood and writing books and articles espousing changes in the church (such as saying the mass in English) that Pope John would later establish. His lectures and demeanor were so elegant and profound that, although I never became a Catholic, I sensed myself as somewhat of an expert as compared to those who had learned theirs in the hubbub of childhood.[10] By the way, James, where is that papal blessing you secured for us during your trip to Rome in 1960? It doesn't matter where you are, we'll pay the UPS. By the way, hope you are well."[11]

There were several omens regarding my chosen industry that I observed but summarily discarded, at least temporarily. Volkswagen of Germany had begun importing Beetles and had reached annual sales of 25,000. What a relief to hear my employer proudly declare that that was exactly the amount we lost each year to inventory glitches. Whoops! Not a particularly gracious statement, besides demonstrating a degree of arrogance. One thing that troubled me in those early stages was our state and federal governments' lack of concern for what would now be called "equitable user fees." It didn't cost any less to register a Beetle but the fee was only about half of that for an American car (at least in Michigan, based on weight). The building and maintenance of highways and other auto-related infrastructure didn't vary between cars, but the governments collected taxes based essentially inversely as to miles per gallon. The government was basically subsidizing imports! Who really cared, because the industry was the only one in the history of modern transportation that was so profitable *that it more than paid its own way including operating infrastructure, for example, and didn't need government subsidies to keep operation viable.*

Another new phenomenon that was only a distraction then, but was to become a recurring and dismal part of a Motown career, was the cyclicality of the business. In 1958 came the first such fundamental downturn since

---

[10] Several years later while seeing my father-in-law seethe when recalling the priest he encountered in similar circumstances, I remember pointing at the cover of the current *Look Magazine* and stating, "I converted mine into a Presbyterian!" We Motown guys have a way of ingratiating ourselves to other people.

[11] This remarkable man succumbed in 2010 at 81 years of age.

WWII, which was magnified somewhat in that Buick, headquartered in Flint and a proud number-three seller in 1956, had slid much further than most during the overall industry downturn. This cycle was to repeat every three-to-seven years and brought with it permanent reorganizations and layoffs, disruptions in product plans and other gloom-inducing events. Over a lifetime, when trying to remember events, I succeed best when I try to relate such events to a house move, a job move, a promotion or a dip in the automotive cycle—1967, 1971, 1974, 1981 and so on.

On my first commercial flight—to visit friends in Philadelphia—posing as an intellectual soon-to-be automotive executive (is this the definition of oxymoron?), I was reading an *Atlantic Monthly* and ran across an interesting article entitled *Speed Kills?*—or some such thing. In it, the author purported that the currently trendy "SPEED KILLS!" campaign didn't convey a totally honest reality.

Rather, it is the *differential* in speed he said that is most dangerous. In his argument, the author used empirical data culled from performance on the Pennsylvania Turnpike. At the onset of WWII, the Pennsylvania Turnpike was the only road of its type, a road with limited access designed for high-speed driving. In order to conserve fuel, tires and other things, the speed limit of the road was posted at 35 mph for the duration. Later, someone took the trouble to determine how such a change might have altered the incidence of accidents as compared to design and formerly posted speeds. Somewhat to his surprise, he found that the fatality rate per mile driven *quadrupled* during those years of lowered posted speed limits. His logical conclusion wasn't that it was more dangerous if everyone drove at 35, rather it was that most people drive in accordance with the conditions of the road at a comfortably feeling speed. Obviously, some people drove at design speed, some drove 35 in the left hand lane and, since the limit was only 35, some who wanted to drive 20 felt safe to do so.

The "killer" obviously became the *act of posting of an unrealistically low speed limit*. Obviously, this nugget of information would cause some angst to my coming years when the Interstate greatly proliferated and the government made several posting "killers" of their own.

Several lessons were learned, however:

- There are often unintended consequences of new laws or directives as it is difficult to consider all possible failure modes, let alone 3rd- or 4th-order effects.
- Intuitive corrections or solutions to perceived problems sometimes don't even point in the right direction. (Consider the golf swing!)
- Numerically calculated technical conclusions or empirical observations are often the best basis on which to make decisions, assuming that one learns to rework any scoundrel's numbers into workable form.

CHAPTER SIX
Still Not a Lot of Honks

Upon completing engineering studies, I went to work full time for Fisher Central Manufacturing Engineering at the princely salary of $512 per month, wrote my senior thesis, graduated with a BME, got married, bought a house, had two children and lived nicely from paycheck to paycheck. There were adjustments to be made: I traded golfing privileges at a private golf club for a wife, such trade-off still being evaluated. Susan's living adjustments were greater. For example, on the first morning after returning from our honeymoon when I had to go to work, Susan was shocked to learn that I ate breakfast before getting dressed; it was also problematic that the toilet seat would be lowered; also, there was less discretionary income than previously enjoyed as a single woman living with affluent parents.

Just as I was starting my first full-time job, the product lines were greatly proliferating. Until the Sixties, there was one body for Pontiac, Oldsmobile and Buick, one or two for Cadillac and Chevrolet Impala, Corvair and Corvette. Being introduced was a whole new series of mid-sized cars for Buick, Oldsmobile, Pontiac (the BOP "A" body). Such introduction caused a workload at Fisher Central Manufacturing Engineering of 62 hours per week for the greater part of two years, thereby generating a period of uneventful living, with the possible exception of mumps, whooping cough, and measles.

When putting an automobile body together from primarily .035-inch thick[12] hot-rolled steel, one needs fairly robust fixtures to hold the parts so that they can be welded together into a reasonably sturdy body. One such "fixture" was the trolley that carried bodies along the line, first loaded with rather large parts such as the floor panel to which were welded various small parts and sub-assemblies. Simultaneously, in another area were put together the sides of the car: quarter panel, rocker panel, door frames, pillars and miscellaneous supports which also were all welded together in a large

---

[12] Approximately the thickness of a stack of eight new dollar bills.

suspended fixture with a profile roughly comparable to the exterior of the side body. As you can now imagine, the two side fixtures were married to the trolley so that the parts that were respectively carried by each could be welded together, giving the body its general configuration and its identity as a vehicle-in-process.

The production-engineering departments were organized to specialize in the type of fixture related to each body component; accordingly, there was an engineering group of twelve guys (no gals yet) for the trolleys and one of fifteen guys for the side fixtures. Naturally, in the normal chain of events there were periodic "coordination meetings" between the groups, as the groups' fixtures "mated" during the process (an approximately five-inch-diameter dowel shoved into a clamping receptacle) and accordingly the pieces carried by each could also be mated to form the core body. Apparently, there hadn't been a ground-up program for a while and somehow the groups were working with different assumptions as to where in space (relative to the body from which everyone worked) the two major fixtures would meet.

Now this, in itself, is minor compared to some of the stuff we'll get into later, but the story is instructive of the problems that would beset the industry over the years. During an intermediate term meeting, the mis-mating problem became obvious to each group. What was the reaction? Nothing! Adjournment! No verbalization of the issue by either side. Back to their drafting boards to continue designing non-functional fixtures (*and frantically trying to ascertain that their department wasn't at fault so their rice bowl— career—wouldn't be broken*). This couldn't be done independently, so another "coordination" meeting was held. How was the mismatch problem solved? It wasn't. Each side gleaned some information about the overall damage done and what the logical fix might be through an exchange of a series of carefully worded questions, but again there was adjournment without acknowledgment by either group that a problem existed. Back to work on the non-functional design. A third "non-recognitional" meeting was held as the schedule to actually manufacture this expensive tooling was quickly approaching, but the two departmental supervisors got together clandestinely, acknowledged the problem, devised a redesign of the fixtures, figured out how many man-hours would be required, and presented a pre-packaged problem-with-solution to their common boss. Up the line, the deal was summarily approved and quietly solved, each ascending higher executive thinking that the "can" might be tied to his tail. Oh well, this was

GM. Lots of resources. Two dozen guys work two dozen Saturdays and problem solved—a problem that might have been resolved quickly, had each side been committed to a common purpose, rather than to parochial interests.

I'm suspecting that a queasy resonance is engulfing the reader. The resonance being that, of the multiple agencies and vendors attempting to introduce the Affordable Care Act of 2010, many knew of or surmised the systemic deficiencies many months before it occurred. Predictably, they also didn't warn of the impending train wreck by passing their knowledge or suspicions "up the line" because, (1) they might be blamed for the wreck or, (2), almost as bad, they could be accused of not being a team player. As a result, the President and several echelons below him were astounded at the seemingly blatant lack of performance.

Permit me to digress about resources. GM spared no expense at GMI. When I talked to acquaintances that went to MIT, particularly about equipment, my counterparts would offer that for a particular experiment the professor would demonstrate how to set up the equipment and how it was to be used. Then the students would make observations and take readings while the process was underway, on occasions being allowed to make adjustments. At good old GMI, we had four or six teams of two, each team being told to go to the crib and get all the components required for such-and-such experimental system.

Particularly profligate was the instructor's deliberate lack of cautionary imperatives regarding equipment or people. For example, "Watch out for XXX or YYY might overheat." Or, "Be careful when you ZZZ or your WWW might not be available to you for a while."

Clearly, GMI held to a learning theory that the experience of finding out for oneself was the most effective method of teaching. When we erroneously created short circuits while wiring a project, we might shock ourselves, burn out the equipment, or both—or even worse.

"Jim, go to the infirmary while Bob gets new equipment from the crib. Don't forget, you guys only have about 45 minutes left to get all your required data."

The reason I refer back to the unique schooling offered by GMI ("The Trained Man Wins!") is that it taught us that we weren't going to design the next jet engine or the next Corvette upon graduation. Particularly, the work sessions interspersed with school sessions taught one that hard work was expected, but that a successful career was built on solid personal growth and experience. We understood that this admirable attitude somewhat favorably distanced us from, say, Big Ten engineering graduates.

While this undergraduate period at the Fisher Engineering Center wasn't hopelessly unproductive, the tasks had very little relationship to real engineering and, although most of the people were pleasant and hard working (after all, they were typical Mid-Westerners), one had the feeling of being lost in a vast sea of recurring tasks not really related to engineering training or how such training, expertly exercised, would be the basis for bigger things. Also, I rationalized, how would a seventeen-year old recognize that Fisher Body would be one of the more rigid and bureaucratic groups of the corporation. Bells would ring to announce starting times, lunch and dismissal times.

Regarding the industry happenings, we attended the wedding reception of Engine Charlie Wilson's granddaughter on the day that the Chairman and the President of Chrysler Corporation, Tex Colbert and Bill Newberg, had a physical altercation in the locker room of the same country club. While we weren't inconvenienced by such activity, we did read about it in the paper, and one did speculate that perhaps the Easterners had a kernel of truth in their assessment of the social graces and coping power of Motowners. It also led us to speculate that perhaps the next Board of Directors meeting at Chrysler might be, well, *awkward.*

"Bill, would you please review for the Board what actions you have taken relative to the DeSoto quality problems—"

Also, there was a book coming out about some alleged drivability problems with the Corvair. The 1960s seemed to have brought a lot of kooks out of the woodwork. What was this particular author's motive? People dismissed him as a kook by saying that he probably disliked big business, like Jack Kennedy. (U.S. Steel raised prices suddenly after Kennedy suggested that they shouldn't. As I recall, he even used the "B" word in describing them.)

The culture of the 1960s, in addition to a tendency to ascribe credence to issues brought forth from individuals of questionable stature, particularly from college campuses, Haight-Ashbury, the Village and the like, brought forth other cultural phenomena that seemed to hibernate for a number of years, only to reappear as mainstream trends in later years.

One of the latter, having automotive implications, was the introduction of the Volkswagen bus from Germany. It introduced the "one cube" noncommercial vehicle to the American public. Although they came and went in limited numbers over a few years, apparently automotive planners noticed in some detail what ordinary people would sacrifice in terms of comfort and styling for the sake of *increased versatile vehicle space.*

Since the 1930s, the industry offered automobiles in primarily "three-cube" vehicles, embodying cubes for engine, passengers and luggage, respectively. Granted, station wagons ("two-cubers") had a following (less than 8 percent of market) but they were built on "three-cube" platforms and didn't allow much additional flexibility or sense of increased space. We'll discuss later how recognition of this feature, and its marketing success, has contributed to the current dilemmas of the U.S. industry.

CHAPTER SEVEN
Frying Pan—1963-1965

On to Montevideo! (Line from Leonard Bernstein's *Candide*.)

I left the GM organization to work for an automotive supplier, American Metal Products, as a salesman in training. At last, I was set partially free in the automotive business.

Let's take a moment to size up the business in 1963. Those American companies making automobiles had been winnowed from over 1,000 during the first two thirds of the 20th century as follows: during the 1950s, Packard, Crosley and Kaiser-Fraser had left the business, leaving, in order of market share, GM, Ford, Chrysler, American Motors and Studebaker. It was pointed out to me that the actual percentage car-market shares resembled a descending geometric series, 50, 25, 12, 6 and 3 percent, respectively. General Motors was actually creeping up when Ford introduced the Mustang. I was led to believe that Chrysler's share was superficially high because of its sales to car rental companies. As I previously mentioned, total volume was about 8.5 million cars (including more than one million Impalas and almost that many Fords)—in addition to one million light trucks.

The companies were usually profitable, somewhat relative to their market share. They were collecting 7 percent of sales excise tax for Uncle Sam under the rules that such tax could not be revealed to the buyer on the sticker or otherwise! This came to an end in the late 1960s but led me to conduct a cursory study of how various modes of transportation contributed to the infrastructure that supported them. As previously mentioned, I concluded that automotive is the only mode of transportation that pays its own way. I think that situation is still the case.[13]

American Metal Products made structural components and seating frame and spring assemblies in Detroit, seating assemblies in Tennessee and truck beds in Louisiana. It later became known as Lear Seigler and then Lear.

---

[13] In the early 2000s the *New York Times* groused that only 20 percent of the Highway Trust Fund was allocated for their subways.

Our products mainly went directly to their assembly plants for installation into vehicles, a small amount were sent to aftermarket operations. Generally, unit price and tooling bids were made for a model year and placed on that basis, expressed as a percent of the specific company's requirement for that model year, with a guarantee of vendor-manufacturing capacity to a higher specific amount. The automakers paid us to make any dedicated and previously quoted new tooling at their expense, for their ownership, and paid upon proof of qualified production of that tooling.

To summarize, the industry usually had three or four suppliers of any given product trying to sell to three or four buyers of that product. In "B" school, they called it a simultaneous oligopoly/oligopsony economic situation, depicting a market with only a few buyers and only a few sellers. As a result, one tried to build up a collegial relationship, or at least a trusting one with certain people that one might or might not select as a friend.

The technological relationship between the vendor and the car manufacturers varied greatly, depending upon the product. On one extreme, the car guys designed the part and requested quotations for eventual manufacture by a vendor. On the other extreme—tires and batteries for example—the vendor was given the performance specifications and he then designed and manufactured the product, shipped it to the car-assembly factories, and even handled the warranty outside of the car-manufacturers' dealer network.

The companies that I worked for made what I would call, "highly engineered products," whereby the vendor's capabilities generally exceeded the customer's in a specific product line. Accordingly, in that profile business it was usually a better strategy to be more competent than your competitors in designing and testing products, suggesting product extensions or new models, and providing input and specifications to be included in the car company's own summary design. The obvious advantage became that your design more closely related to your manufacturing processes than did any other.

While I was happy to understand that most buyer/seller corruption in the industry had been "outed" and solved as a by-product of the quiz show and "Payola" scandals of the late Fifties, of particular help to me was the newly diversified product lines and the inherent complexity they generated in day-to-day business. My understanding was that in historical dealings, an executive from each company would have dinner and negotiate in general the terms and conditions for the next year, the details to be worked out between the respective sales and purchasing representatives. Now, with so many car lines and so many new product introductions, no one executive could keep up with the details, particularly when overseen by the much more sophisticated financial controls introduced by those such as the "whiz kids"—Robert McNamara, Ben Mills and the like. It was my luck that the O.E. (original equipment) salesman that would prosper would be the one that could keep track of the products and the changes therein, could keep his buyer informed about quality issues as they arose, keep track of what the engineers were proposing for the next iterative product design and follow any issues that his company had with the proposed designs.

My company appeared to be on the cusp of recovering from some of the last dealings of the founder. The company had submitted in the early Sixties its seating quotation for the next model of all Ford vehicles, by far the biggest account amounting to about 40 percent of the company's business. While waiting for his invitation to negotiate with his own counterpart over a bottle of fine wine, our founder got a call from Ford's new senior buyer. Such a call was an annoyance, as the upstart wanted to know in hushed tones if our company would consider accepting a contract for 50 percent of the business at the (lower) prices quoted for 100 percent on several of the carlines. The response was, "No, I think I will wait and talk to Ben at the appropriate time."

Several weeks went by and it dawned on someone that "Ben" had not called. Upon inquiry, it was learned that all the new business had been "let" to others and the only business left for the firm was that small fraction manufactured for Ford cars that didn't change configuration for the ensuing model year. The company did salvage some business during "reopened" negotiations, but the volume was way down and the "prices" were less than the previously offered "50 percent of business" level.

Besides seriously damaging the company, the episode taught the very expensive lesson that business in the future will be dispensed based on value, service, quality and diligence as opposed to historical procedures or connections.

In addition to being the negotiator for pricing and other ostensible salesman chores, the "account executive" (which I was to become) was also, theoretically at least, the coordinator of external posture with customer engineering, quality control, material control, product planning, executive contact and quality-recall campaigns with, of course, approval and guidance of management superiors.

My new bosses were excellent teachers and highly regarded in the industry. They let me roam internally for about six weeks and my boss took me to my first account, Chevrolet Gear and Axle, on the East side of Detroit, past the "Hitsville '65" office, down from Northwestern High on Grand Boulevard and the original home of Barry Gordy and the Motown Sound. The reception at Gear and Axle relieved me of the trepidation of being thrown to the wolves. I sequentially met the buyer, the senior buyer and the purchasing agent and all took time to chat a little bit about business, a little bit about family and extend a general welcome. To my boss' credit, from that day on, the account was mine. Never did he call anyone or intercede without my participation, yet he was always willing to discuss problems.

When we had provided extraordinary services during a competitor strike, one of my associates had mentioned to my boss that perhaps I had been too passive when a peripheral player at that customer had tried to weasel during the winding down of shipping requirements. (He was right.) My boss called me into his office, related what he had heard about the meeting in question and asked if I agreed basically with the facts of the meeting as he had heard them? Yes. He first said that this was the one and only time that we would talk about this specific episode, but that one had to take a lot of guff in this business, much of the time deservedly so, as the totality of our company's shortcomings most often fall on our shoulders. Accordingly, when you are right, it is your obligation to yourself and to your company to let the customer know rationally and firmly why your position should be honored, otherwise certain types will always try to use selective memory or other devices to take advantage. People at all levels will respect you for that if you always are truthful and very selectively take this posture. He suggested that I perhaps should have taken a firmer posture in this particular situation, but he then offered that both the customer and company people thought I was doing a very good job. (Note: To his credit he never mentioned this again, but the hierarchy at the customer account rewarded us many times over during the next several years.)

Fast forward eight years. I was by then the sales manager and my salesman had the account. In a social visit I made along with my salesman, the same purchasing agent gave me the high sign, grabbed me by the arm, took me in his office and shut the door.

"You know that job that we negotiated with your company to take that heavy cross-member off our floor and have you manufacture it? As I recall, since we had been running it we knew exactly what the costs were and we negotiated with you to a gnat's eyelash, right?"

"Right."

"It dawned on me the other day that we negotiated with you, shook hands and moved the job. About 60 percent of the cost is steel. Right? Then the steel companies put through a pretty large increase, right? Then Nixon froze the price of everything, leaving you guys holding the bag for the increase in steel, right?" he said.

"Right, but that's the rub of the green, we'll work it out when we can, as we always have," I said.

"I like to stay current on the deals that I make. Why don't you have your guy predate a request for the steel increase, hand deliver it to me and I'll predate a P.O. for a few days after his request?"

As it turned out, interpretations of the "freeze" showed the agent didn't do anything illegal or unethical, yet he took a certain degree of risk during that uncertain time, in order to provide equity. Such actions were not that uncommon in the business as I grew up. It is called a climate of trust and mutual respect. Simultaneous to getting account responsibility, I was given commensurate benefits, including an expense account, a club membership and access to premium tickets for the city's favorites: the Tigers, Lions and Red Wings. What great fringe benefits, I thought. Although these privileges were appreciated over the years, increased business responsibility would create certain tensions when becoming arbiter of who would get what tickets.

Plus, there were considerable demands on my time in conducting an appropriate customer-entertainment schedule. Certain lucky things permitted me to transition into the business fairly easily.

Shortly after I became responsible for the Chevrolet account,[14] one of my new buyers suggested that my dealings at Chevrolet should go smoothly because of my Irish-Catholic background[15] and GM training.

"I'm not Catholic," I responded.

"We don't have to let anyone know, do we?" my new friend replied.

How naïve I was starting out.

I did learn an operating style that both assisted me throughout my career and coincided with my personal leanings. I learned it was always a good idea to do the extraordinary chore for your customers. This would be something having to do with trusting him and accordingly agreeing to some quirky but harmless condition or, even more importantly, putting in a little effort to lessen his workload. I called this the act of earning "chips" that might be "recalled" in emergencies only without compromising honest dealing.

For example, from later in my career I recall the time a Ford buyer called me about 3:45 one afternoon—in quite a tizzy.

"I've been given the assignment of forecasting the price increases on your power-brake product line next year—the added cost of labor and steel. It's due tomorrow morning at 9:00 A.M. I've got to start from scratch and I'll probably be up all night completing this. Whenever an issue like this pops up, you seem to always be on top of it. Would you possibly have any data handy that would help me?"

I told him that he had come to the right place.

"What is the amount of steel price increase that Ford is forecasting as a basis? Okay. As far as our wages go, I'll assume a 3.5 percent increase. Give me about 15 minutes and I'll run these through the good old Riley extrapolator. Oh, by the way, I assume the result you want is the amount

---

[14] One of my bosses suggested that when I walked across Grand Boulevard from the Fisher Building to call on Chevy Central in the GM building, I should look up to the eleventh floor of that building. "Every hour Chevrolet buys enough stuff so that if dollars equivalent to those purchases were piled up, that pile would reach the eleventh floor. I only want this much of that!" simultaneously spreading his thumb and middle finger apart. (I just now calculated, 6"/hr x .0043" /bill x 2080 working hours/year = $2.9 million, remarkably realistic!)

[15] Both of those perceptions were inaccurate. Susie was Catholic, not me, and my father was 1/2 English, my mother was German.

you'll actually pay, rather than the amount I'll request, right? They're created using different formulas, mine being somewhat higher. Right?"

(For perspective, the annualized *increase* being discussed would be about $2 million dollars.)

Sure enough, within 15 minutes I was able to give him his "forecast" of increases due us as a result of the respective changes (as would be calculated by his internal analysts, the level at which we usually settle) for the nineteen part numbers by unit price and by annualized cost using Ford planning volumes. He seemed to be sniffling a little as we hung up the phone, hopefully in anticipation of dinner at home with the family.

Now, in my most bureaucratic moments I would admit that I didn't have the authority to make such a slapdash computation to provide Ford with those numbers. On the other hand, would it have made more sense to let the buyer calculate the numbers, with the chance that he understates them, thereby introducing a new incentive not to honor the real ones when they occur? One tries to do the best one can, whether inside or outside the chain of command.

Regarding gifts to customers, there was a policy that any customer could receive a gift with a value of not more than $25. Through several episodes and many experiences related to me, there seemed to be a phenomenon that when more than a token gift was received, the receiver seemed to have to prove to himself that he was impartial, thereby demonstrating particularly strident postures on normally routine issues. As a result, my posture was to always listen attentively to the customer, as you normally would a friend, present him with an inexpensive phonograph record that his wife coveted but could not find, get hold of a recipe that their favorite restaurant or chef doesn't usually share, write a letter of recommendation for a kid's college application, give the amateur winemaker grapes from your vine, get an underground "fake book" for the dilettante musician. Thus, I attempted to make any gifts of low monetary value, but of high personal and memorial value that would demonstrate a caring and personal relationship.

Even more importantly, I learned to let it be known by your actions that your company, and particularly you personally, are fastidiously truthful and ethical and generally helpful as that is the only long-term characteristic that separates companies.[16]

Riley's second theorem stated that when a new purchasing agent proffered that when you dealt with him over the long haul, you'd learn that he is eminently "fair," hold on to your wallet.

There were yet other benefits. I was established as a businessman around town—just like my father's and father-in-law's friends—because of our mutual business and social endeavors.

One day, I ran into family friend (and eventual Michigan "golfer of the century") Chuck Kocsis in the lobby of Chevrolet purchasing in late morning. Not only was I glad to encounter him, but now it seemed we were on a peer level. As a double bonus, my new "peer" had a world-wide reputation in a reputable and even admirable pastime.

I mentioned to Chuck that I had only one brief call to make and suggested that we have lunch. He offered that he was in a similar situation and that lunch would be great. In those days, the place to have lunch around the GM building—if you weren't an "eating club" member—was Al Greene's across the street in the Fisher Building, which tended to get quite crowded. I suggested we eat there and asked if he had any "connection." The response was negative and that he had eaten there only on rare occasions. No worry, super young exec will handle the situation.

As we left the elevator, I suggested that Chuck stand in the line (Whoops! Long, long line), while I quietly arranged things at the adjacent podium by adroitly approaching and suavely negotiating as appropriate with the maitre d'hôtel. Two things went awry on the way to said podium. First, I couldn't get to it because of the crowd and, second, there wasn't anyone of authority there anyway. On my way back to the line, I started thinking of alternative spots: the Knickerbocker Hotel, Carson's or the pizza place around the corner.

As I returned to the line, the pretentious guy in the tuxedo slowly walking and evaluating the line (acting like Patton reviewing the troops) was just approaching my friend, Chuck. He stopped and enunciated loud enough for the whole line to hear, "Mr. Kocsis, how nice to see you again. In the

---

[16] A similar statement could be ascribed to parents, as opposed to those who manipulate "quality time" and who have sent us some of the current crop. But that's a subject for another book and a half.

future, please have the courtesy to let us know when you've arrived! I almost gave away your table! Right this way! "

As they began walking, the guy, in his most supercilious manner glanced back over his shoulder and said, "Are you with Mr. Kocsis? If so, you may come this way also."

Well, dear reader, forty plus years have passed since then and even yet it would be a stretch to say I've made it to peer level. On the other hand, it's been one hell of a ride.

Perhaps it is time for me to also reveal my "take" on the personalities and operating procedures of the several customer companies. Although I seemed to survive and prosper with all, they all had their own idiosyncrasies.

GENERAL MOTORS

GM was the most organized of the companies. Also, it had the highest-stature personnel up and down the line, and it looked much better from the outside than from the inside.[17]

Purchasing was very professional, and lower-level agents had a surprising amount of authority. Once, a buyer alerted me that I was in danger of losing historic business by admonishing, "Burn the midnight oil. Sharpen your pencil."

My boss and I had lunch with the buyer's superior. We started the story. He asked what his buyer had said. We told him. (Burn, sharpen, give.) We told him the rest of the story. He didn't seem to be reaching for his hanky.

The purpose of the lunch: Did he have words of wisdom about what we should be doing? He did!

"Burn the midnight oil. Sharpen your pencil."

Oh well, it was a pleasant lunch anyway.

The typical GM purchasing guy seemed to get deference while coordinating issues for situations requiring interdepartmental input, which in turn gave deference to specialists in their area of expertise during discussion of proposals and solutions. This led to rational and impersonal conclusions and solutions.

The tendency was to be loyal to quality suppliers—and yet to occasionally market test, when it was obviously a buyer's market or when there was dissatisfaction with a vendor.

---

[17] I later found out that is a usual situation with most companies.

Accordingly, the idea was to buy at rational levels because vendors enjoy medium-level consistent profitability.

FORD

Although purchasing personnel were generally straightforward and courteous, Ford was fraught with prima donnas in many departments. There was a tendency toward internecine disagreement when problem solving should have been the norm.

"The next time that Ford guy tells you to XXX, you tell him to go YYY." There always was a tendency to personalize problems.

To contain costs, they tended to be smitten with analysis rather than market tests. This created opportunities for efficient suppliers (like us) to improve profits.

They were known for waffling on previous verbal agreements, and I soon learned that rather than waiting for Ford to memorialize an agreement in a purchase order or other tangible document, I should write, "To confirm our verbal agreement of yesterday, we agree to XXX and you agree to YYY." And I'd add that if it didn't jibe with our understanding then they should please write, phone, fax, whatever.

CHRYSLER

In spite of considerable executive talent the company seemed to perform at a level less than the sum of its parts.

They were constantly market testing and "cherry picking" in an effort to reduce costs. There was a revolving vendor base. Such a style creates problems when a buyer's market evolves.

Procedural systems were more "loosey goosey." Accordingly, engineers tried to sneak in "midnight" engineering changes for products rather than evaluating and allowing vendors to charge for justifiable cost increases.

In about 1971, I was asked by *Automotive News Magazine* to rate the companies relative to "best" customer for several criteria dealing with modes of doing business. Of 112 respondents, I recall that more than 90 chose GM.

There were also many distressing times. During the last negotiations with UAW #178, Walter Ruether's origins, our company had agreed that the minority of workers known as "skilled trades" be given separate ratification rights on any new contracts. As all boats were rising in those days of the mid-Sixties, this group had become aware that the differential between their rewards and those of the unskilled had been eroding in percentage terms and consequently were taking an adamant stand for recognition on this issue not only with us but with the national union. Such an entitlement clause seemed for the moment, although precedent setting, to be without immediate economic implications and that, in accepting, we thought we would earn a "leather medal" from the national UAW.

During the next negotiation cycle, we had a walkout of short duration (happily from a customer-relations standpoint, with obligatory shipments being more than covered by our inventory buildups) when the negotiating teams arrived at an agreement. Next came the ritual of ratification. Overall, the 2,000 members approved it by about 80 percent. Oops! The skilled guys turned it down something like 47 votes to 32 votes. What was to be done? We turned to the National Union for guidance. They responded, "We're happy with the agreement. Tell the guys to stay at work. Besides, just because they have separate ratification, that doesn't mean they can keep several thousand guys out on the streets."

Our boss responded something like this: "In the first place, we don't think what we say will have any effect on whether they stay or walk out. Secondly, they think their legal rights are exactly that of overriding veto, and we tend to agree."

What was to be done? Upon announcement of the negotiated agreement, the workers had agreed to return, anticipating ratification, and we had restarted the factory. Did we now have to bank the furnaces again? Would they keep coming in, as the national union says, or would the local few insist on another walkout? There was no one to turn to as this was unprecedented, both from the standpoint of what was likely to happen and who were calling the shots.

Finally, after an uneventful week of indecision, our management and the national union jointly recognized that a small but symbolic monetary concession, to the skilled guys only, might kick the can down the road without a lot of economic impact, because of how few employees were involved. Problem solved!

During this period, the U.S.-Canadian automotive trade agreement was negotiated and signed. Heretofore, parts and components destined for manufacturing plants had little or no tariffs, whereas vehicles themselves carried a considerable import tax either way. From a practical standpoint, Canadian automobile manufacturers, then subsidiaries of U.S. companies, for economic reasons had to arrange their product lines for the whole Canadian market and only that market. As a result, I learned at the time that GM Canada was manufacturing the total GM product line, except for Cadillac and Corvette, and a small amount of our GM products were diverted to Oshawa.

Here we're going to use the term "Chinese Fire Drill" (CFD) intended in not a prejudicial manner. In Motown language, CFD means a situation where competent, energetic and fastidious individuals are conscientiously but desperately attempting to fulfill their tasks leading to a final solution or product, but are not provided with the knowledge, material or tools to properly carry out these tasks amidst no coordination; consequently, they have to resort to using trial-and-error methods, as do their cohorts, resulting in a flurry of activity and disorganization with only marginal results, all doing their own thing with the best of intentions. (Note to reader: Please remember this definition, as there are a bunch of CFD's coming up.)

Before the agreement, I understood that GM Canada was and would be expected to be a CFD. On any assembly line would be an Olds station wagon followed by a Pontiac convertible followed by a Buick hardtop. In the U.S., many of the parts for high-volume vehicles would be sourced to several vendors. Accordingly, each vendor would ship to four or five plants. As the U.S. plants would be specialists in their particular carlines, they were able to keep up with incoming quality control, returning outright any parts that they found chronically defective, having enough inventory "float" so as not to disrupt manufacturing schedules. This stuff was known as "red tagged" material. The conscientious vendor replaced it immediately, evaluated the returned material and sorted, reworked or scrapped it and attempted to make amends with the customer.

Obviously, the old GM Canada plant (Oshawa, Ontario) didn't have the luxury of looking at the incoming stuff. Even if they did, they couldn't carry enough inventories of the thousands of diverse parts to return any. I was surprised as one of my buyers expressed his exasperation at hearing that some of his least-conscientious vendors were sending material previously "red tagged" at an American plant to Canada without even having the courtesy of removing the "red tag."

At any rate, the agreement solved many of these problems for the automotive companies and for the overall efficiency of the North American industry, in that Canada was practically able to specialize in vehicles preferred by the Canadian market, importing niche cars as required. A proviso of the agreement, however, obligated the American owners of the companies to ensure that the manufacturing share in Canada would in no instance be less than that which existed upon signing. As those of you statistically oriented already must have noted, to ensure that a series of events never crosses a given threshold, the protocol for those events must be biased away from that line. Given the variations in automotive sales, Canada at that time gained a greater share of North American manufacturing share, as the North American planners had to assure their executives that they wouldn't have to pay exorbitant fines for not living up to the agreement.

Living only several miles from Canada (Detroit looks South on Windsor, Ontario) imparts on one unusual border incidences unknown to the great preponderance of Americans who live hundreds of miles from a national border.

One of my favorite recollections: An associate of mine at the time was a lawyer in the Fisher Building, perhaps four miles from the Ambassador Bridge. One of his workmates asked if he could impose on my friend to run an errand after work. He was having his Maserati repainted and asked if my friend could believe that in the U.S. it would have cost $8,000, but in Windsor a reputable shop would do it for the equivalent of only $4,000?

No problem. He dropped his friend and was heading back across the bridge.

On the Detroit side, "Have you anything to declare?"

"No, sir."

"How long have you been in Canada?"

"Only about 20 minutes."

"What were you doing in Canada?"

"Just dropping off my buddy. He's having his Maserati painted."

"Thank you. Have a good day."

Twenty minutes later comes the buddy in the Masarati.

"Have you anything to declare?"

"No sir."

"How long have you been in Canada?"

"Only about an hour."

"What did you do in Canada?"

"Just seeing a friend."

"Do you have anything to declare?"

"No sir."

"Sir, please get out of the car."

I understand that, as a lawyer, he was smart enough to hire a criminally oriented counsel to defend himself against the accusation that he lied to a T-man while attempting to smuggle about $4,000 of merchandise.

CHAPTER EIGHT
New Boss in Town

There I was, in the mid-Sixties, growing into an interesting and challenging job with attractive perquisites—with loyal employers and a nice family. I'd even gotten somewhat used to the annual new-car start-up frenzy wherein twenty things and demands on one's time borders on being unbearable.

One year during such a frenzy, my boss, on a Wednesday, said, "I've got a meeting with Jamie [THE CHAIRMAN!] next Tuesday. We're going to discuss the content of the data he's going to present at the annual meeting. Would you please work up, as you are skilled in doing, some recommendations as to presentation, style and content?"

Normally a conscientious and ambitious young employee would thank his lucky stars that he was asked to participate and frantically immerse himself in such a request. However on Monday it was apparent that I hadn't had fifteen extra minutes to devote to this project, because I had been consumed with driving to and from places, such was the demand by customers for attention and answers.

I called the boss and confessed my shortcomings.

"I know it's been a frantic start-up," he offered, "do you have ten minutes right now to verbalize how you think your new stuff would deviate from the presentation we made nine months ago?"

Yes. I could do that.

"Thanks, I can finesse my way through that and we'll present the detail later. By the way, can I do anything to lessen your current dilemma?"

"Now that you bring it up, I've got a terrible problem with the Ford guy with that chicken-crap little seat mechanism. Since it's not my regular account, he doesn't seem to trust me, keeps following me around, and insisting that we've got to stop lunch breaks for the workers and stuff like that."

"I'll make some internal calls for info and call the Ford P.A. to get this guy off our back. Don't worry, were almost over the hump."

57

Good boss!

At another time, I was lamenting with one of our manufacturing executives about how our annual "start-up" was persisting way into the fall and into the Christmas holidays. He said that he had been working fifteen-hour days, got home one night at about nine, gulped dinner and was told by his wife that she would put up the decorations on their Grosse Pointe home if he would get the new miniature lights, purchased from another division of the company, to work, as they didn't seem to.

"Here I am," he said, "lying in bed testing these stupid little lights, I'm getting aches in my arms from manipulating them and I don't seem to be getting anywhere. All of a sudden I find myself sobbing with exhaustion and frustration, still trying to get the lights to light so that my wife can do a domestic chore that I should be doing. There's got to be a better way to make a living!"

At this time of my life with pressures growing to secure oneself in a demanding business, one redeeming pleasure was, of course, family. One November evening, after I had had a bad day, I was late and it was sleeting on the drive home. I got to the door and Susan informed me that she was sorry but that she forgot to remind me that it was parents' night at the grade school. She'd go herself but Jennifer was ill and Susan wanted to stay with her.

I took Todd, who was seven (we still held hands in busy places), and we went to the school nearby. I heard that his homeroom teacher was especially good. We entered his classroom. Oops! There were six or eight sets of parents ahead of us. As we sidled toward the our place at the end of the line, I asked him, "Is there somewhere else that we're also supposed to visit?"

"We're supposed to go to the gym. They're having a gymnastic exhibition there."

So we started for the gym, intending to come back later.

Just as we reached the hall, there was a tug on my elbow. It was his teacher, Mrs. Gittens, having excused herself from the line.

"Mr. Riley, I couldn't let you get away without telling you how much I admire the way you are bringing up your children. Let me tell you a story. I'm introducing the kids to musical instruments, only verbally and pictorially, not really my responsibility but something that I think important at this age. We got to the trumpet. I described the instrument and one little girl offered, 'I know of a guy on television who can play the trumpet really, really high. His name is Doc Severinsen.' I was impressed. This girl is being exposed to real things in the world.

"At this point, your son decided to join in. 'Yeah, he can play high, but Doc only screeches out of control in the higher registers. One who really can control it and can improvise at the same time is Maynard Ferguson!' I almost lost it. That and several other episodes like that have convinced me that you have done so much to enrich these kids' lives that you are to be especially commended."

It wasn't such a bad day after all.

Let me bring up one more family experience of a year or so later. Todd, Lauren and Jennifer were now ten, nine and six—and little Julie was 3. We were emerging as a mobile family, able to undertake adventures and entertain similarly configured customer families if Julie was willing to ride on Dad's shoulders.

One Sunday afternoon the Rileys were going to an event without spending any money—as there was not much discretionary money for entertainment. Sounds boring, right? Believe it or not, it was the Count Basie Orchestra playing for the public at Metropolitan Beach. So there! We arrived and there were only about a thousand people—many people were sitting on blankets, or having a picnic, or standing up close to the band. As you might have suspected, your author was an "up-fronter." We could get within three or four people deep from the front, a great place to hear and watch the band. After a few tunes, I decided that Julie and I were going to freelance, her always on my shoulders, and we walked around to the right, up next to the trumpet section.

We stood right next to the fifth trumpeter. In fact, I could read his original one-of-a-kind, manually scripted score along with him. What a thrill for a big band nut! Naturally, I'm swaying along in time with the music and Julie and I are snapping our fingers along with the rhythm. All of a sudden, it's *tacit* on the score for trumpets and our friend the trumpeter noticed the cute little ofay[18] next to him, but she was snapping *on* the beat, really unhip, so he decided to demonstrate the after-the-beat finger snap.

---

[18] A friendly but derogatory aspersion to a white person. The black bands of the day usually had a white person they referred to as this, probably to front for them while traveling in the mid-South.

She made a few efforts to conform, but soon she was back on the beat. He had to start her over again, but it's hard to stop three-year olds once they're started—so he put his hand over hers, firmly yet gently, and coincidentally over my forehead, to get her to reset. This time we were even more animated but, alas, she again resorted to on-the-beat snapping.

At this point we were privileged to get "the look" (famous among musicians) from the Count himself through the crotch of the piano as he was apparently assessing what kind of mischief is happening at the end of his trumpet section. Now, our friend wanted to get the lesson over and done because he's "back in" in about eight bars, so he gave it one more shot. At this point the hand came back, much more firmly but still gently and encouragingly. It's kind of hard to explain, but my knees started to buckle, and for the first time in my life it occurred to me that the Supreme Being might not be Caucasian. We got righted, the hand left and, miracle of miracles, Julie was snapping and swinging off the beat.

I'll bet you're a great teacher, Julie babes, because you learned from the very best![19]

As I have previously mentioned, my bosses and mentors were capable and personable guys; naturally they moved up a notch.

As the remaining marketing operatives consisted totally of several capable but terminally placed veterans and a comparative rookie, me, a new sales manager was hired.

Charlie DeLorean was one of the most mercurial, smart and imaginative persons you could ever meet. His older brother, John had just been made Chief Engineer of Pontiac, under "Bunkie" Knudsen. An uncle had taken the four DeLorean brothers under his wing and encouraged them to learn everything they could about automobiles and to educate themselves to advance their careers in the industry.

My one minor apprehension on being introduced to all 6' 4" of Charlie and working with him for a week or so was that, as colorful and insightful as he seemed to be, one couldn't be certain if his "act" was one of "façade" or one of "sincerity," a quandary others had with me early on, or so I've sensed later in my career. Charlie was well liked throughout the industry and his access to influential people was undoubtedly further enhanced by his brother's position and reputation.

As soon became apparent, Charlie was "real" although remarkably knock-about, to such an extent that one encountering him daily had to pace oneself to his idiosyncratic demeanor. Traveling with him for more than two days was a "trip" in more ways than one. He continually had airline,

---

[19] Julie is now in her 40s and is literacy coach at Hong Kong International School.

restaurant, hotel employees, policemen, boarder patrol, T-men and office managers shaking their heads as to what they should be doing, other than laughing.

They sent Charlie to wander around the company for several weeks. One day he said to me, "Why don't we go see the guys at Fisher Body?"

I briefed him that we had one ongoing project for a seat recliner in their advanced engineering, but that their basic seats were mostly integrally manufactured, other than for a few special models that were already tooled at one of our competitors. I'd been keeping my eye on things, as recently as a ten-days-prior visit, but couldn't be optimistic on our chances for doing a lot of business there in the near future.

"I want to let guys know where I am. I'll make a date and we'll go out there."

A week or so later, we had a date to see Slim, chief body engineer of Fisher Body Division and my former corporate great-great-grandfather.

Huge but sterile office.

"Hi, guys. I've learned that I'm supposed to have purchasing involved when we deal with new potential suppliers, so I have the purchasing agent joining us in a minute."

Greetings all around. Brief small talk about Michigan weather and so on. Charlie got down to business.

"The Budd Company was a good company, but I wanted to find a place that offered products with more proprietary content, where we could contribute more than just being competent metal benders and welders. Not only does it seem more satisfying that one has the sense of contribution and happy customers but, frankly, those products tend to be more profitable for the company. I've spent a couple of weeks just learning the products and capabilities of my new company with an eye for what might be a 'fit' and, to be honest, I couldn't get you guys out of my mind."

The purchasing agent inserts that no one at Fisher wants to look at anything that's not patented. We say we understand. (A story for another day.)

Charlie continued: "It occurred to me during my initiation period that if we were to combine our expertise with yours, we might not be able to revolutionize the industry, but we might be able to make the driving experience a whole lot more pleasurable, particularly from the body-interior standpoint."

Our hosts were beginning to exhibit some interest and I was dying to hear what this obviously gifted pitchman had up his sleeve.

"How so?" Slim asks.

Ten-second pregnant silence.

"Tell 'em, Bob."

Ten seconds of really, *really* pregnant silence followed by about three minutes of almost incomprehensible blather about our innovative invention of the six-way power seat (really old news) and other stuff culled in panic from my recollections. There was an occasional pause, with no help arriving from Charlie or others. I couldn't wait to be somewhere else.

Finally, Charlie winds it up: "Thanks for taking our meeting, fellas. I'll tell John you're committed to sending quality bodies for his nifty new Pontiacs. We'll keep in touch!"

Never was there a follow-on discussion about the Fisher Body meeting. I soon made some deductions. The meeting wasn't to sell them or introduce the Fisher executives to anything. That was a meeting that Charlie concocted to teach Bob he must be prepared to take over any meeting at any moment. That was a meeting for Bob to understand that it surely would be a good idea to prepare pertinent material for an upcoming meeting, even though he's not on deck to speak. During the drive over, it was unforgivable for Bob not to initiate a discussion about the content of the proposed meeting and make an offer to contribute. I learned I was not there to be entertained or to be an honored guest. You know what? The lesson was probably learned better than any lecture he might have otherwise given, undoubtedly enhanced by the terror inflicted and by the elaborate props and extras utilized in the process.

If you were into mind games, Charlie was the Will Shortz of the art. He taught me, when entertaining at golf or other games, the best policy was to negotiate easy when establishing the rules of competition, but to play like a demon in an attempt to overcome the slightly unfavorable rules.

"They respect you that way!"

He was right. I subsequently heard clients demean salesmen who "go in the tank" during competitions, thereby diminishing any pleasure of spending discretionary time with them.

Aha, you're asking, how did Charlie behave while playing social or customer golf, in many people's opinion the ultimate opportunity for mind games?

Let me digress for a minute. Oswald Jacoby, probably the world's all-time best card player said of poker players, "Ten percent of players play exactly like they think. They soon give up the game attributing the unfavorable results to bad luck. Eighty-five percent of players play exactly like they don't think. These comprise the preponderance of players who tend to be small losers. Then there's that five percent that you can't tell how they're playing or how they're thinking. Those are the guys you have to watch out for."

I've made an analogy to social golf behavior wherein 10 percent don't understand the mental component of the game, 85 percent of players understand that there is such a component and consequently attempt to "talk to you" without you suspecting that they are. (They aren't.) At the top of the heap are those 5 percent who instill confusion and agita upon you without you ever suspecting.

Charlie, so far as I could tell, didn't have a conscious plan for throwing opponents off, but he was constantly as jocular and animated as ever, causing a person to wonder aloud how one could play decent golf (mid-80s) without having to concentrate. In one such instance, I overheard him mumble, "It doesn't take that long to concentrate on any one shot." I think I was catching on. From absolute hilarity, before each shot he would suddenly take about twenty or thirty seconds of intense concentration, hit the shot and make funny comments before he even unwound his follow through. I think I've discovered his mantra: Snap into intense but brief concentration for each shot and everyone will marvel that you never seem to have apprehension or concern during your round. How can this valuable information be used to my advantage? We jointly entertained at golf about eight or ten times a year and always in opposition, each with one of the clients.

A story—

We were on the fifth hole at Oakland Hills[20] that abutted Lahser Road when I was preparing to hit a shot from the fairway for which I had some confidence (must have been a layup) when I noticed a Peterbilt truck coming

---

[20] A most difficult hole where T. C. Chen lost his lead at the National Open years later by, among other things, double hitting (two strokes with one swing) out of the green-side rough and taking a snowman, e.g. an 8 on a par 4. This occurs occasionally in deep grass, where one hits the ball and it struggles so much to get airborne, that your club hits it again, waist high, during the follow through.

north. I addressed the shot, felt a degree of comfort, and said, "We're now standard seating on Peterbilt." And "thwap," hit a fairly decent shot. Charlie didn't make much noise but you could tell he was agitated.

"Why in the hell would anyone want to hit a golf shot without taking any time to concentrate?" he mumbled.

I think I was on to something. I put it in my repertoire. I had to memorize a few trivial phrases to use: "I haven't noticed any worms. The ground must be moist." Thwap. "That moss seems to be growing on the north side of the tree." Thwap. My technique seemed to be working as his degree of angst seemed to rise in direct proportion to the quality of shot I hit.

Charlie instilled in me and other young people who would listen the perils of our chosen occupation. The first one I recall was that in our business there were more people with alcohol problems than any other profession. If one had a penchant for it, that person could rationalize that he was obligated to take customers to lunch (true) but needn't continually select those customers who enjoyed three Manhattans in the process. A lack of a likelihood of being detected and stigmatized perhaps added to or enabled the problem because companies often arranged their offices so that salespeople could come and go so that other employees wouldn't covet the freedom from office routine that salesmen needed. This advice didn't particularly interest me personally, as it wasn't my custom and the few times that I did have more than one Tom Collins at lunch I felt as though I needed a nap at three in the afternoon.

Lo and behold, several years after Charlie had gone, I was vigilant enough to suspect I had such a problem in my own department. The personnel department adroitly handled it at my request and the case was closed with minimal disruption to operations because of Charlie's forewarning.

The second piece of advice was that one doesn't dip one's pen in company ink. In this context, "ink" isn't something that you buy at Staples. I didn't see much of this but I did have one undetected liaison in my department that was resolved on reasonable terms.

The one most impressed on my memory was that if one stumbles upon or has otherwise been knowingly exposed to a human frailty of a boss, then one doesn't just try to forget about the whole episode, but, instead, one does convince oneself that such event never occurred.

We had a "wood products" plant in Arcadia, Louisiana,[21] that assembled truck beds for Ford and GM. The main component was southern yellow pine, the specifications for which caused it to be a by-product of the milling process for the principal use of such lumber. The market for pickup trucks happened to be booming in the mid-Sixties and the Vietnam war was upsetting supply lines via its voracious need for southern pine for shell cases. Normally, when one manufacturers a product, one tends to have increased leverage with its supplier as the requirements for a commodity increases, often even leading to modest price decreases. Since our requirements for southern pine were subordinated to requirements of others, we were obligated to secure product from an ever-increasing number of suppliers at an ever-increasing distance from our factory and at ever-increasing costs. As the profitability of the end product was quite high, we were willing to proceed with no strings attached, but our limited local staff had to put in endless hours ensuring that we could secure enough lumber to keep us ahead of our obligations.

Once the crunch was over, the Detroit home office decided to honor the staff in Arcadia and its suppliers by going there and planning a "recognition weekend" in March of 1966. Attending from the "corporate" office would be the group vice-president of operations and his wife, our division president (who we'll call "Mr. Smith"), Charlie as vice president of sales and myself as the primary account manager for this product line and "hod carrier" for purposes of the trip. Charlie asked if they could recommend golfing for the two of us, and one of the vendors got us privileges at Shreveport Country Club. Although we were nominally hosts for this shindig, all the arrangements were made locally, and so our responsibilities amounted to general glad-handing, a few words here and there and staying out of trouble. Although I was increasingly considering myself a somewhat sophisticated and well-traveled businessman, a trip like this would be unusual as 90 percent of automotive business was done within 90 miles of Detroit. So it looked like a fun trip!

We left on a Thursday in late morning. The trip was two stops on prop planes, including one plane change. Smith quickly used his allocation of beverages and so we had to smuggle a few to him, a little awkward but no problem, but the trip seemed interminably long. We finally landed in

---

[21] Ten miles from where Bonnie and Clyde were gunned down by the feds.

Shreveport, rented a car and a reservation had been made at one of the better restaurants down on the riverfront, providing a really pleasurable meal, although it was getting late and I thought how great it would be to get to our hotel.

Charlie, always on the cusp of driver's license problems because of his aggressive (but extremely expert) driving, then announced that he had had one too many glasses of wine. Perhaps Bob should drive. No problem. The three of us left.

Charlie was in the jump seat as navigator, and announced, "I'll try to remember how to get out of this riverfront neighborhood, it's kind of tricky but I think I can even remember a shortcut. Drive slowly up this access road and I'll tell you when to turn left. It's only a few hundred yards. Turn here! Now!"

I dutifully turned and get one car length out of the opening and *smash*— I got hit left front by a single car.

Thankfully, no one was hurt, the police came and I hadn't had too much to drink, the report was written and we were free to go. Was the car drivable? The corner of the wheel opening was touching the tire. Charlie and I tried to pry it loose. Not even close to being separated. Could the car be driven as is? We decided to try. How far did we have to go? Only about eight miles. We proceeded across the river to Bossier City, noted for its hospitality to the U.S. military nearby, although the car was making a hell of a racket and rubber smelling smoke was spewing forth, approximately proportionate to our speed.

"No problem. All we have to do is limp home and we'll have a new car delivered in the morning."

"Let's stop in one of these road houses and have a nightcap" suggested Smith.

Remember, I'm the hod carrier. It's not just a suggestion. Besides, I could have used a drink and listened to a jazz pianist, which is what I tried to convince myself of after the disconcerting episode. We pulled over and went in. There was no jazz pianist, only country music. More disconcerting, to me at least, was that we were immediately met by "hostesses." Introductions were made all around and we were ushered over to the bar.

"Your hands are so soft and smooth," she offered.

Although I was trying to be ahead of the curve as Charlie suggested by his Fisher Body demonstration, I was not actually prepared for this. I made some comment that I didn't have to use my hands for a living, or some such uplifting statement. The other guys seemed cool. How long do we have to stay here, I thought.

We were there about ten minutes, finished our drink and Charlie offered, "Gee, it's been a long week. I think we'll excuse ourselves and come back during the weekend."

Smith wanted to talk to Charlie.

Charlie came back upbeat and announced, "It's been great! But Bob and I are dead tired. See you later."

As we headed for the door, Pearl, the "hostess" with Smith said, "Don't worry, I'll take good care of him."

I don't know what Charlie's proclivities were, but I think he read my discomfiture and orchestrated the exit. Forever, he will be a hero to me. The little "talk" between Charlie and Smith had to do with Smith touching Charlie for $50. Shocking, but no matter, as there were only six miles to a clean warm bed if we could make it.

I discovered that about 17 mph was the optimum compromise between us moving forward at all and the car tending to tear itself apart. It was about 1:00 A.M. in the morning (2:00 A.M., Detroit time) and it would only take about twenty minutes at our selected speed. Finally, a hundred yards on the left was our Holiday Inn, a miraculous sight. When we got within about thirty yards we could make out that there were messages on the marquee. As we got to twenty-five yards we could make out the top line in the largest letters. It said "Welcome Mr. Smith." At that point, we both lost it.

Charlie yelled, "Pull over. You'll kill us both. You're losing it!"

For the first and only time in my life, I thought I might expire through laughter-induced asphyxiation.

After about three minutes, Charlie offered, "Gee, is Pearl going to be impressed!"

We must have sat there for about ten minutes, the combination of exhaustion, a drink or two, and the implausibility of the whole situation combined into spasms of hysterical laughter.

In minutes eleven and twelve, as I was restarting the car and trying to make the last twenty-five yards, Charlie was reminding me that the events of the night didn't really happen, and he asked that I promise him that I never saw the whole episode.

Charlie called Hertz in the morning and said, "That car you rented us last night. It got smashed. How soon can you deliver a new car for us? By the way, I hope it has a better air conditioner than the one we have. That'll be fine."

Subsequently, the trip turned out to be much like we planned, but exhausting. We played 36 holes on Saturday. We skipped lunch on Sunday so we could play 27 and still catch what turned out to be our first ride on a commercial jet plane. As we were playing the last few holes, Charlie was debriefing.

"I think it did some good for morale down here. I want to debunk what I think are their notions that we kind of leave them on their own and that we really are only concerned that their monthly submission of profit is as promised. Remember, this is still kind of a different culture. We're still referred to as Yankees. As for the golf, I really got a kick when you hit your wedge over the outhouse to two feet from the pin, only to miss the putt. It sure has been great getting some fresh air and sun on the body. Thursday night, on the other hand, was something else! What was the name of that broad we left Smith with?"

"Pearl."

"You stupid, stupid bastard! How many times do I have to tell you—"

One couldn't help but learn quite a bit. Charlie's serious moments seemed to come at the end of the workday as we would reconnoiter in one or the other's office during "animal feeding time" at our respective homes (together we had four kids under six). He nominated me and secured for me a company sponsorship to the MBA executive program conducted by Michigan State. Even though it would somewhat complicate life for the family and me for two years, we were approaching likely obligations for kiddies' activities and it was best to get it out of the way now.

Also, I was promoted to sales manager under Charlie's watch, however I later found out that, although he didn't disagree, the result was officially ordained in other offices.

That was Charlie. As he was leaving the company to take over his Cadillac dealership, I finally got up the nerve to ask him, "Did you ever get your four bits back from Smith?"

One last pearl of wisdom, "That's the only circumstance where you're entitled to fudge on your expense account."

69

I always admired Charlie's wife, Shirley, who was also a fun person and must have had the patience of Job. For perhaps twenty years, when Charlie encountered a pianist in a restaurant (not unusual in those days) he would ask him to play, "Do You Know What It Means To Miss New Orleans," his favorite song. Unfortunately, for those same twenty years that song was on popularity hiatus, similar to *It's a Wonderful Life*, the movie, during the mid-Fifties through the mid-Seventies. At any rate, over the years he requested the song dozens of times and *never* did anyone know it. As several of us were preparing to visit him after an official call nearby many years after he left, I thought that a nice "remembrance" token might be a "lead sheet" for "Do You Know What It Means," of which I made about a dozen copies from one of my "fake books." I understand that for the next couple of years, when entering a restaurant or club, Charlie would surreptitiously hand the pianist a piece of paper. Sometime later, he would excuse himself to make a musical request.

"If it is what I think it is, you're wasting your time and your energy," Shirley would suggest to Charlie and subsequently explain the situation to whomever they were with. All of a sudden, all of the pianists could play "Do You Know What it Means." Baffling! After twenty-four consecutive turndowns, there were seven-in-a-row performances. I'll bet Charlie never let on.

CHAPTER NINE
Disdain for Conglomerates

During my early years as an account manager at American Metal Products (AMP), a son of one of the founders—himself a former corporate vice-president and one who felt scorned of chairmanship when he had thought his time had come—left to join a group of "investors" (Parsons Group). AMP itself had a profitable core business, but several misjudged major programs had been holding down earnings and the resulting share price. Surprise! The Parsons Group, after getting control of Commonwealth Bank which became the center of operations, and making a couple of forays into some small manufacturing companies, thought AMP was undervalued and wanted to take over. After the expected rejection of an offer, a proxy fight ensued which, although they weren't unheard of in the mid-Sixties, were fairly rare.

There were very public charges and countercharges, as the combatants were known in business and social circles and they were competing for the same shareholders (for perspective, our company was about number 500 in the Fortune 500). After a few weeks of this, it became apparent that we probably wouldn't remain as an independent company, and that we were *in play.*

The reason this sticks with me is that several months later I heard that all customers were with great interest monitoring our dilemma of being *in play,* with the outcome or even the continuity of our company uncertain. I further learned that GM, otherwise barred by Washington from expanding their empire through acquisition, had drafted a proposal to the federal government requesting they be permitted to make an offer to acquire some segments of our company, offering to immediately resell or otherwise divest itself of most of it, retaining only what was necessary for their manufacturing of heavy vehicles, undoubtedly some of which had national-defense implications.

To save you the sordid details (admittedly the best kind), AMP was taken over by Lear Siegler, a conglomerate company put together by one John Brooks, who scratched together enough funds to acquire the Siegler Heating

Company, a modestly sized maker of Franklin-type stoves, leveraging that to purchase the entrepreneur Bill Lear's aeronautical-instruments business and quite a few other companies. In those days, one suspected that these bosses' "business religion" was more about the conglomerate concept than about the products or the businesses in their portfolio. Then, a "conglomerate" was defined as a company that owned an ever-increasing "portfolio" of companies in unrelated industries that, at least theoretically, demonstrated continual growth and prosperity through the contra-cyclical nature of its businesses, thereby supporting its stock price, thereby making it easy to print more stock to buy more companies.

Mr. Brooks himself was a most impressive figure (think Arnold Palmer), situating the corporate office at the Santa Monica airport, only steps from the corporate jet which took him away for more than half of the year. In addition to visiting his operations and "conglomerating," he loved to play honorary host at corporate gatherings of those internal disciplines that had the most public or employee exposure, namely marketing, purchasing and personnel. His typical trip would begin with a visit to his company or companies that were in the area. At night he would host dinner for the twenty or thirty attending the meeting and then open his suite for a couple of hours. The most interesting aspect of this was that *no intermediate bosses were permitted*. He wanted to press the flesh, tell stories and spend a "boys night out" without the bosses inhibiting the conversations or listening to see if their subordinates are telling tales out of school.

My experience as a twenty-something was an instance in which I was in a group talking to Mr. Brooks and several other peer sales managers from other divisions. One of the guys tripped over his tongue while referring to one of those recurring business phrases. As is my wont, in an attempt to lessen his embarrassment and to relieve the tension, I suggested that he was impersonating Robert Goulet singing the national anthem at the Cassius Clay fight of several years before. (I think it was with Sonny Liston whom Clay [soon Ali] upset to become world champ). Goulet, a Canadian, never realized he didn't know the words until he needed them with about a billion people watching or listening—the humiliation of a lifetime. Chairman Brooks said that he hated to interrupt what we were talking about, but he had a relevant story that he was dying to share with us. The year before he was in the corporate box at Dodger Stadium, when they were only a few games away from clinching the pennant, when down the aisle right in front of him sidles

Mr. Goulet, with no apparent destination. He admitted that he didn't know the singer well but, from the golf club, he's on a first-name basis. Goulet went over to Brooks and started a little small talk, although was preoccupied looking towards the field.

"John, do you know which box is [Dodger owner] O'Malley's?" Goulet asked.

"Right over there. Do you know him?"

"No, but you read and hear so much about him, he must be an interesting guy."

"He is. C'mon, I'll introduce you to him."

They walked.

"Walter, I've got a friend who would like to meet you."

Walter made the immediate connection, and looked frantically to his right.

"Oh, damn, you must have missed the Missus by less than two minutes. No real matter, I'm sure you'll let me introduce you to her some time in the future. Absolutely, no BS, you're her favorite singer in the world. Boy, is she going to be disappointed!"

He was quiet for a moment then his eyes lit up.

"Wait a minute! What a wonderful coincidence! I think we're going to make it to the World Series. Would you please sing the Star Spangled Banner at the opening game?"

There ensued indecisive mumbling. O'Malley didn't follow boxing, didn't know about the unfortunate episode about Goulet and the National Anthem. Brooks told Goulet that as they walked away. Goulet was grumbling that when you go out of your way to meet a guy who's reputation you respect, you wouldn't expect him to try to humiliate you within seconds of shaking hands by bringing up the most embarrassing moment of your life, even though he supposes it was somewhat topical and ironic in that context.

Did Brooks ever convince the singer that the invitation was heartfelt and unrelated to the "episode"? Did Goulet sing? I never did research it, as it would be anti-climactic.

How did the new management affect my business life? Good and bad. Mostly bad. I was slated to be one of the next general managers, even to the extent that I visited a designated division, Vac-U-Lift, with the group general manager, who said to be prepared, that there might be some consideration of selling off the business; but when the appointment happened, as it probably

73

would, I should be ready to take over. This was in April of 1970. I got Susie to emotionally sign on to the idea of moving, but, of course, asked her not to speak of it elsewhere. About July she gently prodded me that although she understood that these things work in mysterious ways, she would like to know whether to renew school-calendar-related events, kiddies' symphony, dance lessons and so on. Thank heavens I told her to proceed as usual.

In early fall, I drove to a meeting at the suburban Birmingham Group office. As we were gathering, Mr. Peppler, my earlier escort to the proposed factory and now Group VP, stuck his head in and asked me to please stop by on my way out. I was somewhat distracted during the meeting as I was thinking that this is an awkward time to make the move, it was new-model start up at my current division and the kids have started a new year in school, but what the hell, it's a significant career move.

That evening when I got home a little early, Susie naturally commented, "I didn't expect to see you home so soon."

"I had a meeting at the group office in Birmingham."

"Wait a minute, I've got to refill the troughs."

Later she asked, "How did it go?"

"Routine. Incidentally, John Peppler stuck his head in the door, pointed at me and said he would like to see me after."

"Yeah? Yeah?"

"The meeting went a little long, but he was still there."

I was having some of my sadistic fun.

"Yeah? Yeah?"

"I didn't get to his office until just now, about 4:00 P.M., just a few minutes ago."

"Yeah? Yeah? What did he say?"

"He wanted to know if I'd ever heard back about that job in Illinois. It got reorganized out from under him and he lost touch. If I hadn't heard anything by now, it's probably a dead deal."

No hesitation at all.

"Did you strangle him?"

The most pertinent point was that they were bringing in a new crew. My one remaining previous mentor who was again, after my promotions, my immediate boss, was replaced with a guy from the original company, AMP, a former personnel director. We now reported to the Canadian guy who told us to operate as usual, but don't do *anything* that would have an effect on the

Canadian business. We had about 45 percent of the newly opened "North American" market for independently supplied seating. Our Canadian operation had about 7 percent. That's about like saying to Coke to do anything it wants so long as it doesn't have any effect on Nehi. How is that possible? To top it off, the Canadian guy then hired an old timer industry "glad-hander" to "help" with marketing for all of the automotive stuff.

Even understanding that my boss didn't have much familiarity with product, pricing, procedures and the like, he didn't seem to be too interested in what we were doing, seemingly more in what he could report to the many bosses. He even abandoned a small but profitable product line for aerospace because he felt he couldn't talk intelligently to the bosses about that product line. I mentioned that tendency to a former AMP executive that I ran into at a Conference Board Seminar.

"Of course," he responded, "haven't you been watching the behavior of your company, Lear Siegler? Of the last eleven guys promoted to general manager, nine of them have roots in personnel, where normally they would come from marketing, engineering or finance. You know why?"

I shook my head.

He spoke something along these lines: "First of all, they don't have any tracks, they've never done anything, good or bad. They're not biased on how the business should be conducted. More importantly, these general managers understand that in very few other companies could they rise to such a lofty position, a very potent incentive not to ignore or try to circumvent the edicts passed down from Santa Monica or Birmingham, as some of those *Motown Guys* try to do."

Let me demonstrate the cloak-and-dagger aura that surrounded the new organization. As Charlie had earlier taught me, every year I took a clean sheet of paper and imagined that it represented 100 percent of the seating market. I then went through carline by carline, model by model of the North American market and ascribed amongst the six or seven suppliers their captured business. The last 20 percent was the hardest, but that probably was the area where several nuggets could be found. The idea was not to rest until you were satisfied that the information was as complete and accurate as you could make it without pulling a Watergate on your competitor's offices. Seemingly a handy tool, what?

This particular year I sent a completed study to the usual operatives, and I decided to include my Canadian boss and associates as we'd been told that any "competition" was past history. I later realized that just the act of adding them to the mailing list and including their information in what I thought was helpful "information only" data, somehow suggested that I was usurping the sovereignty of the Canadian operation and attempting to demean their ability to create their own marketing information. The next time I sat with my two immediate bosses, not a common occurrence, it was suggested that such compilation was probably not such a good idea for several mumbled reasons, none of which made sense to me.

My favorite story about this gang was that the Canadian boss, and for that matter my own immediate Detroit boss, had never been to Chrysler. My boss thought it was important that the new Canadian boss had a symbolic meeting with the historic and legendary purchasing agent of our products, "Bud" Quinlan. An irreverent and hearty sort (think Anthony Quinn with, I might add, the body of Casey Stengel). He, for instance, had a fake plastic urinal on his office wall.

We set up a lunch at the Caucus Club in the Fisher Building for the meeting of the titans; there were about six of us. The meeting was uneventful but cordial and toward the end the Canadian boss leaned toward me and shared in a soft conversational tone, "We spent a long weekend at our place in Palm Desert. The weather was great and Andy [Williams] and Claudine were there, two doors down."

Now, that he wanted to share his personal experiences with me was about as normal as would be the Pope asking me whether it would be better to beatify Pope John or absolve the wayward American priests. I think it was so obvious that Bud was instantly prepared.

"You got a place in Palm Desert?" Bud asked.

"Yes, over by the ___. Have you ever been there?"

"Oh, yeah, many times."

"What do you think of it?" (He was the perfect straight man for Bud!)

"Well y'know, they built all those superhighways and interchanges around Palm Springs and they had all these piles of crap left over. They finally leveled it all off and called it Palm Desert."

My memory goes blank from there, other than remembering the two "suits," whose "brainstorm" it was to have the Canadian boss spend some "quality" time with our purchasing agent, became visibly agitated, undoubtedly because they would be fingered as exposing their mutual boss to obvious embarrassment. On the other hand, I would probably have laughed at

Bud's comments, and they may well have later put the finger on me in private.

Another higher-level mentor not only survived the new regime, but also prospered, being promoted to a group vice president and then a corporate vice president. Because of his talent and experience he deserved it. But I later discovered, somewhat to my disappointment, that such treatment was typical of conglomerate strategies, targeting a talented upper-middle executive who fit their operating style and giving him greater responsibility as a symbol to the newly acquired hired help that the new company consists of other than totally cretin marauders.

Typically within an "Operating Group" of a conglomerate were two types of general managers running the individual businesses: (1) Those guys who were just given a substantial sum in exchange for the new operating division, permitting them to "cash in" on their life's work, and (2) professional managers.

Each organizational "group" seemed to have four or five professional managers and two or three former entrepreneurs. I had a chance "one on one" encounter with this former "big boss," obviously a professional manager and now a group vice president who was lamenting how awkward some of the situations were with subordinate general managers who were former owners of what were now company divisions. In the most interesting one, he described how he had a potential transportation problem getting from one event to the other at one of the group or corporate large meetings.

"No problem," offered his new subordinate, "I'll send my captain with the boat to pick you and your wife up at 6:45 P.M."

Problem solved? Not quite. Marilyn needed confirmation that Bill really did work under her husband, Dave. (He did.) If so, shouldn't they have a larger boat, with a captain *and first mate?*

Same boss, different subordinate. The group's controller tweaked the division general manager that he hadn't been receiving approved expense accounts. That general manager then called his new boss, Dave.

Dave represented to me that his conversation with that GM went something like this.

"There's no way you are going to see my expense accounts. That was one of the main parts of the deal when your company acquired us a year and a half ago. Get this accountant off my back!"

"Just to keep good order, why don't you have your secretary cover up the expense accounts, except where I sign. I'll sign it sight unseen and turn over to the controller so that he can keep track of costs and budget for the future."

"You're not listening! No way are you going to have access to my expense accounts. That was part of the deal."

Dave looked at me, smiled, shrugged his shoulders and said he would just have to wait and see what happened, but he sure hoped that whoever negotiated this as a condition of the deal was still with the company.

Another conglomerate phenomenon: In the Sixties, there was a student at University of Detroit who studied computer science which was then in its embryonic stage. He showed considerable promise and, as a result, the University suggested upon his graduation, as it had decided to outsource the computerization of its business accounts, that he might be interested in getting "seed money" to establish a "computerized data processing" company to handle the University's accounts, and be able to supplement this with other commercial accounts. Of course he would be interested. He established a company and got four or five other accounts, including ours, in short order.

Now, conglomerates were always on the lookout for acquisitions and accordingly told its far-flung employees to be on the lookout for prospects, the criteria mainly being that such company should serve or participate in markets that are believed to have above-average growth. Obviously, it didn't take a Rhodes Scholar to deduce that such a company might interest our acquisition team, and the individual ponying up that gem might get himself, but probably not *herself* in those days, on a fast track.

It was nominated and the deal was struck within months. As I recall, the guy was about 27 years old and the strike price was about 7 big ones (about $35,000,000 in today's dollars), and he didn't come with the company.

Six months later, I happened to be sitting at the white-collar dining room at the company where some of the guys from the front office were lamenting their lot, along these lines:

"That Larry who sold us the company, he wasn't so smart. He never even provided for [computer gibberish]! When you decide you want to [computer mumbo jumbo] you're going to have to transcribe the data by [unintelligible computer speak]. In fact, he wasn't smart at all. I understand all of his former customers are having problems similar to ours. They probably will eventually integrate their data processing, while we, as corporate brothers, will be stuck with their lousy service. No, he was a dimwit."

Since these guys were no further up the food chain than I, I didn't have to bite my tongue (I probably couldn't have anyway).

"I certainly can commiserate with your frustrations. I've had data-processing problems in my own department, but that's only a small element of our business. What I do want to mention is that a reasonable person might question your assessment of Larry as 'not very smart.' Who's bought and is developing a major league soccer team for Detroit? Who's bought a new house in Grosse Pointe and a new yacht? Who doesn't have to go in the office every day? On the other hand, who's stuck with a below-state-of-the art data-processing company? Who's smart and who's not very?"

In 1971, the automotive division was having a pretty good year. We had our solidified pricing before the notorious "price freeze" and the customer orders were holding up. In about April, we were told that the rest of the company, the aerospace segment, was having an abysmal year. We were the last hope of the company having a year that wouldn't incite investors to bail out (the beginning of the end for many conglomerates). Accordingly, the division staff (there were eleven of us) took a detailed look at "run-out" (end of June) and nominated actions to be taken to maximize our contribution to corporate profit. Obviously, these had to be short term and preferably legal. Capital outlays could be deferred, and perhaps plausible adjustments could be made with "fast pencil" financial adjustments, but the opportunity to "manage" profit[22] by companies who primarily manufacture is somewhat limited. (Come to think of it, we did change from LIFO to FIFO to make a one-time "cash-in" on the cheaper "first in" inventory layer.)

Since the cash goes out through purchasing and comes in through sales, these two departments would be the most able to contribute, by arranging for unusual transactions, generally with purchasing attempting to "push back" billings from vendors and sales attempting to "push ahead" billings to customers. As sales director, I was able to pony up about fifteen items and found it would be quite easy to fulfill them, as a few of them were meant only to secure the customer's agreement that they would receive the product a few days earlier than usual, with no impact on their payment schedule. I even think I had a few "chips" left over. Assuming that everything was done according to the book—the only long-term implications were that profits were being pulled forward from the following year.

---

[22] I later refer to this as "cooking."

In addition to studying the profit outlook to determine how it might be improved, we were permitted to study the bonus pool, for how that was formulated relative to profits. The latter study demonstrated considerable personal incentive to fulfill the prospective program. Well, we were quite successful and were acclaimed "Division of the Year." When it came time to pay bonuses, however, a "problem" arose. How could the company pay us bonuses amounting to about half of salary, when most of the company's employees were getting at best only nominal bonuses? We got about 40 percent of that promised at the division level.

One of the criteria for survival of a conglomerate is its ability to generate an improving profit scenario despite the vicissitudes in certain markets or, for that matter, in the economy as a whole. As previously described, the early 1970s were difficult business years. Our strategy was, as a conglomerate, to grit our teeth and forbear. When business receded in general, profits for most companies decreased, wherein our profits remained constant. (This is an example of "cooking!") As a reward, our stock value declined less than the typical company. How did we do that? You've just had an example. During the process, it was rumored that the normally ebullient and optimistic Chairman Brooks morphed into a tyrant. As with: "Anyone who is doubtful that we can't reach the displayed profit goals, please leave the room."

As usual, the business cycle turned around, followed by improved outlook and real profits at most companies. They were rewarded as the stock market favorably responded. Using the same techniques as above, with ever more difficulty, we kept our profits constant. The market expected our profits and outlook to rise. Accordingly, our stock didn't rise with the rest of the market.

Finally, business activity in general got back to the trend line. Profits generally were also tracking at these levels. Unfortunately, we had "swept out all the corners" and our profits started in modest decline. Share values nosedived! Strategically, we should have been husbanding potential earnings when the market wasn't responding, exposing these only so they would be afforded market recognition. For example, my own college fund (pre 401K) had a stock value of 3 5/8, wherein my own personal cost was 11 3/8.

A doubly sad event during this activity was the demise of Mr. Brooks. He had shown up for the annual Society of Automotive Engineers bash, attended the *Automotive News* breakfast at the Detroit Athletic Club, where Gene Cafiero of Chrysler talked about *Listening to the Upcoming Tigers in Your*

Own Company. On the way out, he recognized me and chatted for a short while. Ever the wise guy, I nodded at the rostrum and said, "By the way, I wasn't pleased at the way you handled the Vac-U-Lift divestiture [where I had been designated to be general manager]."

He laughed and said he'd see me that night at the open house after the banquet.

He and about eighty other guys donned formal wear to sit at one of the four head tables at the corners of the intimate banquet for four thousand people. ("Very rare please, and hold the sauce on the green beans.") After the banquet, the chairman and his highest local executive came over to our company tables where the executive explained that John had a splitting headache and would see most of us the next day. John did look preoccupied.

Walking to the routine Friday morning staff meeting the next day, I wondered if the chairman might be visiting, as we were by far the biggest division in the area. Upon arrival, we were all stunned to hear that he had died of a massive stroke during the night. The feeling was one of shock, as I had seen him less than twelve hours before. I attributed his stroke, at least partially, to the frustration he must have been feeling during the financial problems described above, as this occurred toward the end of that cycle. Stroke through frustration, heart attack from over-exertion. A later thought was that, as a tough, self-sufficient guy, he must have been walking around for hours, attending the banquet, meeting Henry Ford, with obvious late-stage symptoms of stroke. A very sad event. Something to reflect on, in personal terms.

A bizarre but understandable event occurred about two weeks after John's death. Mrs. Brooks came into the office unannounced, walked into the former chairman's office, sat in his chair and started writing memos as to how the corporation would be run in the future. When one thought about it, Mrs. Brooks' behavior must have seemed appropriate to her. When John had started "their" company twelve years before, it had sales of $6.5 million annually. In the segue of "our" company from that amount to the current $600 million, John had undoubtedly continued to talk of "our" company, "our company's plane" or "our company's divisions." As their personal financial success in return for John's energies and absences would have seemed, to her, parallel and appropriate to the success of "our" company, he probably had never felt the need to explain to his wife in detail that "our" tangible ownership of the company had been diluted to the area of 3 percent, certainly not enough to unilaterally anoint oneself or another as chairman or issue new procedures. As the people were all skilled at handling awkward situations, the whole thing was handled appropriately, with the widow maintaining her dignity and being assigned to transitional committees until a permanent reorganization was finalized.

CHAPTER TEN
Do Not Spindle

I will take a moment here to review the agonizing introduction of computers during my early years in the auto industry. Two related items that would permeate my thoughts during the Sixties were that: (1) the computer would forever be only a commercially used item and (2) the space program, although more than a pretext for selling Tang, the powdered orange juice, wouldn't ever contribute any substantial technology to further the development and sales of commercial or consumer products. The miniaturization of devices for making computations, primarily as a result of the space programs, has over time probably alone justified such programs.

Nonetheless, it has been a rocky road.

As a high-school senior, although I was pretty much sure that I was going to General Motors engineering school, I was invited to University of Michigan visiting day for potential applicants. They escorted us into Hill Auditorium where there was a breezy hip accordion player (*not* an oxymoron), like Art Van Damme,[23] then came a "sample" lecture having to do with world government.

The highlight of the day, however, was being led into a room crammed with equipment embodied in sheet-metal cases. It was one of the world's first high-capability computers, I think an RCA Univac. At any rate, our hosts explained that the computer could solve 60 simultaneous equations with 60 variables in 60 seconds, something that would take 30 mathematicians 30 years to accomplish. Since I was only able to solve three simultaneous equations, and then with considerable effort, such a claim boggled the imagination.

---

[23] It only occurs to me now, but since I recently learned that he was always based in Chicago and that I haven't encountered a breezy hip accordion player in the intervening 63 years, perhaps it was the man himself.

In my early days in sales, Doug Roby, an AMP salesman and son of a former company president, was returning to our shared office after calling on his Ford account.

"I'm so mad I could mutilate an IBM card!" he exploded.

In those days of the early Sixties, one was exposed to IBM cards, on which one penciled information relating to hours worked, sales made, deals blown or whatever specific information was required, then passed it along to where it was "punched" according to the data and inserted in an IBM central processing machine.

"DO NOT SPINDLE, FOLD OR MUTILATE!" expounded each card.

It didn't specify the penalty for the violation of such order, but one sensed that it would be severe—much worse, for instance, than seducing the boss' youngest daughter.

As you might guess, such an absolute order didn't go down very well with yours truly. My hero became a guy I had heard about who really didn't violate any of the three commandments. What he did was better. Somehow he got hold of a manual "puncher" compatible with the subject punch-card system. In those days, most household bills were accompanied by one of these cards, on which one was expected to pencil in the amount of the remittance and return the card with the check. This guy punched obscenities and false remittances into the cards and mailed them back. When they were processed through the computer, this information was delivered to the surprised operator. Apparently, the technology was ahead of applicable law, and no provider ever dreamed that anyone could communicate directly with his computer. The last I heard, he had irrevocably snarled 26 accounts.

In MBA school they showed us what a useful tool the computer could be, particularly for optimization calculations. This would be applicable, for instance, if you were scheduling the work of a factory making a variety of products that required changeovers of equipment, particularly if the factory had the ability to make the same products on different machines or different production lines. One could plug in the total requirements and product mix for the next month: For instance, put in some constraints, such as when raw material was available, how many hours used in changeovers, minimum runs and so on. The computer would search all 180,000 permutations and print out the schedule that demonstrated the lowest manufacturing cost for the month. Remarkable! What a powerful tool.

In practice, however, results were often less than satisfactory. Perhaps it seemed that way to me because I was exposed only when things went awry. One morning my phone rang at about 9:30 A.M. It was Cadillac calling.

"We're out of axle tubes. If you don't deliver soon we'll have to send the first shift home at noon and pay the second shift four hours even though they don't have to come in."

Thank heavens we were only five miles away because it was really a no-no to not deliver to schedule, let alone being so far behind that there was not any inventory.

In somewhat of a panic, I called the production control guy.

"Tell Cadillac they've got about three skids worth on their floor. Tell them to look for them. Plus we have about six skids on our floor; we could send those."

We couldn't find either, but we immediately set up for manufacture, which was 24 hours away. Finally, I was able to piece together the actual situation. Cadillac, over the past several months, had returned to us the equivalent of three skids of parts, an event that wasn't plugged into our computer; so they really didn't have any. The six skids on our floor really didn't exist either, or rather they were only theoretical skids; the computer deduced how many parts were made, less an expectation for scrap and startup, by the amount of material the process had ingested. We had experienced an abnormal number of "cold-shut" forgings and so the six skids were really scrap metal. One minor mitigating factor was that Cadillac itself had slightly under ordered due to their own computer glitch. We finally sat down with our people to resolve the issues.

"No problem!" they asserted.

"Yes, problem," I offered. "We didn't perform for a new customer to the extent that he had to lose production and pay for no work. I don't know how many tens of thousands of dollars it cost him, and I won't ask because we might then be asked to participate."

In the early Seventies, the Detroit election bureau hired a computer whiz to streamline the antiquated voting system. After the citywide election, it was noted that this didn't check out and that the result was implausible—and what happened?

I can only suspect it went like this:

"No problem!," he responded, "we'll simply adjust this and feed it back into the loop."

"Who's the mayor?" someone asked.

"Unfair question," responded the administrator.

Many years later, on a commute from New York, I couldn't help but hear a computer technician talk about his call to fix a customer's problem.

"They didn't have enough permanent memory, so the data wasn't being entered properly. I soon found and fixed the problem although, unfortunately, they lost all of their personnel records. Now I didn't think it my place to bring it to their attention or even respond when they found out so I became very animated when the computer was fixed. I kept calling people over to see how well it was ingesting new data to the extent that they just told me to leave. When they call someone at our company about their loss, we will respond, 'No problem. Of course you've provided back-up as suggested.'"

Since the early Sixties and through a dozen or so administrative assistants, I've always encouraged candid give-and-take. The only phrase I don't want to hear when we were discussing an issue or problem and outlining our plan of attack? You get the idea.

I wondered if I was the only one noticing these things. I finally read an article by a noted economist who stated that from the beginning of the computer industry (1955?) until 1991 there was no discernible efficiency that could be ascribed to the use of computers. There was no improvement in the ability to print airline tickets, insurance policies, run factories or railroads. Now we know that during that period the computer could perform some remarkable tasks. The answer must be that counteracting this were myriads of employees who were attempting to get on board while instructing their computer to print through the bottom of the sheet, canceling two days work with the press of a button and other such counterproductive activities.

His theory tends to be borne out by the data of the Clinton years, where the unit costs of material and labor were rising at a rate of about 5 percent annually; efficiency improvements were 3 percent, generating an inflation rate of 2 percent (it's almost that simple) and, very much like the auto industry of the Sixties, just about perfect and finally inferring a beneficial contribution by the computer.

While we're on the subject of computers, I recall being able to smooth talk a Sears employee into letting me buy a scarce "Pong" game for the kids for Christmas, 1975. This game was a milestone in that it was a computer-like machine which was "interactive," in that it requested a human being do a specific task in a specific time, otherwise the machine "won." At the time, it was considered such a milestone that subsequent years would, like the Gregorian calendar, present computer-like products with their year of introduction "after Pong" (AP), not totally unlike Detroit's penchant for attaching a year designation for their vehicles. For instance the "home" computer from IBM with the "Chicklets" typewriter keys was introduced in about 8 AP. Why isn't Apple referred to as 33 AP? I guess the personal-computer industry became so utile and large that its image needn't remind us of its origins that might now be considered a primitive and trivial machine.

CHAPTER ELEVEN
Ground Zero

We're rapidly approaching the events that lead to the current dilemma. Although you already know much more than you care to about the joys of living and working in Detroit, it is probably best if we pause for just a moment to introduce other factors that made the industry what it was in the Sixties, how products were viewed by Americans, how their view of the manufacturers seemed to be somewhat less than that of the products and the status of labor relations. I will also set the groundwork for issues that are about to impinge in no little way on the business: The economics of import/export as well as the recognition of a need for improved vehicle safety and more care for the environment. Lastly, we will reveal the premises and criteria that will be used here to evaluate the events and the motivations of the players themselves in our overall attempt to adjudicate the same by attempting to sort the rational from the irrational. (Unfortunately, not too many ponies uncovered!)

You undoubtedly have your own impression of the origins of the domestic automotive industry. Mine is one of a laissez faire, or unrestricted, environment, with the most successful pioneers working primarily out of Southern Michigan (Ford, Durant, Dodge) and wildcatters and the Rockefellers developing oil, oil supply and its delivery system. Accordingly, from the beginning of time until about 1973, the industry evolved in America under the premise that neither the cost nor availability of gas and oil was a key factor in vehicle design or the facilities to build them. Henry Ford devised the procedures to build cars from interchangeable parts, and the efficiencies generated permitted him to start paying his workers wages enough so that they could buy their own cars, and his company was so successful that he made his first (and last) billion by 1920. GM evolved as an amalgam of Oldsmobile, Buick and Chevrolet and took over as Number One in the Thirties.

We needn't belabor this, other than to offer the notion that, from the origins of the business until the present moment, most Americans became almost irrationally attached to the automobile and to the freedom and versatility it provided in their lives.

I recall that the newly emerged Ralph Nader referred to it as if it were a narcotic, one of his few statements that I tended to agree with, happily. Even into the Sixties and beyond, buyers were in increasing numbers specifying air conditioning at about $300 when they would never consider spending that amount for air conditioning their home. They would avidly sign up for $150 hi-fi sound systems when few would do so for their home. Kids were planning the hour when they would get their unrestricted license. Since the mid-Fifties, the industry paid attention to amenities and styling, particularly in the interior. Pontiac and Dodge successfully shed their grandma and grandpa images, with hot new high-powered engine offerings. In the early years of the industry, some marketing genius started identifying cars with "years" and so cultivated a "status" culture not only in model but also in freshness. I was surprised to learn then that in working-class neighborhoods some used their cars, particularly convertibles, as substitutes for porches or gazebos in which to "hang" in leisure time, cranking it up every few hours to get smokes or ice cream cones or whatever.

By the end of the Sixties, Americans were well on their way to two-car households.

Generally, government officials supported such tastes on the part of Americans, certainly the Interstate system planned in the Fifties by the federal government signaled that auto (and truck) transportation would continue to be a major source of individual transportation. Undoubtedly redundant here, but it seems that almost no imposition of taxes or cost could wean Americans from their automobiles;[24] accordingly, the auto industry has always paid its own way. We needn't belabor the situation of the other modes of transportation, other than to again note the *New York Times* has taken umbrage that only 20 percent of the automobile-generated trust fund is being allocated for mass transit. In one of the first paradoxes of the current economic distress, where public officials are expected to discourage certain forms of transportation such as cars and private planes, budgetary problems are dictating that public mass-transit systems be cut back, as their subsidy for

---

[24] In the Seventies, when gasoline was approaching $1 per gallon, Ford conducted a study which indicated that demand for gas would be constant up to $2.50.

operating costs amounts to somewhere between 48 percent (New York) and 85 percent (Charlotte).

Adversarial in nature, the relationship of the UAW and the automakers, established through extremely hostile episodes of the 1930s, had seemed to settle into a routine, although somewhat disruptive, minuet.[25] Every three years, the union would select a company with which to negotiate a "master" agreement. If there were a strike as an incentive to spur the quality of the offer, the vast resources of the UAW would provide substantial support to striking workers. When the "master" was settled, this would be shown to other manufacturers as the model, and modifications would be made only to accommodate unique situations at the other companies; consequently, the whole "top tier" would be settled for several years. Suppliers had their own ritual, being obligated to provide "standby" inventory to support shipments to customers in the event of a strike, and then working off that inventory, which meant in turn that their own associated disruptions of plant scheduling on others was inflicted down the supply chain.

Never, to my knowledge, did any such settlement exhibit wages, benefits and work rules that were fully offset by improved efficiencies; consequently, the excess was passed up the supply chain, eventually to be accepted and paid by the retail customer, rationalized as "inflation." Did the manufacturers create industrial hari kari by acceding to union demands, as hindsight now seems to indicate? The question, in my opinion, is not relevant as they had little choice. As long as both sides recognized that costs could be pushed on to the retail customer, it was implied that to incur the lengthy strike that would be required to alter the current mode of doing business established a motivation of union busting as well as the temporary and potentially long-term loss of market share and investigations by the National Labor Relations Board (an independent and then powerful Federal entity created to enforce that no employer abused its presumed negotiating advantage). The federal government generally applauded the precedents set during these negotiations, such as living wages, medical coverage for all employees, eleven vacation days and generous pensions. And, if you recall, LBJ just hated strikes.

As the legend goes, he would insert his "help" into negotiations by summoning the combatants to Washington, talking turkey to them and

---

[25] It is interesting to note that, in the Fifties, Alfred Sloan, GM former Chairman and management guru, referred to this ritual as unsustainable.

inserting them in a room to iron out their differences. Upon no such "expedited" settlement, the President would blame "distractions" as impeding the process. Accordingly, he would send them back to their room and sequentially and inexorably remove these distractions: telephones, sleep breaks, table, meal breaks, chairs and finally, lavatory breaks.

Then LBJ would say something like this, "You boys can be justly proud that you have settled your differences. I'm just glad that I could be of some help."

Here we should probably recognize the fourth hypothesis of my MBA school: "Increased volume covers a multitude of sins."

In spite of ever-increasing imports, the domestic industry enjoyed several spurts of prosperity, at least economically, under the old labor/management "system," until the second gasoline crunch and Carter's "malaise" of 1980. UAW membership, already 1 million by the end of the war, increased and reached a plateau during the 1970s at about 1.5 million, the erosion starting in the 1980s to the 2008 level of less than .5 million. During those 50 years, wages of UAW workers rose 2 1/2 times in purchasing power. Recently, even the union has seemingly acquiesced that this level is, unfortunately, not sustainable. Many of the contributing reasons will be discussed later.

Mr. Nader ("the professional scold") hypothesized that auto-centric behavior was past, that the new generations would seek drivers' licenses only when the need for such could not be avoided. They would have more altruistic and noble pursuits. After a few years of penitence due to recognition of such covetous "guilt" (no convertibles or pleasure driving), I think Americans reverted to their usual habits. Don't take my word for it. The next time you encounter any fourteen-year olds, ask if they have thought about and can tell you the year in which they would get their license. Most will respond with the month or the earliest specific date at which it *will* be secured.

Not unexpectedly, such adoration for their vehicles hasn't seemed to transfer to vehicle makers. In the first place, by definition, they are considered Goliaths, not a sympathetic embodiment. The marketing system dictates that eyeball-to-eyeball customer contact is undertaken by independent dealers, an unpredictable but mostly truthful lot, albeit including 10 percent bottom feeders to which most people become exposed during at least one faith-jarring episode in a lifetime. To many among us, compared to an auto dealer, Bernie Madoff seems like Warren Buffet. As we previously mentioned, there is a natural tension between auto manufacturers and the Eastern establishment—with Detroit brandishing its financial (and other) independence and New York publicly wondering if hinterland cretins should be independently making decisions that have so much impact on economics and lifestyle.[26] Washington is generally cooperating with the industry because it serves a common constituency and it contributes to its own sustenance, although as the opportunity will arise, it will morph into a somewhat adversarial "advisor" in creating automotive specifications and performance standards.

On the personnel front, Bunkie Knudson, executive vice president of General Motors and son of a former GM president, was recruited by Henry Ford II in 1968 to become President of Ford Motor Company, shocking most of the industry and horrifying many of the young Ford executives. Bunkie "holed up" for the first few weeks, further frustrating otherwise apprehensive Ford executives. The story is told that Bunkie finally called for a staff meeting at 9:30 A.M. one morning that summoned all of the eager next-level executives. He himself showed up sometime after 11:00 and announced, "Now you know how your subordinates feel when you corporate princes don't show up promptly on working days."

He then left the meeting.

I recall how easy it was to approach him at the fall vendor open house, even though my Ford account manager was a college friend of his. I gathered at the time that he deliberately wasn't "knock-about" with Ford employees, or for that matter, much of the pool of Ford vendors. Mr. Ford fired Knudson nineteen months later, stating that the Knudson presidency just didn't work out. Although I understand that Mr. Iacocca was delighted, he had to wait another fifteen months to formally be named Ford president.

It only occurred to me now, but in those days there were a multitude of very capable "car guys," or, as Mr. Iacocca used to say, "buck sniffers." They were moving around the industry or dropping out at that time and there still seemed to be a stable of them in the wings. Unfortunately, that would change in the next decade or so.

The industry wasn't helped with its own aforementioned swagger or when George Romney met with considerable success at American Motors

---

[26] *Travel and Leisure Magazine* has defined the Detroit "renaissance man" as one who plays golf *and bowls!*

with the refinement of Nash and Hudson into a company specializing in low-cost and fuel-efficient Ramblers. Several constituencies, such as pioneer environmentalists and habitually frugal Americans, signed on. Further, when AMC stock greatly appreciated, he got much favorable press (as a latter-day David?) that he opportunistically used to tweak the other companies about their "gas-guzzling dinosaurs." As it turned out, his business model was based upon so much frugality that it wasn't sustainable. Salaried employees brought in their own toilet tissue and had to empty their own ashtrays and wastebaskets. Wages were frozen for years at a time, and when Romney became governor, his successor, Roy Abernathy, had to relieve some of the employee tension, to the detriment of costs. Although Romney's operating style at AMC didn't last, it is *exactly* the frugal style, along with his exemplary personal stature and credibility, that one would desire in a governor. Accordingly, when Susan gave birth to our second child, on the way home from the hospital we dropped the infant with grandma Riley so Susie could cast her first ballot ever for George Romney.

A personal note about my dear Susie and her mother Lois: It was May of 1961 and her mother had tickets for opening night at the Metropolitan Opera in Detroit for a production of *Faust*. Susan's father, Carl, although generally a social animal and prominently known industrial designer, didn't particularly want to go, so Susie was recruited. She was not yet 21 and 5 months pregnant with our first child and she looked sensational for the quasi-formal event as the two elegant ladies left for the opera. Who needs guys! (And this is even before the women's movement got into full swing.)

Susie reported that the production was sensational, although she detected some definite nodding among the mostly automotive executive guys in their cute penguin suits a little after eleven o'clock, a condition that seemed to abate after midnight when "sins of the flesh" were depicted. Sometime during this, Lois remembered why it was useful to have guys along; they have pockets into which they reach and pull out cash for incidental expenditures. Who was going to pay for parking? Lois was lamenting this during the second intermission when, lo and behold, there was neighbor George Romney. Embarrassed, Lois meekly approached but was enthusiastically greeted by his whole party. She confessed her problem and he couldn't be more honored or pleased to help as he graciously ponied up a fin. Now, more than fifty years later, Susie still remembers this as she always tries to make sure that I have a few dollars in my pocket when I'm out and about.

The domestic market was served primarily by the domestic manufacturers, in the ratios described in the earlier chapter. Volume of the niche Volkswagen import had seemed to flatten, although another potential threat seemed on the horizon as several Japanese manufacturers had started to export to the United States. The first attempt was a 1957 Toyopet Crown, which went from 0-60 in 5.7 eons. Japan continued to doggedly capture market share with improved vehicles and attractive pricing. I recall us laughing when we heard that Honda was going into the automobile business. Here in the U.S. we had winnowed out more than 997 domestic manufacturers and this manufacturer of wussy little motorcycles thought it could compete?

At a school rest break while chatting with Rene VanSteenkiste of the Budd Company, I happened to think out loud, "Might it be possible that the quality 35-mm U.S. camera-business scenario (Germans first in, Japan later dominating the market) could be replicated in the automotive business?"

"You just wait!" he responded.

Let's talk briefly about the economics of exporting, particularly in the case of Japan. The country's industry was pretty much decimated by the end of the Second World War. Here was a country of about 120 million industrious people living on an island the size of Montana with few natural resources. The strategy as conceived by the government and adhered to by the populace was to produce an efficient and growing industrial base to ensure future prosperity, with emphasis on the "future" part (consumerism could come later). The remarkable nature of their industrial recuperation was demonstrated to me in the early Sixties when our own company started buying Japanese steel for our usual manufacture. Here were the steel companies of Japan, buying ore from Chile, making world-class quality steel in Japan, delivering in Detroit and beating U.S. Steel, price-wise, in the process. Remarkable!

At that time, one could extrapolate the Japanese success in primary industrial materials into serious competition in other industries if they were to use such skill and determination to expand into other product lines. A unified policy of securing world-class technology, selecting industries to attack, offering and delivering quality products, pricing aggressively so as to penetrate markets, making huge investments in capital and education,

94

skewing foreign policy efforts toward issues of trade, limiting the leverage of labor by inhibiting anything but local unions and a myriad of other well planned tactics would enable the Japanese to compete in many selected industries.

I might add here that the posture of the Japanese relative to business and ethics, at this juncture, was above reproach. As part of the strategy was securing world-class technology for the purpose of speed-to-market entry, they sought out and secured the very best (that they couldn't legally and expediently copy), accelerating by years their emergence in several key industries. Although they were skilled negotiators, they fastidiously honored agreements regarding such technology. One of the legendary stories has to do with a major corporation, Mitsubishi as I recall, who diligently kept fastidious records during WWII, sought out the American licensor afterward, presented a record of their royalty indebtedness incurred during the war and pledged to work this off as Japan and its industry got back on its feet. Some of the Japanese companies that I later became acquainted with had been happily paying up to half of the already meager profits as royalty. The name of the game there? Growth and export in fundamental industries driven by attention to share of market. The name of the game in the U.S.? Growth and profitability, preferably with a string of ever-increasing quarterly earnings in order to maximize stock price, which in turn, (1) permits one to purchase companies on the cheap with highly valued stock or (2) defensively makes it expensive to have potential acquirers make a run at you. (This activity is strictly covered and Japanese companies' backsides are protected from corporate raiders by laws and oversight in Japan.)

By design, Japanese companies earn relatively low profits related to sales. As their cost of capital is also low, supported by government policies, their return on invested capital is more comparable to worldwide norms. Let's assume that their planned return on sales is 5 percent (probably on the high side). "Fixed" costs included in such total cost are normally applied to sales in one's home market. These are costs that don't fluctuate with the volume of manufacturing, consisting of amortization of plant and equipment, engineering, marketing and administrative costs among several other things. Even in an industry that is not very capital intensive, I would suggest these costs amount to about 25 percent of total costs. Accordingly, if a company has excess capacity and maintains constant pricing, an *incremental* sale would have a profitability of more than 28 percent related to sales. To calculate the total delivered cost for an export transaction, then transportation, tariffs, transaction costs and foreign marketing costs must be subtracted from this profit. If tariffs are low (approximately 0 percent on autos), it can be surmised that export sales can be perceived as even more profitable than core market sales and why there may be temptations to lower pricing in order to secure market share offshore. That's why "anti-dumping" laws on imports (selling at lower prices than at home) are virtually universal around the world. Also, most countries offer preferred tax treatment on exports, a "below the radar" further inducement for exporting.

A young plaintiff lawyer, the previously mentioned Ralph Nader, had burst on the scene with his book *Unsafe At Any Speed*, a highly critical assessment of the operating performance of the Chevrolet Corvair, particularly in the context of safety. The Corvair had a peculiar rear suspension that underwent particular scrutiny and, although I wasn't qualified to adjudicate the merits of Mr. Nader's arguments, there was no *All My Sons* determination of deliberately subordinated foreknowledge of problems or lawsuits related to such. "What is his motive?" was cocktail party conversation among the twenty-something set. Was he signaling his peers to accept Corvair contingency cases? Did he just want to take a piece out of General Motors like JFK did with U.S. Steel? Did he have political ambitions? Did he want to secure authority to force automakers into modifying designs? Was he a true altruist citizen? All of the above? After fifty years, one can conclude the following: All of the above, except for the statement preceding it.

The book caught the attention of people involved in the industry and, seemingly to a much lesser extent, of the general public. As could be expected, of course, it *really* caught the attention of General Motors. Now Mr. Nader probably anticipated a situation which was lost on GM: Less than 20 years removed from a world war, there were probably about 4,000 former marines in positions of varying authority within the corporation who knew just how to handle just such a situation (and draw everlasting paternalistic ardor from the corporation). Secure information that would undermine the credibility and/or reputation of the enemy! Sure enough, soon a General Motors connected operative was discovered trying to get the "goods" on Mr. Nader. Now, this was really newsworthy. Mr. Roche, President of GM, publicly apologized to Mr. Nader. Nader became a "cause célèbre" and brilliantly handled a campaign, primarily through news conferences, purporting that he was a self-ordained "consumer advocate" and that he would attempt to influence policies that would protect and empower the otherwise helpless consumer.

At the time, America was a relatively safe country in which to drive, although our fatalities were amounting to about 55,000 per year. The AAA would customarily encourage people to drive safely, and drive the point home by stating, "This Memorial Day, 45 people will die on Michigan highways." (Usually an accurate forecast.) It was difficult to argue that there shouldn't be some organization overseeing and helping to evolve a beloved American activity that resulted in the deaths of tens of thousands of its citizens annually. Accordingly, it seemed rational, particularly amongst the *brouhaha,* that such task be assigned to a Federal department to study traffic safety data, and devise and recommend safety improvements to vehicles. Such was established as the National Highway Traffic Safety Administration.

The traveling MBA school served dinner before classes, partly as a practical logistical matter and partly to encourage collegial discourse on academic or public issues. One evening I was expounding[27] on the issue of automotive safety. My argument was that Americans tend to focus intensely on certain issues, argue all of the ramifications and titillating potential moral or legal implications, then move on to another issue to the extent that the former is virtually discarded. My examples were that the issue of Communists in the government and whether Joe McCarthy was a good guy or a bad guy shouldn't have much to do with how the issue should be handled. The issue was pretty much dropped when he was revealed to be a putz. When Ford demonstrated a rather elaborate case for vehicle safety ten years before, people talked about it along with the pros and cons, then moved on to other issues. Most recently, we had just been through an extended dialogue about bomb shelters. Were they a good idea or not? Should that be a sanctuary for your family alone? What if your neighbor, bereft of a bomb shelter, indicated he wanted to share yours? What are the moral issues? What if he tries to force his way into your shelter? What means are you ethically and legally permitted to use to deter him? What if his "force" includes firearms? We, as a society went on for a long time on this and the hypothetical nuances, only to drop the issue completely. I think that the latter

---

[27] Motown guys tend to be good at expounding, although the subject matter sometimes leaves something to be desired.

was related to the successful negotiations regarding the Soviet missiles in Cuba by the Kennedy administration.

"This will also soon be forgotten or minimized," ended my expounding.

I happened to be sitting with guys who were only familiar faces.

"I think you've completely misread this particular situation," one offered. "This issue now stands that a Federal Administration has just been established. That Administration will hire what are hoped to be capable people, a *budget* will be established and funded, there will be short-range and *long-range* plans created. Career paths will be formulated with the most ambitious of the new hires. I think this one will be around for a while, unless something unlikely and unforeseen occurs sometime in the future, as Federal Administrations do not usually demonstrate a tendency for self-immolation."

Okay, so at least I stopped expounding for a while.

Although this is probably obvious, my training has imbued me with virtually obsolete linear thinking. That is, when I evaluate some phenomenon, there normally is an investment of some scarce resource (money or energy, mostly) to secure a stream of benefits or big payouts in the future of even scarcer commodities (more money or energy or status or safety). For example, when the proposal of windmills for generating electricity rather than for pumping water arose in the early Eighties, the first and easiest evaluation consisted of: How much total energy was expended to manufacture the windmill? How long would it take to recapture that energy through generation of electricity by the windmill? (Called the break-even point.) When the latter answer was seventy-five years, it automatically fell out of my purview. (I was pleasantly surprised recently when I learned that this had fallen to the range of five years).

I will admit that I'm in the minority, but one of my pet disappointments is that those people whom I encounter that are most ardent about conservation, improved lifestyle or earth-preservation issues seem not well grounded in science or mathematical models. For instance, when someone in 1981 espoused the idea of putting windmills up around the perimeter of the United States, they typically didn't seem able to tell me what benefits would accrue, other than "touchy feely" ones and general ones relating to imported oil and so on.

We've tried to be reasonably objective when trying to position all of you in the mindset of the Sixties (now there's an oxymoron!). There probably was some unacknowledged apprehension and irritation on the part of domestic auto-industry professionals that, in turn, didn't help their external demeanor. At a meeting where a *Free Press* reporter was lambasting Ed Cole, then GM chairman and in my opinion a totally reasonable and charitable person, that he could tolerate even one missing nut or bolt or spot-weld without resigning, Mr. Cole responded, "How could you not understand it? Sometimes I have trouble even getting the gist of an article in your paper for all the typos."

I mean—there was almost hysterical press indignation.

There probably existed apprehension about the new government department and how they were going to fit in. There was the notion that Americans tended to buy for their personal self-interest, not necessarily "American." Perhaps most of all, many of the industry operatives were veterans of the two recent wars. They were sensing, probably correctly, that their potential overseas competitors were being unfairly thought of by the (car-buying) public as "Black Forest Elves" or "friendly understated monastic Japanese" as compared to their own perception as characteristically "cigar chomping fat-cat purveyors of gas-guzzling smoke-belching dinosaurs." In their minds, at least, these characterizations didn't fairly correlate with the way the parties conducted the wars or the way the sequential country occupations undoubtedly would have been handled, as demonstrated by each of the competitive party's prior performances when such situations arose.

"Have we done such terrible things," they asked, "that the other guys are perceived as sentimental favorites?"

CHAPTER TWELVE
Management Chores

It was July 21, 1967, a Friday on which I'd been given my first real promotion. MBA school and its time pressures were gone for the summer and we'd long planned for a babysitter for the three kids and a weekend with Susan's parents on Harsen's Island. I was now automotive sales manager, my responsibilities had expanded to all of the automotive manufacturers and a solid sales team seemed to have accepted my new role. What could possibly have dimmed my outlook?

Such optimism extended into the following Monday-morning drive into the office. As I was breezing down Northwestern Highway it occurred to me that the going was too easy for a Monday morning, even though the teachers were out for the summer. One of those new Monday holidays must have slipped by me, I thought. Oh well, I'd go in anyway and review, in quiet, the issues I'd been working on so I could turn them over to Jay—who was my successor on the GM accounts. It got even spookier, as there were *no* cars by Wyoming (seven miles from the Detroit civic center), where the traffic usually began to back up, and there were no people visible on any street or overpass (think O*n the Beach* by Neville Shute). For five minutes or so, I'd been listening to "drive time" radio, WJR, and J. P. McCarthy who commanded more of an AM audience than the whole television spectrum. A commercial ended by saying to be sure to get there by 5:00 P.M. tomorrow as that's when the sale ends. McCarthy himself said something to the effect that although the station had received no official guidance, it probably would be better if people remained near home. Next commercial, "[Big boat horn blast.] It's on the half hour. There goes another Bob Lo boat from the foot of Woodward."

What the hell was going on? I asked myself. Oh well, I was approaching my exit at Livernois (five miles out) and I figured that I might as well go to the office and get organized.

I got to the main factory and safely got inside our small satellite sales building next door. Naturally, I called plant protection to see what was going on and got the details. (It's the Detroit riot, stupid!) I called home to see that they've gotten the word and are safe. Okay. I finally got time to think. Now the radio broadcast makes sense. The Saturday episode is 36 hours old and known to all but those imbeciles who can't perceive what's going on around them. Why would the premier radio station belabor such a horrific episode Saturday night and then Sunday without fermenting further animosity or racial mistrust? And it hadn't had time or personnel (located at the midst of events, in the Fisher Building) to revise its programmed commercial messages? (Incidentally, not the last seemingly "parallel universe" I would encounter.)

Now that the confusion and immediate concern for family had abated, was I in immediate peril? Apparently not, since everything was quiet. I made a few calls, including one to our scheduling and shipping department, which was working since most of our customers from the Detroit plant weren't within the ten-mile or so radial area that seemed to be hunkered down. I noticed that I had a lunch date with a Chevrolet engineer at the tech center, and so I called to see if he was in. Sure was and he'd be glad to be picked up at 11:45 A.M. I sorted through a few papers, called Charlie to see if he wanted anything brought from the office, heard a few reports of gunfire off in the distance and mentally sorted through my route options to the tech center.

Imagine fighter-pilot directions: the tech center is at about 1:30 on the far NNE side.

It took me seconds to recall the three or four alternate routes and deduce that they would all take me through three or four potentially bad places. Accordingly, I got in my car, closed the windows and locked the doors and headed safely out Joy Road in the 9:00 direction.

The next three days were filled with concern and dismay, particularly since we had three children under six. Although we lived a considerable distance from the danger zones, there were rumors that émigrés from Flint and Toledo were nearby asking directions so that they might participate in the demonstrations. After two days of authoritative disorder, President Johnson sent in the National Guard (and Cyrus Vance) on that same Monday. My own particular concern was that ordinary citizens had for two nights seen their more unruly neighbors not only creating havoc in the streets, but were also returning home, undeterred, with color television sets, cases of liquor and champagne and designer clothes. For all but the most upstanding citizens it had to be a temptation to replicate such unchallenged misbehavior, if only for the sake of fairness. Now we were sending in Federal weekend soldiers to restore "order" against those exhibiting the least egregious behavior when the most aggressive participants would be home resting after two arduous nights.

Thankfully, the riots were largely over within a week, as they were a spontaneous eruption of frustration, aided by a few agitators and excellent weather. Sadly, however, while the uprising highlighted issues that needed serious attention, the city has never come back. A city proud that its population had the greatest ratio of families living in homes rather than apartments or government-subsidized housing now had burned or boarded up houses in many formerly viable neighborhoods. A city that had opened up most of its neighborhoods in the Fifties and Sixties had no "ghetto" that could be cordoned off in order to minimize the disruption. Ironically, those small businesses in the neighborhood of our factory were untouched during the riots, whereas on a normal weekend several windows would be broken or the drug store or dry cleaners would have theft or burglary problems. I later found out that Kelsey Hayes and several other businesses in the area were equally untouched.

For the next six months, dinner-party conversation often evolved around, "Where were you when—"

One of these stories even more bizarre than mine was about a couple that had a summer cottage in Canada. Their child had been running a moderate, but concerning, fever over the weekend. As they were coming across the Ambassador Bridge, they thought it might be a good idea to stop at the emergency room of Henry Ford Hospital to get him diagnosed and medicated. This should not be a problem, they surmised, as it was rather late on a Sunday evening, and it was right on their way home. But, unbeknownst to them, in was in the proximity of many of the problems. They stopped and got in the waiting room. There were a lot of people there. Oh well, the figured, they're already there; they might as well stick it out. Where it took me only minutes to realize something was abnormal, it took them an hour or so, when the nurse, who they later determined was performing triage,[28] came through, looked under a blanket at a wound of over a foot long and cheerfully said, "Oh good, most of the bleeding has stopped. Hang in there!"

---

[28] The skill of determining the order that patients would be taken in, so that no curable person would die and so no resources would be wasted on those who would die anyway.

After several similar offerings by the nurse, they finally started catching on. "We should have caught on sooner, when we saw people waiting who were bleeding through their blankets," offered the wife, "that should have given us a clue as to the shape of the people being treated inside who were given priority. Needless to say we took the kid home, gave him a few aspirins, and weaseled our way into the pediatrician on Monday morning."

Commerce shortly got back to normal, although it was a busy time for me since I was meeting a lot of new people, particularly at Ford, our largest customer, and Chrysler.

At Ford, the buyer (lowest-level purchasing) of our largest-selling product line (spring-and-frame seating units) was not noted for a Christ-like demeanor, but was more noted for a Napoleonic[29] one, although I considered it more Caligula-like.

Soon, I blessed his renowned reputation when word came back to my company executives: "Just because you send in here a smart, fast-talking kid boss, don't think you'll be able to—"

My bosses knew I had gotten his attention.

I was playing golf with our chief engineer and customers at his club, Plum Hollow, when afterward in the locker room I was approached by the vice president of sales of a competitor[30] whom I had met once, but knew mostly through his reputation as a square shooter and envy of all my former bosses regarding the remuneration and perks received while administering only a small fraction of our own business.

In the demeanor of a wise and benevolent uncle, he espoused, "I understand how frustrating it must be for a guy of your profile to deal with a guy who has 'our favorite Ford buyer's pretensions and convoluted logic,' but before you try to take dramatic actions that, incidentally, might use up some of your own well deserved coin, let me offer this for your consideration. [He hadn't broken any law yet!] Here's a guy that spends his time meddling in other Ford people's responsibility to prove he is the seating 'czar' to the extent he has little time doing his own job regarding paper work

---

[29] Archaic usage, Susie uses the noun "Short," as in the sentence, "He's a Short," perhaps not indicating the proper respect for a confident man of small physical stature.

[30] I'm still idealistic and well versed on the legalities of anti-competitive behavior.

and particularly regarding purchase orders or justifiable changes for same. As you have undoubtedly heard from your predecessors and Ned, he's always nine to twelve months in arrears in initiating purchase orders for new parts. As you've probably also heard, because of his procrastination, about 25 percent of all of the prices he issues are erroneous. Now, you might think that he's taking advantage. Not so! If you study these, you'll find out that they are random, caused by his belated issuance [much like you would have if you balanced your check book nine months in arrears] and as likely fall to your favor as his. He will eventually correct errors in his favor if you walk him through the traceable steps, and actually be appreciative that it was kept between the two of you. Now, regarding those errors in your favor: Some of these are the result of conversations of ten months before, such as, 'I'll probably have to give you $.25 less for this but you've got the business so go ahead and tool.' Or when you respond to his prodding that you might be able to give him $.50 on the Lincoln package two years out if he gives you the tooling and first order now. When you receive purchase orders with numbers in your favor, you must have him change those that can be immediately traced as erroneous, but on the grey ones such as I talked about, you can evaluate each one and decide whether it is ethical and appropriate to confirm it."

Further keeping one honest, at the same time complicating these transactions, it is common practice that purchase orders and amendments are issued that sometimes affect billings and payments for such made as far back as a year; accordingly, a bad judgment you have made can have significant implications as corrections accumulated over a year drop right to your current gross profit/loss line.

My increased responsibilities coincided with the first directives of the newly formed National Highway Traffic Safety Administration (NHTSA). The industry has been around for a long time and it has been historically unusual for an external culture to impinge on its own. At that time we had two parallel "new" cultures: (1) the safety culture which is absolutely mandatory and (2) the computer culture that conventional wisdom demands a company stay abreast of, otherwise it is feared that competitors taking advantage of such technology will shortly "out-efficient" you right out of business. Since there is very little history in either culture relative to the industry, naturally young "hard chargers" introduce these into whatever a discussion is about, knowing that they are as experienced in these as anyone and inferring that they are modern soon-to-be managers comfortable in the current idioms. (Remember I was an old codger of almost 30.)

As a result, many meetings, particularly those called to solve timely problems, didn't seem to have flowing ideas in either English or Motown. Shortly after a meeting would convene, one of the youngsters would offer, very, very seriously, "I can conceive a scenario where this issue might have safety implications."

I couldn't resist. "Thanks, Herman, that's quite a relief. I was afraid we were dealing with a functional problem here."

Everyone, except Herman, would "get it," smile, and we would continue to conduct our business.

As many of you probably recall, the first directives called for seat belts for all front-seat passengers, then headrests and integral shoulder belts. One of those first autumns during start-up, I was happily cognizant that there were very few related problems, when I got a call from Jack Hughes, one of the senior purchasing agents at Ford.[31]

"We've got serious problems. Grab some prints and meet me at Wixom in 45 minutes. Come by yourself; I'm trying to contain what's going on."

When Mr. Hughes calls, one usually does what one is told.

So I dutifully grabbed my stuff and headed toward the Wixom plant, sole builder of Ford luxury cars Lincoln and Thunderbird (newly a four-seater). I was apprehensive on several counts.

First, the product line comprised seat frame and spring assemblies. We'd been a developmental innovator and the leading independent supplier for years. Imagine, if you will, the Lincoln front-seat cushion. It had a frame slightly narrower than the distance between the front doors. Inserted in this were perhaps 20 wire springs, each of which was fastened on the rear frame, creating an approximately 4-inch-wide zig-zag pattern forward across the seat top while creating the seat profile, the front having a rearward "V" so as to provide "flex" at the front of the seat. You've picked up that these individual springs are kind of complex. When you're manufacturing and shipping thousands of assemblies a day, there is a concern that the whole factory might turn into one humongous Chinese Fire Drill. (The prevention of such is one of the important techniques we developed.) On the few

---

[31] He's the purchasing agent who offered the former chairman 50 percent of the business at 100 percent pricing levels.

occasions where I saw a bin with tangled springs, a lift truck appeared shortly to remove and scrap them, by far the cheapest solution. Historically, there had always been tidy blueprints showing the components and how they were arranged. As you can imagine, there had been real-world variations due to the inherent instability of the components. Now that quality control is more highlighted due to its effect on safety, along with the rest of the seat suppliers, we had been having problems defining what realistic variations should be permitted consistent with quality for assembly of the seat padding and covers and performance. Charlie used to say, "It's like trying to put a micrometer[32] on a marshmallow."

Second, usually when parts are assembled in the final-assembly area, they have different origins. When the mating parts are internally manufactured, the supplier is naturally less likely to be given the benefit of the doubt or, similarly, is given the blame for the problem. Since Wixom, or at least Ford, did its own "cut and sew" of the seat upholstery and padding, I feared encountering some of this, real or imagined.

Jack and I became versed on the problem as interpreted by Wixom personnel. It was pretty vague. The front-seat backs didn't seem to be going together properly. We walked over to look at prints. We looked at the title block, "∇." Uh, oh, that new symbol, nicknamed "inverted delta," meant that the product depicted on the print *really did* have legalistic NHTSA implications. Not to panic. We looked at their first assembly attempt. There were some peculiar metal parts (must be on our seat) in the middle of the top that were creating funny looking bumps right through the seat covers. I made a few discrete calls. Eureka! Our seats had been changed to accept a headrest. The plant didn't even know about it.

One of Wixom's floor operatives offered, "Oh, that's what those things are for; they just got in; I thought they were some unusual small cushions or armrests, with a flat piece of metal coming out one side. Now I understand. They're headrests."

I needn't and didn't get involved in the restart, and Jack thanked me for participating and contributing. In fact, it appeared as though we were the only solid citizens in the CFD, as it was certainly inferred that our seat had the right specs, wherein neither the seat cover nor the factory operatives did. This story stuck with me as similar situations seemed to recur over ensuing

---

[32] A precise measuring instrument.

years. Granted, Detroit was not particularly happy about taking orders from the federal government, and feedback about product feasibility *and introductory date* generally were received as sniveling by the government operatives. A predictable and highly publicized example happened several years later.

The Michigan legislators passed a law with an aggressive introductory date, requiring children's pajamas to be flameproof. Several manufacturers recommended that the date be deferred in order to ensure that all systems were up and running, particularly since a new chemical was involved in the process.

"What, you're arguing that innocent children should be killed or burned so that you can take your time getting this ready?" the politicians railed.

Predictably, no timing relief was offered. As you may remember, nobody accounted for the fact that the hurriedly prepared and ordered bag containing the toxic fire retardant resembled that of a cattle dietary supplement. Sure enough, for a considerable period, cows were fed this stuff that contaminated their milk and the beef, both of which were in the food chain for a number of months. When the problem was finally diagnosed, about 10,000 cattle had to be slaughtered. The then Michigan governor, Bill Milliken, offered that the episode seemed to equally contaminate his governorship despite his accomplishments and popularity on most issues. Only for my own curiosity, I recently researched the issue and discovered that female children born of mothers who were pregnant at the time exhibited premature menstrual activity, the effects of which are still unknown. What the hell, as this is being written, your governments are giving themselves timing relief on their several-year project to have non-HD television stations turned off, primarily because they are way, *way* behind in arranging for boxes to convert existing sets. Bulletin: The vaccine for the swine flu was rationed because shipments were delayed for unforeseen reasons. Thank heavens the people responsible were easy on themselves.

Shortly thereafter, my boss Charlie left the company to take over his own Cadillac dealership in Cleveland, obviously leaving me with some trepidation as, even though I've been responsible for products comprising 90 percent of the company business, I wondered if the company wanted to commit its total marketing to such a neophyte. They hired a semi-retired respected former sales manager to come in several days a week to be mentor and "seat-warmer" for me. What more could one ask for? Particularly since I

107

still had another year of MBA night school ahead where, once I got into the week, sometimes my obligations became more that I could possibly handle. I found myself dictating my school assignments over the phone from customer waiting rooms and sometimes didn't even have time to proof for typos before turning them in, thereby giving at least a subliminal message to the grader that perhaps I didn't take these assignments too seriously. I told you, these were good bosses.

As luck would have it, shortly before Charlie left, he was scheduled to attend the annual fall Society of Automotive Engineers conference at the Greenbriar in West Virginia, only to break his arm shortly before the event. Lo and behold, the Rileys were tapped to get on the train in Detroit and to get off at White Sulfur Springs,[33] a short walk from the famed resort. Although not much of a "chore" as purported in the head of this chapter, the seminar did have morning sessions. The former military general, acting as assistant head of NHTSA, spoke on the relationship between the automotive community and the newly formed agency. The message was that the industry should not be distrustful of the safety group but rather, his group should be considered a partner in ensuring the motoring public the safest possible means of private transportation. So far as procedure, "We will never specify the nature of hardware requirements. All of our rules will be centered around performance. Only when we have proved to ourselves that means could be available *at reasonable cost* would we move the performance specs closer to what we feel is ideal."

These words were somewhat encouraging, but I think there remained trepidation on several levels. If, for instance, one wanted to undermine the commercial airline industry one could perhaps make the case that all passengers should be required to be fitted with parachutes. The jets were fairly new and we didn't really know how durable they were. Also, there were all of these nuts currently high-jacking planes to Havana and potentially shooting holes in the fuselage; think of how much safer passengers would be. Of course, such requirement would render commercial aviation unfeasible— not to mention that its carefully crafted and subsidized financial model was soon learned to be much more fragile than ever dreamed of in the Sixties.

---

[33] We thought seriously of giving our fourth child the middle name of Greenbriar, or C&O, but thought better of it; as you know we called her Julie instead.

On another level, people gravitating toward employment in the new administration undoubtedly thought they were doing important work. Certainly some of them might let their idealism and enthusiasm espouse specifications that are not as attainable as they might seem. As I will later discuss, if such a situation or misjudgment occurred, the process would become so politicized as to force NHTSA or later, EPA, to be almost completely immovable so as not to appear to be "caving in to Detroit." I'm only surmising, but I believe that the process got, and remains, so politicized that the SAE, the non-legal automotive standard-setting organization for the industry, elected to put its new home office in Pittsburgh, a place bearing little relationship to the industry, so as to ostensibly straddle the two factions and not appear to be indebted to either.

I was finishing my MBA and a brilliant young economics professor kept asserting that for optimum economic performance there be only two parties to any transaction, the buyer and the seller. If a third party is inserted, *no matter his motives,* resources become misallocated (more broadly, things tend to get screwed up). Certainly, one must have overseers to prevent charlatans from prospering through undetectably shoddy products, or a Food and Drug Administration and a Department of Agriculture to oversee the plethora of products arriving from an almost unlimited number of sources. To rationalize a third-party intervention, the test should be a comparison of the anticipated benefits to the loss of economic efficiency. Otherwise, a good assumption is that the consumer is the best judge of what is best for himself, particularly with tangible goods or things that are a matter of taste.

We should state here that the directives put forth by NHTSA are not retroactive. That makes considerable sense, as retrofitting cars is, almost by definition, an inefficient use of resources. Unless there was some great urgency, none of which I recall, the starting date coincided roughly with the start of a new year's production, the trigger being when manufactured. During one of the early summers, General Motors endured an unauthorized local plant strike just before the end of the model year. Accordingly, about 130 cars, I think Chevy IIs, never got through paint as the plant stopped for a number of weeks. When things got settled, the plant had to change tooling, conduct an expedited pilot program, dust off and finish the damn Chevy II leftovers. Oh, and by the way, they had to get a deviation or waiver from NHTSA as they technically weren't "manufactured" in time to capture the old rules and were now technically considered "NON-CONFORMING" vehicles. Now, remember there were still several thousand of these exact vehicles in dealer lots and showrooms and hundreds of thousands of Chevy IIs running on the highways, all of which were considered "CONFORMING" or "GRANDFATHERED" and therefore could be legitimately sold as new or used cars, as the case might be.

NHTSA turned down the request for deviation on the 130 cars.

"*No problem,*" was the GM solution, "we'll sell them in Canada."

Oops! GM shouldn't have acted so publicly. Canada then had to say that it wouldn't approve import of such "non-conforming unsafe vehicles." Things were getting somewhat serious. Perhaps the totally rational safety "helpers" weren't so totally rational. On the other hand, maybe the country's resources weren't needlessly scrapped after all, perhaps there's an environmentally friendly barrier reef off Key West or similar place enabled by the placement of eleven dozen 1968 Chevy IIs.

Something only occurs to me now, as I have learned to think like an entrepreneur rather than a loyal company man that was part of my training. There was probably an opportunity to secure the Chevy IIs and never attempt to get them licensed, but use them to create sort of a Western U.S. equivalent of a Viking funeral. One could easily outfit the interior to accept the departed loved one, create some device to hold the gas pedal down and launch both over the South Rim.[34]

---

[34] At the same time recreating the scene from *Rebel Without a Cause.*

CHAPTER THIRTEEN
Executive in Training

Things were moving along and I was being exposed to situations that they don't teach you in "B school" or, for that matter, probably some that aren't experienced in most people's lifetimes.

Ford Motor had established a special group to investigate and develop a heavy-truck turbine engine to replace the historic diesel engine. We sensed a potential fit in that in our history one of our skunk-factory[35] people had developed a technique for manufacturing rotor and vane assemblies for jet engines. This is tantamount to fastening a multitude of curved fan blades (vanes) onto a large metal ring (rotor). As one might imagine, it would be quite a complicated process of welding the vanes to the rotor considering that exotic alloy metals are used and that all of the surfaces are curved. This process, later known as "stabbing," brought a specific spot in the rotor up to a critical temperature then quickly thrust the vane right through the rotor, creating almost a seamless assembly that enabled a very straightforward means of testing for structural integrity. Since it was a niche business, we didn't do much with it, but we recently had secured all of the rotor business for the new Boeing 747 and the business had always contributed cash to the company.

Our thinking was that since we had proven skills in working with exotic aerospace materials, perhaps we could secure a toehold in this proposed turbine business by cooperating and participating in pilot model development. Unfortunately, our automotive guys, my group, didn't have proper product knowledge to handle the account and our aircraft guys didn't have any contacts or interest with Ford.

Accordingly, we hired a highly reputable manufacturer's representative, who not only knew the technology surrounding the business, but also was a reputed "drinking buddy" of the anointed Ford heavy-turbine czar. This was handled mostly outside my purview as I had little to contribute and was

---

[35] An advanced and uninhibited development laboratory.

preoccupied with other matters. I was nonetheless copied on the monthly reports and knew we had secured several orders for one-of-a-kind pilot or test-engine parts, a propitious sign. All of a sudden, there was a dilemma.

A meeting was called to review the issue. It seems the "czar" had been participating in the recently established adult-luncheon circuit. He had become smitten with the hostess at one of these eateries and approached our representative asking that, as a buddy, could he possibly loan him a sum of money so that he could "tidy up his affairs" (dump the first wife) and ride off into the sunset with this wonderful creature he would cherish to his dying day. Our rep, in turn, requested that we be a backup for the loan. It wasn't an awful lot, about $5,000, but that seemed like a lot to me in the Sixties, and more importantly, the whole episode and request was tawdry. We asked our rep what he would do if we rejected the proposal. He reasonably responded that although he knew this guy for many years, he didn't have other business with him at the moment and would think about it, but he probably would walk away. He was proposing that he lend his buddy the money and we become payer of last resort. We decided to indemnify him against a loss on the loan.

Fast forward two years. There was still a breath of life in the turbine program, but things weren't moving very rapidly. Our rep reminded us that he was still holding the bag on the loan to the czar. The esteemed czar apparently wasn't going to be coming forward, therefore, shouldn't the rep be allowed to collect from us? Have you approached him directly on the issue, we asked? No, and it would be awkward for him to do so, maintained the rep. Enough of that, we said. Figure out a way to graciously bring up the subject, and if things don't go well, we'll pony up for the loan. We got feedback. According to the czar, it was an extremely bad time to bring up the issue. To his dismay, the princess he married didn't seem to be as innocent as he had supposed. In fact, she had actually been exhibiting more affection for buying clothes or improving her standard of living than she had been exhibiting affection or support for him. He didn't know what he was going to do. It certainly wasn't an appropriate time to be discussing this.

We paid the money. I, obviously, made a mental note. Again I commended the bosses for letting me observe and participate in this debacle, without having to decide the issue or be responsible for the outcome.

One day, two guys from the FBI came into my office.

"Can we talk?" they asked.

This could not be good.

I could think of no reason to immediately make a mad dash for the border (even though it was only four miles away). Of course we could talk. I thought it was maybe related to a situation of a few months prior when we had let the local police use our second story as a staging area for a drug bust across the street. It wasn't. They asked me to acknowledge that I had hired a young woman several years earlier to work in one of our small sales departments. It seems that young Detroit women who weren't ensured of a Saturday-night date sometimes went to Windsor, Canada, where a lot of Vietnam War draft dodgers were ensconced. Apparently, she and several local girls had been carpooling to the occasional party. One of the other girls was a daughter of one of our factory foremen, allegedly not an inherently attractive woman. Quite unexpectedly, this woman announced that she was engaged to one of the Windsor guys. Several weeks later, she maintained that the engagement was broken and that she was pretty upset. Several weeks after that, she seemed to have disappeared, as her usual behavior never expressed signs of meandering. Her parents called the authorities. Without giving away anything regarding any investigation, the FBI revealed that they suspected foul play. They'd talked to my employee and maintained that perhaps she hadn't understood the gravity of the situation. (I was starting to catch on.) If, in fact, there had been foul play, it seemed logical to assume that the assailant might deduce that this secretary was the only conduit as to where and with whom the girl had been consorting. Therefore, it took not a big step to surmise that such a person might think that it would take only one more rub out for him to be free for life.

"She may be in considerable personal danger." (I was afraid they were going to say that.)

For the first time in his career, Bobby fix-all didn't have all the answers and would admit that a specific task was beyond his job description.

It's surprising what one can do when forced against the wall. I did talk to the girl with her boss after thinking quite a bit about it. I explained that nobody thought that she had done anything wrong but if these guys were really bad, they might try to make things hard for her. The interview ended with her stating, "I don't know why they keep wanting to talk to me, I didn't know Cindy all that well."

The FBI agents were right; she just didn't get it.

I went to talk to personnel. John (bless him) said that this problem was more up his line. Why didn't he handle it—and call on me only if he needed my help on some specific thing. If I ever say anything bad about personnel guys, I'm not talking about John. I went about my business.

Several months later I stopped in personnel walking back from lunch.

"Thanks for stepping in, John, has there been any resolution on the problem?"

"Oh, long ago. The former fiancé decided she had become a pain in the behind and did her in. His trial was more than a month ago and he's incarcerated for 25 years or some such thing. They don't coddle over there as they do here."

Does it dawn on you how much I'm saving on movie tickets? I get the feeling that I'm a participant in these dramas with convoluted plots, in some cases even demonstrating more human fallibility than you see even on the silver screen. Unfortunately, they mostly are *film noir* situations; there are very few *Luxury Liner* or *Holiday in Rio* plots mixed in.[36]

Now that I was on staff, several of my cohorts, including the general manager, encouraged me not to get intimidated by the financial guys and how smart they appeared at the staff meetings.

The conversation went something like this: "They talk about their deviation analyses and their random-access programming and their optimization studies, but they don't know squat about our products or our processes. Take them out on the shop floor sometime and ask them to show you the forging machines. Ask them if this is an axle housing or a torsion bar. They don't know anything about the nature of our business."

Although never shy with my own opinions, I made a mental note of this.

As there are relatively few key buying influences when selling original equipment systems for the auto makers, one tries to create an environment in which negotiations are based on shared values and mutual respect, while maintaining arms-length dealing. Those that have "gamed" that system, rather than really lived by it, have on occasion implied that they really enjoyed working with the other party, and if that party ever decided or was required to make a professional move, they knew of at least one place to

---

[36] I'm grousing because I had no shoes. My apologies. Many of my almost contemporaries were living through the horrific Vietnam experience. My hat is off to them.

which they could turn. I was early on taught that this behavior was unacceptable and leaves either (1) a false sense of security to the other party or (2), to the most sophisticated parties, leaves the impression that they are being "bought."

One Thursday I was working in my office and there had been a winter storm watch. I checked home to assure myself that the kids were safe and that we didn't have any unusual obligations. All of a sudden, it was my senior buyer from Chrysler on the phone who had just been a victim of R.I.F.[37] He was naturally quite upset and wondered if there was perhaps a place in our company for him. I'd only been dealing with him on what you might call a peer level for a couple of years. He had been square with us and we have had several pleasant evenings and golf games as couples. Probably, over the years, one of my predecessors had suggested this call. I knew that our own company wasn't in a hiring mode. It was also known to me that the act of hiring one of his professional profile might start the phone ringing by others, only to be met with rejection. I knew this guy would function better in a purchasing situation rather than a sales one. On the other hand, I did commiserate and think it appropriate to provide emotional support. Remember, he had just been cut off from his associates of quite a few years and I think he was entitled to a cathartic discussion amongst people with whom he wished to confide.

"What a shock," I responded. "You've obviously caught me cold, so there's nothing that I know of offhand. I tell you what. Let me make a few phone calls [I mentioned the names of a few higher ups in the company that he was acquainted with] just to get the situation sized up. I would feel better discussing this with you in person. Would you consider meeting for a quiet dinner with Susie and Alice later this evening? Let's think of something convenient—wait a minute, how about the Red Fox?[38] I'm only a mile west and you must be within two miles the other way."

Arrangements completed. Boy, my Susie puts up with a lot.

We got there and our guests arrived shortly afterward. There was hardly anyone in the restaurant because of the snow. Obviously, both of them were

---

[37] Let go because of a Reduction In Force.

[38] The same place where Jimmy Hoffa was to be stood up for lunch five years later, or was he?

shaken and her eyes were red. We got a drink and both of them started talking a mile a minute, which was good, otherwise I would have been expected to talk.

Two servers approached the table.

"Excuse me," said the woman server three or four times, each time more emphatically. "This is really important! I'm Brenda, your server this evening and this is John. John is a trainee so don't expect to see him delivering food although he will usually be with me."

Fine. Brenda and John left.

Our guests continued. A little later Alice was in a particularly bad patch, explaining, "For more than ten years we had hoped to join a private golf club and with your help and introductions were able to join Detroit Golf Club which we just adore. I don't care what happens—"

"Excuse me!"

"—somehow we'll tough it out although I know the job market can't be—"

"Excuse me!"

"—very good. If things get really bad, we'll sell our home before we drop out of that very special place."

Her head fell into her hands.

"Thank you. I may have left the wrong impression with you. Although I told you about John, I neglected to tell you about James, who will be your carver this evening, as the need arises. I didn't want you to be confused. Enjoy your cocktails! I'll be back in a moment."

And she was true to her word and returned. And returned. And returned.

"I'll let you know the specials"

"I'll deliver the explanations when I deliver the complimentary appetizers."

"I'll make sure you know about our special butter when I deliver the rolls"

"I'll take your orders."

"I'll find out whether you want walnuts or blue cheese on your salad."

"I'll finally introduce James."

"And—I'll demand to be front and center about eight more times within the next hour."

It must have been the first time in my life that I ever experienced a parallel universe, that is, two completely detached activities being

116

superimposed and alternately espoused in an urgent or highly emotional manner. I will say though, I did later have a similar sense, although vicariously, in some of the British plays such as *Absurd Person Singular* or *How the Other Half Loves.*

I was able to report that I had talked to a few of our named executives who wanted me to extend their sympathies and who had promised to keep their eyes and ears open.

I also have a suggestion about living for my dear readers. When an eatery says, "We don't just serve dinner, when you come here you receive a total dining experience," turn tail and go to a place where they just serve dinner.

The company was as good as its word. I was promoted to top sales guy after a year. The next year was quite successful as we captured more than our share of our traditional Ford business. As a kicker, we got a windfall from Chrysler when Rockwell exited as a competitor in the seating business and we were successful in our offer to "turn on a dime" and take over its business —no project cost, same landed price, no sweat.

However, our general manager, one of my last links to the company when I was hired, was let go and replaced by that former personnel manager —which put us as we described in our earlier assertions about conglomerates.

The company, now known as the previously discussed conglomerate Lear Siegler, bought into the "touchy feely" management style so popular in the late Sixties; accordingly, we had a highly reputable consulting company regularly send its psychologist to do a "360°"analysis on key personnel, one attempting to assess relationships of each individual on a boss-subordinate-peer basis. I recall the first interview where he sincerely and quietly asserted that he would like to give me a test, but only if I chose to take it, and that, in either event, it would have no impact on my status within the company. Sure, I've been taking competitive tests all my life. He warned that I would have only fifteen minutes. I took the test. It was an insult.This test was so simple that Mohamed Ali would have aced it and gone into officer's training school.[39] I finished in six minutes and took another minute to look for errors.

---

[39] As many of you might recall, Ali didn't do well on his Army induction exam, which was passed by 95 percent of inductees. His riposte? He gleefully and laughingly responded, "I always said I was the greatest; I didn't say I was the smartest!"

I shoved it at him. Wouldn't I like to take a little longer reviewing? I'm was catching on only then. The test itself was meaningless. He was assessing my approach to taking the test, my demeanor while taking it and so on. He looked at the test.

"How'd I do?"

"Pretty good, only a few wrong."

He reached down to put the test in his case.

"Excuse me, that surprises me—"

I think he marked me type A.

Over the next several years, I found these guys quite helpful, but only in this context: In talking about a certain situation or relationship, I would assess about 80 percent of what they would say would be accurate, but something I already knew. The next 15 percent would be absolute baloney that they must have dreamed up to justify their exorbitant fees. But there was 5 percent that was profound, things that they could explain that I would never deduce, because they came from a background, a set of values or motivations, that are different than my own. If you could pluck out these nuggets, in certain cases it would greatly improve personal interactions. The "rules" for talking to the consultant were that you were to be as candid as possible with him, and he would act as your surrogate when talking to other parties. He would subsequently generalize your issues in order to rationalize the situation in his own mind and separately offer what he felt were appropriate postures for each participant.

One day, when showing up for an appointment, my interviewer confessed, "I'm not really myself today, I've just come from my sessions at Bendix and they're extremely trying, as their means for motivation of employees is not "carrot and a stick" but more like "pushing with a rope."

I didn't understand exactly what he was talking about then, but I came to find out later.

You must recall our Ford buyer and also our Canadian associates. I was not shocked to learn that my "Canadian cousins" didn't revere the Ford purchasing guy either. On top of that, when the new U.S.-Canadian auto-trade agreement enabled Ford to centralize its North American purchasing operations in Dearborn, it created all sorts of personal inconveniences and a sense of insignificance on Canadian suppliers who naturally felt more comfortable in dealing at Oakville and Oshawa, Ontario. (When I first learned about this, I had guys roaming the halls there daily, and I told my new boss who suggested I not inform my Canadian associates as I would probably be tagged as "the messenger.")

"Let them find out the bad news on their own!"

Several months later I was chatting with the Canadian salesman (remind me to tell you one of his most unusual experiences), to commiserate with him and see how he was coping. Specifically with regard to our mutual Ford personality, he maintained he was going along okay, but he was taping all of his conversations as he thought that he would shortly have something so incriminating that he could plead for his rotation out of that job. Clearly, not my style.

About six months later my boss, the general manager, asked me to stop by to discuss several issues. Not an unusual occurrence, as he was always meddling with sporting-event tickets.

"I've got several tasks for you. One, your Ford friend is giving everyone fits. I want all calls with him to be taped, so we can assess if he's dealing fairly with us, or making inappropriate remarks about our management. Buy as much equipment as you will need."

(Less than a second pause.)

Two!

Being just as quick as the Dickens, I picked up that the lack of pause between the first task and the second obviously meant there would be no toleration of discussion regarding the first task. The next several tasks were trivial, reinforcing my thought that they were only intended as barn-door closers on the first.

I went back and thought. Obviously he had gotten the idea from the Canadians. First, I thought it was unethical. Second, I thought it was against the law, but I could find that out. Now any red-blooded American might take extraordinary steps if his children would go hungry or his wife was being accosted. But, what would be the benefit of this? Some of our "suits" thought they had been bad-mouthed? Third, *It was stupid!* My boss was told by his Canadian boss to tell me to do this and he dutifully did. He wouldn't dare to follow up or even bring it up again.

I went and talked to my account manager, a senior guy who became quite agitated.

"Oh it's those Canadian guys, they think they've got so much under control," he said.

119

"Calm down, I've already decided we're going to stonewall it, I just wanted you to know the lay of the land so that you don't unwittingly start talking about our cousin's shenanigans."

A week or two later I encountered the "shrink" who was going to see one of my guys.

"I've got a real one to throw up against the wall. Please see me when you have three minutes."

Do you want to know the learned psychologist's reaction to my real dilemma? I wish I could tell you, but even I can't remember, other than he really, really didn't want to hear what I just told him. I do remember that he flannel mouthed me to the extent that he completely flunked.

What about the Canadian cousin's escapade? As I previously said, the moving of the Ford purchasing function for Canadian production from Oakville to Dearborn created agitation for most Canadian suppliers. Our guy had come over on a Thursday, intending to finish his business about Friday noon and drive the four hours home as he and his wife had a dinner date. Well, perhaps someone left him waiting in the lobby but, anyway, things ran long and, instead of getting away at noon, it was mid-afternoon. He was already way behind and he was trying to beat Friday traffic.

He got to the Ambassador Bridge, one of the two Detroit connections to Canada, and was reminded that it was undergoing repair and that there was only one open lane in each direction. He thought something like: Oh well, better just line up and hope for the best as the tunnel goes through downtown Windsor.

He was crawling along with the traffic and got about half way when the VW "Bug" ahead of him stopped.

A young woman got out.

"What the hell is going on now?" he said to himself, but much later admitted to being momentarily distracted by the attractive blond woman. She left the door open, walked in front of his car, took about twelve more steps across the idle lane and the walkway to reach the railing. One leg over, the other leg over, and she was gone!

Can you imagine the rush? Panic!

I've got to get help, he thought. He opened his window signaling the oncoming lane to let him get past the VW. No such courtesies were extended but he forced his way through amidst a gaggle of horns and epithets. At last, he got clear sailing to the Canadian side and the authorities. He finally pulled up to the guard completely out of breath, although he hadn't taken so much as a step.

"The girl—the girl—out of the Volkswagen and over to that side. Both legs over in seconds. She doesn't jump but she's gone. I can't believe it — she never stopped—I had no chance to—"

"How long have you been in the United States?"

"You don't understand, the girl in the VW, gone—no hesitation—just gone! She got out of the car and — it seems so unreal—"

"Let me put it this way, when did you come to Detroit?"

"Yesterday, but I wanted to get home early and look what I got into—the girl got out of the car and—"

"Have you anything to declare?"

"No, but you'll give it to the authorities—wait a minute, will they want me as a witness—are you going to call a tow truck? Should I be filling out a—"

"They're starting to back up behind you, sir, off y'go."

"But we're going to have to —"

"I'm going to have to ask you to proceed, sir"

This was unreal, he thought. (Imagine, if you will, the *Twilight Zone* theme song.) He pulled over to think (in the area where they ask you to stop when they suspect you've got contraband Jack Daniels). An extremely good policy when one is flummoxed.

And so he thought: How come no one was interested? I guess when I saw that guy's badge I assumed he had general law-enforcement interest and authority. Not so, obviously; he was only interested in Black Jack and pot. Certainly someone of authority must be interested. Maybe I'll try to find the nearest police station.

He did so.

Boy, were they interested.

Although he was relieved and glad to tell what he saw to real authorities, now he had the opposite problem.

"What color were her eyes? Nail polish? Moles or scars? Other uniquely identifying characteristics? Color and type of shoes? Pleated or un-pleated skirt? Hair?"

Four times he went through the routine with four different officers. He finally got home around 2:00 A.M., but he couldn't have eaten anyway. Later, he did receive correspondence from the Windsor Police informing him

121

that the woman had been found downriver and that his help enabled them to close the unfortunate case in an orderly manner.

About this time, the boss told me that the niche aerospace business was under critical review. In corporation speak that means he was going to drop the sucker. What could be his motive? What prompted him to initiate this? I finally discerned what was happening. The "Lear" in the company name refers to the Grand Rapids aerospace instrumentation business and the largest division in the company. Accordingly, many of the company executives, including our group vice president and the chairman, speak aerospace while we speak Motown. When my boss spoke with a superior, he was always grilled about our aerospace business and specifics of new aerospace programs, both commercial and governmental, in terms of code names and acronyms that he didn't comprehend. For his own credibility and his career's sake, he decided that it would be easier to exit the business than keep up to date on these programs, although he did try to give the business to a sister division, with no takers.

The macro-economic talk in the early 1970s dealt with the fear of inflation, as the "fed" had made some adjustments in its money supply to more closely correspond and react to economic activity. The boss asked me to make a brief presentation for discussion at the next divisional quarterly staff meeting, emphasizing how our business might be affected and any potential solutions. While I theoretically understood economics, I wasn't qualified to gin up my own theories, so I found what I considered to be a particularly sensible article in *New York Times Magazine* and used that as the basis of my presentation. In those days, inflation was defined as either "cost push" or "demand pull." We were definitely in a "cost push" scenario and so my recommendation, after a statement of the problem and some analysis, was to "freeze" wages. My theory was that, in our highly integrated economy, all variable costs consist of wages if one considers the whole supply stream. This theory and proposed action was received, I felt, with "a grain of salt" at the meeting. No one contested the logic but governmental action of that sort was unprecedented.

As luck would have it, in about six months after my presentation, Nixon froze wages *and prices* because of his and his advisers' concern that, without some sort of dramatic action, inflation might rise to a level as high as 7 percent After about thirty seconds of gloating to myself because of my prescience, it dawned on me to semi-panic and that I'd better check the status

122

of my pricing with the various customers (about $75 million worth) because the rules were that prices were frozen at the level of published pricing or *executed* contracts as of the date of the edict. It turned out that we were in a pretty good position. Some of the pricing had anticipated increased future costs and was guaranteed constant for the coming year. That applied mainly to GM and to Chrysler and, to my barely muted satisfaction, gave Chrysler heartburn as they had insisted that we estimated cost increases and submit prices containing those at the risk of losing business. I think the unwritten rules are that when you submit a bid to secure business you may well want to represent such a bid as constant pricing plus variable cost increases for the purpose of plausibility, but since it is really a market test on the part of Chrysler and an arm's length bid to secure business on your part, it's not technically a price increase that you're negotiating with an existing costumer. To their chagrin, they had *issued* contracts reflecting these increases long before we started shipping under them and consequently, before the "freeze." Their own aggressive purchasing policies enabled us to get our Chrysler business re-priced "under the wire." Theoretically, at least, they had accepted our price increases and were barred by the government from passing them along to their customers. Obviously, they didn't see it from quite the same perspective, but we soon worked out our differences.

At any rate, having become a self-anointed expert in optimizing pricing systems, we stayed on top of the government rules. As it turned out, you were permitted to pass along your actual incurred increases in labor and material, as compared to that in your previous pricing, but could not include a contribution to profit (the government implied they were more afraid of "demand pull" inflation by introducing this procedure). First, of course, you had to demonstrate your intentions to the Federal Government and get approval. We went to the local Federal Building the first day that the PC-1s were available, that being the form that was used to petition the government for permission to raise prices. To my dismay, one was required to petition the government by presenting a computation showing how you arrived at your new pricing and supply underlying support, such as a labor contract showing wages being increased or suppliers' price changes before the "freeze" and not yet being included in pricing. Another "required" part of the computation was to subtract one's own productivity improvement during the interim the existing prices were in effect. We spent 36 of the next 48 hours to get these in before the crush. To my delight, however, was the condition that unless one had received notice within thirty days that such pricing was disapproved by the "price board," one was permitted to price at the submitted levels. Noting that it takes a magazine about six weeks to change your address and about the same time for the IRS to return your overpayment, it seemed that we would be tethered for only thirty days, which turned out to be the case. Not that it got us much of anywhere during the confusion throughout the industry, but I secured some sadistic delight in accompanying my guys to specific customers where we had submitted price increases months before.

Conversations went along these lines:

"I'm sorry, guys, you're entitled to an increase and I think I indicated that you could have one, but my hands are tied," they may have opened. "But the government says that it's illegal for me to issue a purchase order with a new price on it because of the freeze."

"There are provisions where the government will allow price increases if the seller gets approval from the government."

"Yeah, but that's way down the road. Nobody knows much about that. That'll have to be ironed out in the future."

"We've got good news for you. We have run the gauntlet. See, here are our receipts for our PC-1s. As of yesterday at 3:20 P.M. we were allowed to charge you what we told you several months ago. So far as having to show you something from the government, to misrepresent that we hadn't gotten injunctive instructions from the government when we actually had would put both of us in the hoosegow for at least six months. So, you see, you are permitted to give us the price increase as requested in our submission of August 21, 1971."

"Put aside the price freeze. *Would you believe* that I can't pay you the price increase because—"

As it turned out, the cost and pricing actions of 1971 were not a seminal event in the history of the industry, although they generated confusion throughout, until at least 1974. I'll always remember that blinky little birdlike guy that explained the price board during the announcement in 1971. Wait a minute! It couldn't be. Is that the same guy now trying to get the darter-snap arboretum for West Virginia? (At least it was until he succumbed, still as senator in 2010).

After the dust had settled and the wage/price freeze was history, several notable economists stated that the exercise was categorically ineffective. Why? If any price freeze is actually effective, there will emerge a black market, and none seemed to appear during this particular period. Although inflation did not increase, they maintained that that was the normal course of economic events. It is my belief, however, that the freeze gave management a pernicious mindset to keep its pricing current rather than periodically catching up, perhaps leading to Jimmy Carter's inflation of 12 percent during the "malaise" later in the Seventies.

CHAPTER FOURTEEN
Transition

As you've probably sensed from my presentation of the "conglomerate" style and the general behavior and demeanor of my insecure bosses, I concluded it was time to move on. Although I was on the chairman's "Hi-Po" list and I'd had eight productive years, the conglomerate itself seemed to be hiccuping and there were probably not going to be many divisional openings, as they seemed to be backtracking on the need for business diversity.

I was recruited as automotive-industry manager for an aluminum company, Harvey Aluminum. It had just been sold to Martin Marietta, who had hired what I considered to be outstanding young management, and they had the presence of mind to hire an "automotive" guy to handle that particular part of the business. They saw the automotive industry as a fertile field for aluminum applications, particularly because of its ability to decrease weight, thereby increasing fuel mileage. During the interview process, they remarked that I seemed to be particularly "well read." I didn't seem to remember that attribute as being bandied about in Motown.

In the two weeks between my acceptance of their offer and showing up for work, the company name was changed from Harvey Aluminum to Martin Marietta Aluminum.

I spent a couple of weeks at the home office in Torrance, California, for product and organizational familiarization. My sense during the recruitment process was more than confirmed regarding the capability and openness of my new management. I was less than enthused, however, that the prevalent product lines had generally become commodities, such as sheet, plate, extrusions, foil. When I had a cousin in the business during the Forties and early Fifties, I sensed the excitement of a new material with several admirable attributes being applied to new fields.

"They're going to be making canoes out of this stuff."

"You don't even have to paint your house anymore. They're going to use it for aftermarket house siding and paint it and cure it so you'll never have to paint again." (In terms of aesthetic appeal, this one didn't have "legs.")

Sailor Rex Marshall told you on television how pliable and easy it was to use Reynolds aluminum foil in the kitchen to preserve food, much more adaptable than waxed paper or cellophane. Heat transfer properties were excellent, so that pots, pans and griddles would be made from it, although much later there were allegations that this contributed to Alzheimer's. The 1958 Chevy Impala had colored decorative anodized appliqués in the door panels. (That application was dropped, as they couldn't control the color within zillions of angstroms of the specs.)

Actually, I was more concerned with the regularization of the support functions such as rapid turnaround on quotations for new business, timely delivery of pilot and production samples and production scheduling rather than the maturity of the industry itself, as it was understood that my charter was to influence and secure specific designs of automotive components, with an emphasis on fabricated products made in our Adrian, Michigan, extrusion factory. I was going to be the guy to lead them into the automotive industry and a stable of quasi-proprietary new products.

The first apparent application to attack was automotive bumpers. Aluminum extrusions were capable of making car-width bumper "blanks" of complex open or closed cross sections that could be shaped and machined to a specific car design. Not only was there a weight savings, but also these savings came in the overhung front or rear mass, an extremely desirable situation from the standpoint of vehicle handling. We were too late for the Chevrolet Vega application, but were able to secure business from Chevrolet (Corvette) and Pontiac.

I encountered the cultural challenges that I sensed would happen but only could specifically identify when they actually occurred. The aluminum company had an ordering process wherein the customer submitted a purchase order for a specific material within the stated specifications and in a specific amount to be delivered two to six months in the future. Naturally, running an automobile assembly factory is a much more fluid situation. Chevrolet, as a result of their sheer volume, adjusted schedules weekly, and the current week sometimes fluctuated because of acts of nature, local strikes, product mix changes, overtime and other sorts of variables. Those immersed in the industry appreciated these updates as they could continually tweak schedules in order to home in on actual requirements and minimize inventory. My Adrian plant manager called for a command meeting.

127

"These guys don't know what the hell they're doing. They keep zigging and zagging so you don't know what's happening. We're going to have to get them shaped up!"

Not likely. Having grown up with Chevrolet, I devised a statistical system wherein I demonstrated to the factory how to adapt to the changes so as not to shut down the Corvette factory, at the same time running their own scheduling in an efficient manner.

In a similar episode, our 'Vette bumper called for several self-tapping nuts to be embodied in the bumper.

The same manager called in a swivet,

"Since these are shown on the print as specified by Chevrolet and we can't get delivery from the vendor because he has Chevrolet orders ahead of us, we assume that Chevrolet wants to insert them themselves, so that's the way we will ship the bumpers, without the rivnuts."

"No!" I replied, "We're obligated to ship to the specs on the print. I'll call the sales manager there to get parts for us, otherwise we'll have an Adrianic fire drill."

The marketing and management people continued to impress me, however, with their understated actions. They had put together a new sales staff with a diversified ethnic profile in the early Seventies, long before that became common. If there was a seminar or conference somewhere that might become awkward for one or more of the parties, they ate with the highest executive or, in the case of shared rental condos at a mates-included seminar, they would bunk with such executives.

During one of those programmed training seminars, we were obligated to undertake role playing in set-up situations, bringing the negotiation, or whatever, to its logical conclusion. Not being rocket science that required a lot of intense concentration, some of the guys had fun by impersonating celebrities or other characters, a distraction not frowned upon by the trainer and the department head. The most memorable one was of Peter Lorre trying to sell widgets to a male cross-dresser.

Several serious issues arose, however. The new Martin Marietta management didn't think it appropriate that a home office for a product such as aluminum, used mostly in the heartland, should be based on the sunny shores of the Pacific, and moved the headquarters to Washington, D.C. Not only did they pledge allegiance to where they thought more and more of the economic influence of the country would migrate, but it was also easier to "clean house" of some of the holdover Harvey employees by explaining that the company just moved away.

Secondly, a series of events made aluminum a seller's market almost overnight. The production of aluminum is electricity intensive, and the northwestern states that supplied such electricity via normally inexpensive hydroelectric power had incurred a drought, thereby permitting the release of electricity to gluttons like aluminum-reduction factories only on a standby basis. Now, the vaunted sales department automatically became overstaffed. A company didn't need many prospectors when you could sell all of the aluminum you could make on the basis of, "We'll let you know the price when we ship it to you." Although they slimmed down the general activity in the Detroit area, I was assured that my automotive activity would continue, as it embodied a long-term strategy for providing products with proprietary content in a large industry that may have been on the verge of substituting aluminum for iron or steel for several significant applications.

During this bush-beating part of my career I nonetheless attempted to stay in touch with the industry in general. At the annual Greenbrier seminar, a study entitled "RECAT"[40] was presented that evaluated all of the safety items mandated to date, including their actual and economic performance. As of 1973, the only item to pay off[41] was the seat belt. I should mention here that this was about the time that GM introduced a version of the much talked about "air bag" that would cause so much brouhaha in the future. The car was the Oldsmobile Toronado; the air bag was of large design, covering from the hips to the head, of which only a few thousand were sold. Of interest to only me and a few other involved associates in the late Eighties was that the seat belt company that we later controlled had made an alternative proposal to use a canister of highly compressed air instead of exploding chemicals to force out the bag. When our customers professed skepticism when trying to introduce such a concept fifteen years later, their doubts centering about being able to maintain such high pressure over years of repose, we found several of the unused prototypes from the early Seventies activity. The

---

[40] An acronym created by the think tank authors of the report, the full phrase being lost in the mists of time.

[41] At $1 million per death averted and $300,000 per injury averted.

pressure readings were 3,000 psi. The technology was adopted 20 years later for heavier vehicles.

During this period, one of the landmark events of this fifty-year history occurred. In early November, 1973, President Nixon gave an address to the nation explaining that because the oil-exporting nations of the Middle East had embargoed shipments to the U.S.A., we would need to reduce our short-term usage of petroleum products by turning down thermostats in our homes, lowering speed limits, using smaller cars and minimizing recreational driving. Since he was on the subject of petroleum fuel, he also offered that our long-term usage of such fuel would have to be reduced as worldwide reserves only amounted to seven years. He also reminded us that oil was not a renewable resource, that most of it was formed millions of years ago, and that once it was gone, it was gone! Within weeks, he had signed the bill for the Alaskan pipeline and had called for oil independence by 1980.

I thought about this at home that same evening and in my own cynical way of thinking came up with several items of disquiet or observations:

- Why would the president possibly commingle the short-term potential dislocation of the supply line with a caveat that long-term world supply of oil is at the precipice of collapse? These two issues are only remotely related, the first one politically initiated, the second being a statement of global geology.
- Thank heaven that gasoline is not an easy commodity to hoard!
- Speed limit of 50 mph posted on the interstate system? Could create potential death traps.

Hindsight has made me believe that this one address caused *all further operations of the domestic automotive industry to be considered as Away Games!*[42]

The domestic industry was created and had evolved amidst a seventy-year environment of inexpensive and plentiful fuel to propel our vehicles.

---

[42] The National Football League has statistically proven that the home team has some quantifiable advantage over its opponents; I recall perhaps maybe 3 or 4 points. I use the phrase in the context that all foreign competitors have grown up in a scarce gasoline environment, ergo they enjoy a "home field" advantage under scarce gasoline rules.

This, combined with the comparative vast distances between our cities,[43] caused automotive companies to concentrate on vehicles capable of carrying families for many miles in relative comfort. About 1,000 companies that didn't provide these features, as adjudicated by the American buying public, were winnowed out of the business by the end of the Sixties.

Conversely, companies in countries that might want to export here got their DNA in quite different environments. Government policies kept gasoline prices at several times those in the U.S.A. The road systems, particularly in urban areas, were not conducive to large vehicles, and the ancillary costs of operating vehicles were quite high, and favored the smallest vehicles.

To decide that the U.S.A. would henceforth operate under Europe/Asia policies relative to automobiles (gas taxes excepted) as a result of a supply-line hiccup seemed to me then and now as a premature action.

First, permit me to critique in some detail the actions by Nixon/Kissinger during those few days in November.

The embargo was precipitated by the Organization of Oil Exporting Countries (OPEC) as a result of American willingness to supply arms to Israel during the Yom Kippur war of the same year. Critics other than I pointed out that the governmental actions relating to the embargo were the first time in American history that, when an offshore entity threw a hissy-fit at an American policy, the U.S. government reaction, rather than attempting to mitigate by using the usual steps of diplomacy, economic leverage or leverage induced by American allies, instead adjusted *internal* policies to conform to such precipitous external actions.

Gasoline and crude oil are generally fungible commodities. We perhaps could have arranged for one of our allies to order and trans-ship to us. (To this day, U.S.A., Canada, Mexico and Venezuela, when taken in aggregate, are self-sufficient in oil.) We were led to believe that to do so would indicate that America was unethical or wasn't playing in the spirit of the game. The impression is gleaned on the part of the general public that OPEC behaved as a benevolent uncle or international institution that was displeased with our misbehavior and we are obligated to follow its punishment until we could gain our way back into good graces. OPEC, in fact, was a renegade consortium of countries attempting to monopolize the production and sale of

---

[43] London to Rome, all across "old" Europe, is less than 900 miles.

oil. If an American were found attending an OPEC meeting in another country, he would be immediately jailed upon his return to the U.S. If an OPEC meeting were held in the U.S., all participants would be incarcerated and severely punished. Such monopolization is strictly forbidden in the U.S. or by U.S. citizens and such behavior is dealt severe penalties. Certainly, we should have made attempts to disrupt OPEC actions or OPEC itself by, perhaps, encouraging non-OPEC countries to select one or two OPEC participant countries for worldwide boycott, as many of OPEC countries get most of their public money from the export of oil. OPEC is not a trade association or cooperative. It is a group of countries whose sole charter is to collaborate and control the production of oil to optimize revenue at the expense of others.

In MBA school I learned one good long-term feature of cartels such as OPEC. They inevitably break up as a result of diverging interests. Imagine my intellectual horror in hearing network commentators lament the "bad news" about the arguments erupting within OPEC or the possibility that OPEC itself may break up. How in the world would we continue to get our steady supply of gasoline? A lot cheaper, that's how. In my darkest moments I wonder (and am afraid to find out) if our most recent favored trading partner, Mexico, is permitted to fraternize or correspond with OPEC within the terms of NAFTA, our special commercial agreement with them.

Now let's talk about the finite supply of oil. I agree that it must be finite.[44] The issue is the absolute amount.

Permit me to make several of my perverse arguments. Let's talk about the unbridled production of chewing gum. Since the amount is constantly increasing and I'm pretty sure it doesn't degrade, at some time in the future we will be up to here with used gum. The effects on quality of life—I don't even want to go there. Here's an even better one that I'm just passing along. This one is about trash, just normal bulk household trash with no chemical or leaching implications that would have to be handled separately. An investigative scientist looked back 500 years, figured how the generation of trash *per person* has grown over those years and extrapolated this 500 years ahead. Then he found out how many *people* were on earth then and how many there are now (generating trash), also extrapolating that out for 500

---

[44] In contrast to water, which is perpetually recycled and consequently never substantially diminishes on a global basis.

years. He then created a trash generation curve, which you could readily understand would be geometrically upward in nature. He then aggregated all the trash under his curve and attempted to compute where we could put it. Let's assume we put it all in one place and will constrain the pile at a certain height so as to be able to put golf courses or condos on top after 500 years, say one mile high.[45] What area would we need to contain this pile? The size of Montana? The size of Rhode Island? Actual: a cuboid, one mile high and 20 miles on each side. Next problem?

I carried the article around for several years but can no longer find it. If you do, along with my O-blood certification, please send it to me.

When Nixon made his revelations, the amount of oil calculated to be available for pumping was seven-years worth, certainly implying that things would become dire by the turn of the century. The second crunch came in 1979 and I looked again, seven years. I looked again at the turn of the century when my computer didn't implode. Again—seven years. I haven't looked recently, but if I had to guess, the next time I break a mirror, I'll have two contemporaneous problems.

If you want to create hysteria, try taking the total amount of consumption of any commodity and then announce that you are going to allocate it amongst the states. That's exactly what happened during the first gas crunch. You will absolutely short five or more states, each of which has a large city with camera crews, more than willing to capture the mile-long lines and feed it to the networks. On top of that, control the price so that the hysterical people can accuse the dealers of "gouging" which has taken on a legalistic connotation. Once people realized that gasoline wasn't something that you could fill your garage with, they had to make sure that they got their fair share. To ensure that everyone got something, the government suggested that no one be given *more* than half a tank-full. Lines immediately doubled as the most avid waited in line for hours to get less than a gallon top-off. To re-adjust, the government suggested that no one be given *less* than half a tank. Rumors spread that you couldn't trade a Cadillac or a Lincoln for a Volkswagen, straight up. Nissan had found the going very difficult in the U.S. and was about to pull out with its Datsun vehicle, subsequently deciding to stick around for a while.

---

[45] Much like Fishkills, that makes me inclined to get to Kennedy Airport via the Verrazanno-Narrows bridge rather than via the Walt Whitman.

During the few months after the "crunch," the retail price of gasoline went from about $.25 to about $.55. Most top managers of manufacturing businesses intensely dislike operating in an inflationary environment because of the difficulty in passing along the increases in costs for incoming materials, thereby squeezing their profits. The hysteria created there enabled retail prices to climb faster than the price of a barrel of oil and such a phenomenon has been replicated in subsequent disruptions in oil supply, as proved by the profits of the major oil companies. When the price had settled at about $1.25 a gallon after the second disruption, an observer of the industry noted there still was $.25 "hysteria pricing" in a gallon of gasoline. I recall being vilified by suggesting that at a dinner party attended by several oil-related operatives (even more satisfying than the good dinner). Sure enough, after a small adjustment in the OPEC hierarchy, indicating that they didn't have as much control as previously perceived, the last two bits came out of the price.

In Motown, we were reassured that relief was coming as several American oil companies owned considerable reserves just across the river in Canada.

"Wait a minute," was Canada's response to hearing that in public. "Just because you have title to some oil that is in our country doesn't mean we're going to release it for export."

Even I didn't espouse that we start WWII I/II over that pool of oil in Canada. Things would work out if only our government didn't really take some precipitous action in its oversight of the crisis. I escorted the Chrysler guru of government relations to a speaking gig and suggested to him that I had deduced that the government had deliberately "shorted" gasoline to the media centers—such as L.A., Chicago, Miami, Philadelphia—so as to bring home the message about the shortages. He responded that it fit with their message that gasoline was, and would, become a scarce commodity, but that they were so disorganized that the seemingly staged hysteria occurred only by happenstance.

The action that really touched my funny bone was the idea about lower speed limits. Here we were just finishing the most substantial freeway system in the history of the world and we were going to strangle driving at 50 miles per hour (maximum speed was shortly set at 55). Ostensibly, this was done to save fuel, although as heavy vehicles were most efficient at speeds higher than this, savings were minimal; it seemed to me as a compulsory "sacrifice" as recognition of the shortage. In any event, the speed change to save gasoline in cars assumed that the value of one's time was about $2 per hour. A Detroit paper had followed the president of General Motors from Detroit to Lansing at about 75 mph and proudly and gleefully reported how wanton that GM president must be in the face of the crisis. He didn't bother to explain how he could rationalize his own performance following for the full distance at the same 75 mph.

Shortly thereafter, the government proudly announced that its gas-saving policies were also paying a "safety" dividend. (How many ways can the government be right on the same issue? It brings tears to my eyes.) I can certainly understand it on those three-lane jobs, with the "passing" lane in the middle. There never should have been such a perilous highway in the first place, but I knew that wasn't the case on the Interstate System. Conventional wisdom seemed to convey the phenomenon that people would always cheat a few miles per hour over the "safe" posted speed. Since there could be risk of severe penalties as one approaches 20 mph "over," the posting of the speed limit a 55 will cause people to drive at a "safer" speed. Wrong!

In the Nineties I had the pleasure of hearing a presentation by a PhD physicist who had studied the relationships of safety to speed, in detail, through empirical means. First of all, he pooh-pooh'd the idea that most motorists will exceed the posted speed limit into "unsafe" speeds.

"Baloney," he asserted—or something along these lines as I remember it, "if that were the case there would be mayhem daily on many roads in states such as West Virginia and Colorado. In certain stretches, I would challenge anyone to drive at ten miles over the speed limit and not go over the edge. People generally drive at safe speeds. It's only when speeds are posted at a significant variance to my calculated "safe" speed does mayhem and dismemberment occur. My safe speed? Take the 85 percent of drivers out of the middle of actual drivers. Take the median of those middle 85 percent and that is the safest speed for that stretch of road." [Note to reader: Aren't you sorry that you don't carry helpful information around like I do?]

I approached him afterward and told him of the "baggage" I had carried around for 40 years about the Pennsylvania Turnpike during the war. He hadn't heard of it but said he would look it up, particularly since it confirmed his work with about four years of actual data.

He also had other bits of useful information, for example, that the fatality rate goes up four times between midnight and 4:00 A.M. Our daughter had a young family in Columbia, South Carolina, and they drove to visit us for the holidays. (After all, I do live with a grandmother.) As the conventional wisdom convinced them that to have a child un-tethered while driving could lead to instant death or dismemberment, they would only drive when they knew the children would be inactive. Accordingly, they elected to leave home at 10:00 P.M., when the kids would go to sleep, and drive all night. Now I haven't commissioned my acquaintance to study it, but I would suspect that that is not even close to the safest way, considering that they are driving at night and that freeway driving is so fast that the main goal must be to avert any accident through alertness, as the survival rate for an actual crash at 70 is very low. NHTSA would provide a genuine service if they delivered real-world practical suggestions for family travel.

Incidentally, NHTSA finally admitted that their "safe" speed of 55 mph on the exurban interstate system didn't provide the safest situation after all, what with civilian "enforcers" driving in the left lane at 50 or 55 mph and other such mischief too numerous to mention.

I got a call from an obscure flesh peddler in Lansing, an unusual venue for an automotive-related recruiter. He was looking to fill a marketing position with a major automotive supplier whose identity he wouldn't reveal right away. Given my situation, I asked myself, "Why not?"

After talking with me and to whomever else he talked to, probably some in the industry and his client, he revealed that his client was Bendix. What the hell, being incentivized by being pushed with a rope must be better than with a whip, chains and food deprivation.

Although my office would be in Detroit, my bosses and the group offices would in South Bend, Indiana. (Ironically, the corporate office was in Southfield, Michigan, about three miles from the sales office.) I went to South Bend for the interview. They had it set up somewhat like a driving pool. For each hurdle I successfully crossed, we added that person to the group to visit the next interviewer. Naturally, I didn't want to expose the same pair of ears to the same shtick over and over. I found myself changing the story in subsequent meetings so that it became almost as convoluted as Chapter Six hereof. I finally grabbed hold of myself and realized that changing my basic story for amusement purposes as we went up the food chain could lead to an amusing story of how I blew the interview.

We wound up in the office of Jim Treacy, the group vice president. The straightforward interview seemed to go well, and he said "okay" in a task-accomplished sort of demeanor, extending his arm to pass along the dossier.

"Wait a minute!" he said, drawing back and re-opening the material. "Oh, I see, you attended General Motors Institute, I'm assuming therefore that you have no predilections against Notre Dame?"

Pause.

Those of us who grew up in the midwest in mid-century tend not to have apathy for Notre Dame. You either love 'em or hate 'em. In 1949, my dear parents advanced my musical education by moving me up to a Strasser wooden clarinet by spending $135 dollars, almost a king's ransom at the time. (That reminds me, it needs a pad job.) They were pleased to do this and were proud of my accomplishments, but were somewhat apprehensive that I would be taking it to school daily, and who knew what perils the Strasser and I would have to endure. At any rate, I understood that its health was equally as important as mine and, if it became lost or damaged, undoubtedly my own manhood would also become inoperative. As a pre-teen, I was starting to become interested in sports, co-incidental with Michigan State under Duffy Dougherty emerging as a national football power. In a show of misplaced exuberance (seems to happen a lot at Notre Dame), a group of ND students took a marauding run through the in-formation Michigan State Marching band. Never in my young life had I heard of such a depraved act. People and instruments were scattered everywhere, including my next-door neighbor, Tom. What type of animals could have conceived and carried out this horrific and heinous destruction? That sort of thing tends to leave an impression. It's a good thing that I completely forgot about it after 25 years. (Grrrrrrrr!)

The pause didn't last very long, and I couldn't resist.

"Jim, I have the greatest respect for Notre Dame's resourcefulness and inventiveness for gaining advantage over its opponents. I'm referring, of course, to roughing up the Michigan State Marching Band, inventing the fake injury at Iowa to stop the clock and physically intimidating the officials at Syracuse to get yet another shot at the winning field goal."

No pause.

"I don't remember the Syracuse episode," said Treacy.

"I think that happened while you were stationed in Europe, Jim," offered my future boss.

That Treacy was an okay guy. Unfortunately, he was to move on in six months.

My dear Susie had barely forgiven me for leaving those great aluminum guys thirty-five years ago, and they even offered to bring me to Washington in a planning position. But I felt that it was probably better to get back into a more familiar role. Ironically, our respective corporation's paths crossed in later years in a much less collegial manner.

CHAPTER FIFTEEN
Bendix Revealed

Only after I hired on did I realize that Bendix was the largest U.S. independent automotive supplier. I had known the name since childhood as it was stamped on the brakes of my 1946 model bicycle. Although I had known a few Bendix people over the years and knew they were significant players, they didn't seem to mingle at the usual industry-wide events, which I later attributed to the fact that most of their upper-middle managers resided in South Bend.

My two-month orientation was generally uneventful other than participating in meetings that involved forward-looking programs and existing problems. I was delighted with their market participation in brakes, steering, motors, electronics and other highly engineered products. Bendix had been the inventor of hydraulic brakes in the Twenties and subsequently power brake, disc brakes, fuel injection and many other complicated functional parts. Not only were they skilled at design and engineering, they were also preeminent in devising methods and designing "test stands" to qualify or reject acceptable products in-line with production, simultaneously quarantining and keeping track of the defects in rejected parts. For instance, the test stand for the hydraulic-brake booster checked for twelve performance characteristics and had a red light for each of these characteristics. It also included an integral bin that required a deposit after a red light or the production line wouldn't run.

In spite of the few usual mature and consequently laggard product lines, notably the decades old drum-brake line and perhaps the master-cylinder line, the product mix was quite profitable, none more so than the friction-material (brake-lining) product manufactured of asbestos, resin, rubber bands, cashew-nut shells and all sorts of exotic ingredients, where we enjoyed a considerable market share.

Almost best of all was the fact that the working-level people of the automotive segment of the company were truly committed to the business and the prosperity of their company and their customers. As I came on board,

139

there was a strike by the UAW against Kelsey Hayes, another old-line supplier with whom we competed for market share of the brake business. The two of us shared all of the Ford disc-brake business and, although we both had the capacity to handle more than our given share of such business, a paper analysis and our contractually committed shipping capabilities demonstrated that we weren't close to being able to support all of Ford's requirements on a continuing basis. The Bendix plant and group management took on the task as a challenge to absolutely maximize production by optimizing or augmenting the scarce resource (MBA school's number-one principle). They had stand-ins during meal breaks. They had a special operator exchanging rejected parts with repaired ones in order to optimize that bottleneck final-assembly and qualification operation. They worked weekends. They performed maintenance on third-shift weekends. We were able to keep up for a number of weeks until the strike ended, a very good insurance policy relating to continuation of business with a major customer.

The above extraordinary manufacturing operations were undertaken on a customer-paid, "reasonable cost no object" basis. One of my first tasks was to gather up incremental costs from the plant and put them in plausible form for remuneration from the customer, something that was quite easy for me.

Bendix, historically a revered manufacturer of automotive and aerospace components, was in the process of "modernizing" its management and rationalizing its various businesses. It had just promoted Mike Blumenthal, a remarkable individual success story, to chairman, and he created an "office of the president" consisting of three executives. Mr. Blumenthal was born in Germany and as a teenager fled the Nazis with his family, winding up in a Shanghai detention camp, where he correctly envisioned that North America would be where the action would be after the war. In that Shanghai camp he disciplined himself to master English. Accordingly, after the war he found his way to America, and five years later was teaching economics at Harvard, having received his PhD from that vaunted institution. Occasionally he would conduct a "state of the company" meeting for gathered Bendix employees. His early comment about the automotive business was that it was "surprisingly profitable" but that henceforth we would be more analytical as it would be imprudent to continue to rely on our "luck." At the time, the statement was vaguely ominous but, hey, my compatriots and I can be just as analytical as those Harvard economists. What I didn't count on then was the effort necessary as to appear to be "analytical" in his context. It occurred to me then that Mr. Blumenthal's attributes, although greatly admirable, didn't seem to fit the Motown scene. We will discuss this in more detail later, but first let me tell you my favorite Blumenthal story.

The surviving Detroit automobile companies were so successful that they had a foreboding that the federal government was watching and hovering over them regarding domination of the transportation sector or complete integration of vertical supply lines. General Motors knew that if it even thought of buying a supplier of any importance, it would be punished for attempting to further monopolize the business. Ford was the government's dilemma, as it wasn't generally as integrated as GM, which integrated before the anti-monopoly laws had any teeth and, consequently, was grandfathered with regard to several important component businesses. Occasionally, the government would let Ford expand out of "fairness." Ford bought Autolite Company in 1961, the main product line being spark plugs. Shortly thereafter Ford was sued by the Kennedy Administration under the Clayton Act, contending that Ford's ownership would further minimize competition in the already concentrated spark-plug industry. After an extended period of legal posturing and appeal, Ford was ordered to divest itself of Autolite by the court, which also proscribed some conditions of the sale. Although there were a half dozen or so potential buyers, Bendix was the winning bidder, negotiating an accompanying ten-year supply contract, a confirmation of its pleasure doing business with its largest customer. It was 1973. Neat. Done.

Now, Bendix was an extremely efficient and fastidious dealmaker, but it apparently didn't include its Fram Division in the negotiations and its executives weren't familiar with the high volume "direct-to-customer" aftermarket business. During the negotiations, the Autolite employees were mainly inaccessible to the Bendix acquisition team. As I understand the whole story, when Bendix took over, they appropriately adopted mainly a "business as usual" posture to the Autolite team.

Nonetheless during an early meeting, one of the Autolite operatives offered, "Of course you secured ownership of the part numbers in addition to the Trade Name and Trademark."

Oops! Bendix hadn't, but argued that the trademark is the main marketing tool.

"Not in this particular business," the operative countered, "the control of the part numbers and lists are what make direct customers and most importantly, mechanics, tick."

Then ensued the internal legalistic review of the situation. Did Bendix have the specific right to use the current part numbers? It had the right to use everything for a certain period, approximating the period required to exhaust inventory, literature and other things that would change as a result of Bendix ownership. What about after that? As the agreements were silent on the issue, it was unclear. Should we have asked Ford? We could've, but since they had just introduced their own new family of products, Motorcraft, and were still in the late stages of getting organized, we would probably have caused them to focus on the issue, most likely generating a "no" answer. It appeared that the most rational way to proceed was to simply presume that Bendix had such rights. As no change was expected for a period that would be months out in the future anyway, Autolite would continue to use such numbers until such time as Ford started asking questions, if ever, and at that point deal with the problem.

Autolite continued to use the existing parts lists for an extended period with no apparent problem. Consequently, it bestowed upon itself a sense of entitlement. Considerably later and all of a sudden, Ford did start asking questions. Bendix pushed back.

After Mike Blumenthal settled in his office in Southfield and his home in Ann Arbor (naturally, there are automotive cretins habituating Grosse Pointe and Bloomfield Hills), he was reminded that, as chairman of Ford's largest supplier, it would probably be appropriate that he at least make some overture of acquaintance to Ford's chairman, the iconic Henry Ford II. (Notice that his name is on the building; it seems to make a difference.) At this stage in his career, it was unusual for Mike Blumenthal to have to behave as a supplicant, but he dutifully called and left a message that he would like a brief word with the proprietor, at the proprietor's convenience. The proprietor called back. Mike thought it would be a good idea to meet over a meal and discuss any issues on the proprietor's mind.

The thinking goes that Ford began thus, "Mike, I respect your reputation and I have had fond and intimate business ties with Bendix executives going back to WWII, but we've now got that festering mess about the spark-plug numbering system. Please do me a personal favor before we discuss getting together, get that mess cleared up!"

End of conversation.

Remind your kids that when the commencement speaker talks about "tremendous trifles" or "the want of a nail," the message isn't just bloviating baloney; otherwise, as chairman in the future of the 50th largest company in the universe, he or she might be humiliated by a tirade from Bill Gates.

During my first few years at Bendix, Chairman Blumenthal and other analytically oriented executives seemed apologetic or somewhat embarrassed that the annual report showed about 80 percent of our earnings were coming from the automotive sector. Undoubtedly his not irrational view of the industry was that it was mature, it was at the apex of one of its cycles, there were too many external overseers and there were too few customers that were inordinately influencing one's business. To top it off, the most influential and successful players didn't seem to be particularly analytically oriented.

Incidentally, I heard it several times from several different Ford executives that one of the guys from Ford finance kept a running tab on the financial performance of vendors, from a very practical standpoint of who might not survive in order to plan for replacement and, from a not so practical standpoint, those that consistently outperformed the customer, Ford. The latter, of which Bendix was the most constant, were entered on the Ford financial crap list. Never seeming to have any practical effect, we considered it to be a badge of honor, something like being on Nixon's enemies list.

You will recall my earlier lesson about the accounting (analytical) types and their application to our business. I had earlier observed in staff-review meetings those operating managers who could tap dance over the numbers, drawing inferences and pointing out third- and fourth-order effects of the numbers posted. Not infrequently, these managers were replaced due to a mystifying lack of profits. Contrastingly, there was the old time "arm-chair" manager, who seemed most uncomfortable with the modern format of his monthly presentation as he had difficulty in ascertaining whether an improvement in floor performance was associated with a decrease in inventory—and the like. These guys operated by primarily keeping a daily vise-like grip on about four indicators, for example, how many people on the floor, quantity of goods signed off by quality control for shipment, how much scrap, and quantity of goods actually shipped. These guys often surprised us by unremittingly delivering performance consistent with the operating plan, despite that they usually had the oldest plant with the oldest equipment and the most mature work force and the most mature product lines with the most militant union.

Sure enough, the oldest Bendix plant, located in South Bend, with more than one million square feet under its roof and $100 million in sales, had such a profile. For my first several years, the plant consistently delivered quality products and performed in accord with plan objectives. Then, the general manager was prematurely retired. The succeeding general manager was replaced within a year, then replaced again, then I lost touch; although about that time I learned of the impetus for dismissal of the original general manager seven years prior through two eye-witness executives of separate disciplines reliving their common experience in the back seat of my New York taxi. At his annual profit-plan presentation, that ensconced original South Bend general manager seemed to give short shrift to the part about hiring and promotion of women and minorities, at least in Mike Blumenthal's estimation, and didn't seem to rectify this with enthusiasm and certainly not in responding to pointed questioning. Apparently, Mike let it be known that he would be disappointed if he had to suffer the presence of this guy in the future. I was dismayed about the story and I was dismayed with the cavalier attitude of the two executives, probably in the context of how cows must sense when they see a neighbor giving less milk and then they see that neighbor taken away. The same with chicken neighbors laying fewer eggs— enough! You get the idea.

About five years later I learned that the plant had been closed. How could that possibly be? I, of course, knew that there had been a second gas crunch during the Carter years. I knew that there was a belated "southern strategy" on the part of Bendix, building new plants in Southern states for lower wages and younger, more resourceful rural employees and transferring products out of Northern plants.[46] Even so, it was implausible that such a resource would justify abandonment. I otherwise had an out-of-the-ordinary trip to South Bend and ran into some of my old compatriots, who might shed

---

[46] My experience consistent with about a dozen observations reveal that the substantiation studies for new Southern plants usually embodied highly optimistic assumptions, including improved efficiencies due to better floor plans, ability to cast off cost obligations at the old plant, and so on. A knowledgeable sage once told me, "After several years struggle, total cost savings amount to difference in wages, difference in fringes, (Δ wages, Δ fringes) *if you're lucky!* The most egregiously optimistic studies, when put into operation, might even warrant the parent company making an extraordinary phone call: to the poor house requesting a reservation.

some light on the situation. Some administrative and engineering functions remained there after the manufacturing was moved elsewhere.

Between several observations of former associates and my own prior observations, there seemed to have been four or five key company players (who I could identify), including that long-standing general manager, who had over the years created what I would call a minuet with the union and four or five of its interacting operatives. Although the relationship ostensibly seemed to be adversarial to the partially informed observer, there had apparently been built up a mutual respect, or at least a respect for the other side's dilemmas. Each recognized and seemingly had empathy toward the pressures of the other's constituency, in the case of the management, upward, and in the case of the union, downward. Accordingly, several of these operatives met surreptitiously behind coffee machines or in maintenance closets, giving each other heads-up on potentially disruptive issues, suggesting symbolic give-and-take opportunities, goading the other side into solving issues—for example, grievances, attitudes, work loads, and so on. These management techniques aren't taught at Wharton Business School, although they were used extensively in the auto-manufacturing business. As these few operatives peeled off, I understand that the new (more analytical) management lost control, having serious problems with productivity, quality, scrap rates and most other metrics that permit a manufacturing operation to survive. I'm also suggesting that that phenomenon has been replicated in many places throughout the mature industry and that, in operations, relationships trump analysis every time.

CHAPTER SIXTEEN
Environmental Queasiness

Simultaneously with my joining Bendix in 1974 was the domestic industry's first struggle in trying to conform to the Environmental Protection Agency's automobile-emission standards.

There were primarily three types of contaminants found in automobile exhaust: SO_2 (sulphur dioxide), NOX (nitrous oxide) and CO (carbon monoxide)—in addition to the usual particulates. Each required a different treatment to minimize its presence in the exhaust. The EPA standards defined permissible effluent in grams per *vehicle mile,* regardless of vehicle or engine size. One would have thought that the U.S. governmental agency would have anticipated the dire consequences for the domestic industry's engine capabilities and created a system, for example: grams per (1) vehicle weight or (2) engine cc's or (3) official miles per gallon or (4) horsepower—anything to segue the industry into gasoline economies in an orderly fashion and spread the turmoil amongst competitors. The solution caused Detroit to temporarily add all sorts of valves and restrictors, in addition to the introduction of catalytic converters, to be able to get any vehicles on the road. Such government-directed programs and the simultaneous elimination of ethyl additives (lead) in the fuel forced such slapdash and panicky engineering programs that the usual power-plant performance intrinsic in domestic automobiles was somewhat compromised.[47] Undoubtedly, most of you can recall those cars that were determined to chug along long after the ignition had been turned off. As I recall, this was also the same time when drivers were forced to fasten their seat belts before the engine could be started, giving rise to those resourceful "valet" parkers who postured as if they were driving a flying carpet.

One of my favorite engineering "unintended consequences" recollections has to do with the introduction of the catalytic converter to mitigate NOX

---

[47] And probably was the main "straw" that temporarily "broke" Chrysler's "back." More on this later.

and CO problems. Everyone knew that these devices ran very hot when they were operating, and so a shield was added to isolate ambient equipment and people from the high operating temperatures generated by the catalyst. To their horror and dismay, Ford engineers encountered a vehicle operating situation wherein in very special environments, such shield was still hot enough to ignite sparse dry spiky grass under the car, or dry leaves—not a particularly good way to entice a repeat buyer, especially since Ford didn't offer asbestos seat cushions. Into the solution mode they went. They devised a method to introduce a pattern of "coolant" holes in the shield to solve the problem. It didn't exactly solve the problem, and created the added problem that even if one was aware of the situation and alert enough to drive the car away, the edges of the holes behaved as a scythe, snipping off enough grass so that the fire accompanied the car as it was supposedly driven out of peril.

For purposes of mileage efficiency, the domestics hurried a few "stand-in" cars, such as the Pinto, Chevette and Dart, which did nothing to enhance the reputation of Detroit's small-car capabilities, particularly in competition with imports' highly refined and tested offerings in this suddenly important market segment. Subsequently came the very highly publicized issue of the Pinto involved in a crash that perforated the gasoline tank. I think this was the nadir of Detroit's formerly high reputation in customer satisfaction and engineering excellence, although the damage would be felt to the present.

At any rate, you're dying to know the effect on importers. *Virtually nothing.* Since the crucible for establishing NHTSA and EPA rules is "reasonably attainable technological capability," the standards were derived from the import cars demonstrating the best performances relating to the effluence of these contaminants. While Detroit was frantically trying to get qualifying cars on the road, European and particularly Japanese manufacturers were happily improving their general efficiency and the quality and presentation of esthetic characteristics ("fits and finishes"), to the delight of the automotive press and apparently the American public.

In our own shop, Ford had contracted with Bendix to provide an engine air pump to improve the combustion process and thus minimize exhaust contaminants. Ford, in a pinch to meet EPA requirements, ascertained that it must reluctantly provide such an air pump late in the development cycle and accordingly took a license of an appropriately sized one from the developer, Saginaw Steering Gear (Division of GM). GM licensed Ford to buy such air pumps from vendors of its choice. Ford, in turn, contracted Bendix to facilitate and manufacture for all Ford light vehicles.

As we were preparing to start up the air-pump manufacture, I got a call from the financial guys.

"Were going to need a forecast for *aftermarket* sales on the air pump!" they demanded.

Not to worry, super Bobby's going to get right on it. This part was all new to the industry and so any general information regarding demand would be useless. And aftermarket demand is usually mostly dependent upon durability of the component.[48]

We had access to GM testing that demonstrated remarkable durability, considerably better than the specifications on such testing results required in the ongoing quality-control system. We also needed to check potential demand generated by repair of collision vehicles. We discovered that if the air pump was damaged in a collision, it would probably be found stuffed in the rear-seat cigarette lighter. No car left, no air pump needed for repair. Next, we wanted to ascertain the propensity for the owner to repair or replace the part after it failed to work. No problem. I had access to several of the industry's preeminent engine analysts in my own company.

I approached one: "How might the customer driving experience change when his air pump fails?"

Now there were several answers, depending on the nature of the failure, but the general response was, "Well, his power train will immediately perform in a much more responsive manner. His gas mileage will go up. His car will drive more quietly, with perceptively less vibration. That's about it!"

He'd probably want to know if there were additional air pumps that he could disable.

It was time for Bobby to segue into number-crunching mode. It dawned on me that to not replace one's air pump might put one's vehicle out of conformance with EPA standards, as were 99 percent of other vehicles currently on the road. It also dawned on me that those specs were so new that there was no equipment available to check them. Third dawning: If the government was really interested in cleaning the air in an expedient basis, why didn't they start by pulling the blue cloud belching old timers off the

---

[48] If one doesn't wear out, who would ever need a new one!

road.[49] It must have had to have something to do with politics or plausibility on the part of the public. If you're inconveniencing the Goliaths or making them less competitive, that's not a real problem because they've gotten rich on the money of the citizenry over the years.

Later, I responded to financial.

It went something like this:

"I've got a number for you regarding air-pump aftermarket. I needn't go through all the numbers with you, but since Ford will put a little more than two million air-pump-bearing vehicles on the road this year, I compute that we will sell about 3.7 units in the aftermarket. Why don't we round it up to 5."

Now let's take a look at our activities in manufacturing the subject air pump. Normally a manufacturer of engineered assemblies understands how the performance of the end product is affected by the manufacture and assembly of the component parts, through years of experience through which one learns where to "tweak" when things seem to be getting out of control. As the air pump was not of our design and therefore a completely new animal, at least to us, we didn't have the benefit of experience and started by being careful to make the component parts within the indicated tolerances.

Imagine, if you will, an assembly slightly larger than a softball only resembling a manual wall-mounted pencil sharpener receptacle in shape with a pulley wheel on one side in place of the pencil-size selector. Within this item is a leaved rotor that spins rapidly when the item performs its usual function. What type of product are we describing? Correct! A siren. That was our dilemma over the first few months, trying to make enough acceptably quiet and functional products so that Ford didn't have to temporarily buy from GM or another competitor. Without even trying to ascribe blame between design (GM) and manufacturing (us), we were frantic to get acceptable product shipped so that we could start amortizing our considerable investment in specialized air-pump equipment.

On one of my frequent trips home from our Newport News factory[50] on the then overtaxed Bendix air fleet, our Automotive President Bob Hungate,

---

[49] Later, most states did that.

[50] The former Bendix radio factory, converted to making electronic products and air pumps.

a very talented and rational "automotive guy," shared his frustration with the start-up of our first high-volume electronic fuel injection (EFI) product line for General Motors. We were one of the early developers of EFI, and actually had shipped production units to Chrysler and Chevrolet in the late Fifties. Poised to capture the market for a significant new original-equipment product, Bendix had been historically frustrated at how slowly the industry was accepting the product that offered greatly improved control of the fuel as it is injected into the engine with all of the accompanying benefits. We were somewhat selfishly pleased that the government's edicts provided a "killer-app"[51] for introduction of the system but, as Bruce Willis might say, "The timing was a bitch!" We were counting on EFI to be a major product line because of its inherent benefits and the fact that production costs would decrease with volume and experience. Bob was lamenting that although he had quite a few concurrent "fires" to extinguish during this particular start-up, his presence and participation at the factory was justified to express "interest" to the customer in the context of it becoming one of our core products in the future.

He explained it like this: "I sit there all day properly and symbolically wringing my hands. We put EFI controllers (in effect, a simple computer) down the final "assembly and test" line and the test stand rejects exactly 98.5 percent of them. We can ship right away 3 of 200 that we send down the line. What's even scarier is that the defects seem to be random. If the rejects were mostly because of one characteristic, we could focus on fixing that particular characteristic during the production process, simultaneously repairing off-line those parts rejected for that characteristic, re-testing and shipping. Because of the randomness of the rejections, we are at the verge of losing control of what assemblies have been rejected for what characteristics."

It only occurs to me now, but fuel-injection units with random defects might have been considered then as another candidate for overwhelming the earth, replacing or at least surpassing chewing gum as the greatest contaminant.

It occurred to me then that a lot of talented executives were spending a lot of effort in solving urgent short-term problems promulgated by slightly

---

[51] A scenario wherein a new product that has been languishing is the obvious solution for new circumstances. Otherwise static inertia and financial issues can delay improved products for years or decades.

askew specifications or slightly ambitious introduction timing embodied in recently published governmental edicts.

We get through the tough start-ups of 1975 and I was pleased that the Rileys were to be included in the Bendix entourage at the annual Society of Automotive Engineers fall meeting at the Greenbrier resort in West Virginia. We traveled down with the Treacys, Mrs. Hungate and several other couples. On the ride to the resort from the airport, the people were organizing the weekend.

"—and we'll have to be done early because of the formal party on Saturday night."

"Formal party?" offers Treacy.

One of the other guys starts getting on his case: "Jim, don't tell us you didn't bring a tuxedo. You need to read about the events and be prepared, otherwise, you're going to embarrass us all."

This was one of those times I was sorry to be with the gang or in close proximity as I didn't want to share Jim's embarrassment or, even more important, to somehow be associated with generating it. When the others were out of earshot I told Jim that the probable reason they were "prepared" was because they remembered the Saturday-night party from their previous visits. Besides, I seemed to recall that the Greenbrier rented tuxedos in their haberdashery. I recalled several others being caught in the same circumstances.

The good news for Treacy: The Greenbrier did rent tuxedos. The bad news for Treacy: They only had brocaded "black on satiny brown" tuxedo jackets. Now, this bad news didn't relate to the fashion value of his tuxedo. The bad news was that there were ten or twelve guys at the party of perhaps 200 couples, all wearing the same peculiar brocaded tuxedo that announced to everyone that they couldn't get their act together, something like the "A" that the Puritans made certain women wear. Jim showed up at Bendix table number two and, sure enough, he was seated with his previous tormentor.

"Jim, I know you've been busy but, see! Your oversight has caused you to secure the same psychedelic tuxedo as the other idiots who forgot to bring theirs. You'd think if you had to rent some sort of cockamamie outfit, you'd at least arrange to get something *different* than all of those other idiots. People can obviously see that you're one of those guys who just tried to cope with their embarrassment. Such might not be the case if you'd been able to get something *different.*"

This time I was happy to be seated at table number three with the Hagenlockers of Ford and the Schocks of my department. I was also happy that Treacy wasn't at table number one, where the Hungates were sitting with the Iococcas and several other "suits."

Otherwise, it was a very pleasant evening and the food at the Greenbrier was exceptional as usual. Although the format was European plan, where the food charges are included in the room charge, everyone ordered as if everything were ala carte. Then the servers aggregated the orders of each item on one plate for the table. As the main course was being served, a roar went up from table number two, much like you'd hear at Augusta when someone made an eagle on number thirteen. After the uproar subsided, I discretely went over and saw what had happened. As it turned out, carrots were one of the favorite selections at number two. As the server was to begin serving the six orders on the plate, she proceeded to dump the whole thing down Treacy's front and into his lap. Without a moment's hesitation, Treacy jumped to his feet and proudly announced, "I'm different!"

As I have previously told you, that guy Treacy was okay, although I was to find out within two weeks that he was to be elevated (?) to chairman of a new company that Bendix was spinning off as per the obligation to the anti-trust department from the Fram acquisition of years previous.

We had other developments happening rather quickly. We had enjoyed over the years half, or about $10 million annually, of General Motor's master-cylinder business, the component that distributes hydraulic pressure to operate the brakes, so we felt the re-quote would be routine. Our Buick account rep wasn't known as a Mensa, but he was absolutely honest and hard working and was respected as such by customers and the company alike. Our quotation was $5.08 each.[52]

Our rep turned in the quotation and got feedback. At $5.08 we would be awarded nothing. At $5.00 we would be awarded 50 percent of GM business, as usual. I suggested a few nuanced questions to be asked of the Buick buyer

---

[52] How can I remember specifically $5.08 each 34 years later? Have you ever struck out, bottom of the ninth, two on and two out? Have you ever missed a four footer to lose the annual handicap cup? Do you remember who your teammates were? Do you remember who your opponent was? I remember! Charlie Brown remembers! Robert Goulet remembers!

and asked our rep to go back and make certain. He did. What was to be mis-interpreted?

Let's critique the account representative's performance. He made our presentation for continuation of the business. He got feedback that revealed price elasticity within a gnat's eyelash (1.5 percent price differential between 50 percent and none of the business). Most importantly, he prevailed on the customer to hold his placement of business until we'd had time to review and submit a new quotation. His grade, A+, at least in my considered opinion.

I went back to the bosses. I said the information previously received was 100 percent accurate. There was otherwise a lot going on. The business was old, as was the equipment. The division was forecast for growth in new products so we could probably use the space for these new products. We'd promised the corporate office that we would finally generate "discipline" in our pricing rather than letting the customers jerk us around. That was okay by me as no one seemed to have an emotional attachment or enthusiasm for this business. We stood firm. We got the heave ho. No one seemed to think it was a big deal.

Now fast-forward six months. It was time to generate a financial plan for the coming year. We made a sales forecast of all products (no GM cylinders) by number of units and price per unit. The financial guys married the forecast to the number of man hours, machine hours and purchased parts to be required, in effect creating the real or actual accounting costs related to the sales. The calculations were merged into a financial plan.

Panic! What happened? The bottom had fallen out. There must have been some error in computation.

We did it again. Same result.

What happened? The accounting types have a dread that the typical sales guy will give away money that is rightfully ours. Accordingly, they establish estimating "costs" to be used for quotations at a level higher than real costs or what they feel represent a typical cost for a certain type of operation. Imagine a master cylinder. It's a cast cylinder a little smaller than a toy kaleidoscope wherein a hole is bored down the middle and such hole is finely machined so that a piston (attached to the brake linkage) can move back and forth creating pressure. In addition, ancillary machined holes are required to let the brake fluid flow in and out. In short, there's quite a bit of metal machining required, amounting to several minutes per unit, as opposed to parts that are formed of sheet metal by stamping— ka-chung, ka-chung—

153

that, at most, take several seconds. As we previously stated, the product line was old, so old that the expensive machining equipment had been long since depreciated. Ergo, the real "cost" of machine amortization was zero. Unfortunately, the "typical" machine amortization cost per unit, as used in quotations, was about $2.00. Accordingly, profit in our new financial plan was lowered by the modest profit realized on this *plus* $2/unit of master cylinder business lost times 2 million units, half of GM production. The $4-plus million dollars annually, that we had been enjoying for profit and machine amortization with the GM business, vanished. The real cost for the machines, zero, remained the same. The plant did about $60 million in business annually so the $4 million unabsorbed burden fell right to the bottom line as a reduction in profits. In effect, the decision not to accept the GM business caused the division to lose 7 percent return on sales, thus rendering it marginally profitable.

All of a sudden, the division, having been a constant profit producer and logical source for our new and exciting products became a "red circle" plant, qualifying it for special "executive scrutiny." In the shuffle, Bob Hungate was removed from the direct reporting line of this division, an indignity that I suspect sat very poorly with him. Within a year or so, he retired.

Why did I feel so personally responsible? I should have known better. Having previously worked for smaller suppliers who were less rigid and more accurate in their cost estimates, I should have suspected that certain machining costs would be loaded on the cylinder business because of the inflexible Bendix cost-estimating system. I should have asked for a review of "real" costs. But, I was new to the company! No sniveling, Riley; you blew it. Normally, for carryover business, it wouldn't matter at all what a cost estimate might be. This was different because we casually walked away from business. The fact that we didn't discover our own disaster for six months was unforgivable.

Henceforth, I took the time to check quotations based on cost estimates to see that all elements were plausible compared to whatever "comparables" were at my disposal. At a later meeting with a "post-analytical" executive boss, I was explaining a quotation proposal based on a cost estimate, and a parallel one tweaked by me because of some implausibility I had found.

The boss stated his position: "You sales guys have always complained about receiving inspection costs being applied against purchase price rather than direct labor."

Incidentally, I'm defining a "post-analytical" executive as one who looks for direction from above, isn't very capable of making analytical evaluations anyway, but has promised never to question anything that his bosses or his accountants tell him.

"I don't have a problem making such a representation to the customer," I responded. "I don't have a problem with that. I do however think it undesirable that we fool ourselves."

I never was one of his favorites, and it was just when my kids were about to start college.

The 1975 model year started out badly. Top management expected that sales for the year would be down approximately 10 percent from forecasts. Apparently unwilling to ride out the surmised storm while operating at historically high profitability levels, we were called for a command performance in South Bend.

"Anyone wishing to talk rather than listen at this meeting, signify by saying, 'I resign.'"

They were going to cut all departments by 10 percent. Now, I admit I have a certain perspective, but original-equipment sales expenses for large suppliers were significantly less than 1 percent of net sales. The staff had been carefully selected, trained and encouraged to build a trusting relationship with major customers. To eliminate two of the ten guys that service about $400 million annually in sales, would detrimentally affect some accounts in unpredictable ways. We were instructed that all personnel must be notified, starting Thursday, and be completed by the next day, Halloween. By the end of that day, we were obligated to call the full surviving staff together and to announce that the inquisition had been completed, to assure the retainees that their jobs were safe until the highest ups had another swivet.

This is, and should be, the hardest job for anyone to do in his or her career. At least it was for me in the three or four episodes I lived through. In that particular situation, one of my unfortunate targets was on the road, his return being uncertain, depending upon negotiations at International Harvester in Chicago. Since time was short I called his home, on Wednesday night I believe, to see if he was home or when he was expected. I unwittingly stumbled on the fact that he was no longer living there with his wife. Oops! I found out his arrival schedule from the travel department on Thursday and met him at the airport. I didn't really have to say anything. This hip guy was pleased to ply me for detail on the overall RIF activity over drinks at the airport bar.

Apparently feeling sheepish about the perhaps petulant reduction in force and concerns regarding the continual loyalty of the obviously excellent middle management staff, top management decided that they would initiate a new mid-level bonus program. It was so hurriedly put together that they notified the potential recipients before they had a chance to notify the "regular bonus" participant bosses. My guys started asking questions, to which I responded, by shrugging my shoulders, and letting them know that I'm not yet in the loop but "how can it be bad?" I would get back to them when I knew the details.

I didn't realize how bad it would be until I *did* get the details. I learned that the corporate staff had written each participant a letter revealing the joyous news that the corporation had initiated for its loyal staff a new, no-strings-attached, Christmas bonus in ranges from $0 to $1,500 (1975 dollars). Undoubtedly, the guy who knew he'd had a bad year would be expecting about $1,250. Several days later and to my horror I got a list of those eligible and the total amount of the pool. If I divided the total pool by the number of the participants, I would come up with an average bonus allowance of $450. I had several stars and leaders who did yeomen's work under stressful conditions who must get somewhere near that maximum. That means, for the other very good recipients, for their good work and loyalty, we proudly would give them a check for $375 and a D on the implicit grade attributed to the magnitude of the check. Several of them justifiably and in a somewhat tactful manner implied that the company probably needed the money more than they did or that they would have been happier with a simple pat on the back.

A related quickie. The manager of our friction-material sales was a legend in his field. For more than thirty years he had lived and breathed brake pads and linings. I don't know this, but he probably didn't enjoy Woody Allen movies. So heavily was he involved in the product that he had a separate small budget for road testing in Detroit where he carefully monitored his own results to the extent that he participated in tweaking formulations to incorporate his findings.

"Hey guys, reduce the cashew shells by 40 percent add three extra rubber bands and cure at 383°."

How some guys get their jollies is a wonder.

Since I had no special interest or skills relating to the product line, I had little to offer and because of the almost obscene profits made by his segment through a strategy of engineering potential competitors out of industry-wide specifications, I felt my best service, as boss to him, would be to keep prying corporate and group inquisitors away. I generally did that and let him know that was our working strategy, and our relationship was excellent. Several months in, while discussing a certain budgetary or personnel issue with him, it dawned on me that he must have thought that our "arms length" relationship excluded me from exposure to his departmental budgets and personnel records. Obviously, our informal relationship didn't extend to my not having knowledge of these operating details, that were sent to me from above and which in many instances I helped create. Yet, as he seemed to take pride in his independence, was so conservative by nature and seemed to take pleasure in revealing what he felt were these intimate details with me, his trusted boss, I didn't disabuse of him of his mis-perceptions.

I had three or four regular executive bonus-roll employees and contributed in assessing how the bonus money should be split up, and naturally was exposed to the final numbers. On the first year, this manager came in my office, winked, put a piece of folded paper on my desk, and left. I opened the missive later to find out it was a sharing of the amount of his own personal bonus award, of about $6,500. Of course, I already knew this and routinely tore up and discarded the paper. The next year was an extremely busy time. As he was ready to go home, I waved him into my office even though three or four of us were meeting on some issue or another. He just wanted to drop a piece of paper on my desk. Wink. He did. I caught on. He was telling me that he had gotten his $7,500. The meeting went on for hours more. As I was cleaning off my desk (thank heavens I did that at least once a month), I reached for his paper, glanced at it, and started to make a movement to discard it. Wait a minute! He had made a transcription error, it said $750. I called him at home. He said that the number I saw was the number he got. I sensed that he had been sitting home in the dark, seething that his bonus is the smallest he had received in 22 years. I told him that there must be some sort of error, that I understood that most bonuses are up slightly and certainly he is regarded as he has always been, one of our most productive employees. I suggested that he not cash the check until I got to the bottom of it, and vowed to immediately cut red tape until I do.

I diligently undertook my task. I felt like a soccer mom whose kid had just been red carded out of the game after two minutes. No boss available. No boss' boss. I finally got hold of one of the corporate presidents, the automotive one, in Southfield. I explained the problem, apologized for calling at 6:45 P.M., but I had a suffering employee, who he knew well, who thought he was being abused by the company. He responded that the higher number sounded about right, but he would have to get into it, particularly since the books were closed. I called my guy right back, told him whom I talked to, that he was looking into it, which seemed to assuage him quite a bit. He eventually got his proper six bits.

I should have listened to the psychologist years before and suggested to Bendix when I signed on that perhaps they should specify a sturdy steel rope with which to push when attempting to improve employee morale.

Since I had done such a great job in bringing prices up-to-date for the company in 1974, during the jittery fourth calendar quarter of 1975, someone high up got the idea that we should get prices up-to-date before the end of the quarter. In fact they were so caught up in the idea (no Christmas until all increases are collected), that Bob Hungate came in for a day to demonstrate diligence and help by making higher-level calls as appropriate. Practically, it didn't matter when the prices were agreed upon, as they would take effect October 1, three months prior, in any event; but that's a nuance that corporate accounting or management couldn't comprehend. I felt it foolish to go around picking up owed chits that I had earned with great effort, for no net advantage, particularly when the customers were attempting to put out their own fires as the downtime approached.

Mr. Hungate came for the day and started to realize the difficulty of trying to compress complicated dealings involved in justifying increases, particularly when the other side had other urgent priorities. At any rate, we bought him shirts and underwear, got him a hotel room, and he stayed for three days. During the second day, things were getting hectic when a personnel guy called for Hungate. One of the secretaries let him know of the call by note and she was immediately and aggressively rebuffed by gesture, as he was otherwise occupied on the phone. When notified, this personnel guy asked who runs the sales office and asked to speak to him. I excused myself from the main meeting.

"Bob, I'm Sam from corporate personnel and I desperately need to talk to Hungate."

I explained the situation and that he'd stayed over and that we'd gotten two guys on hold who we'd been desperately been trying to get hold of since yesterday. He understood but wanted my assurance that I would have Hungate call him at the very first opportunity. He'd be sitting by the phone. I agreed. When no one was waiting on the phone, I reminded Hungate to call Sam. I got a rather firm rejection gesture. The meeting went on until about eight and we perhaps saw daylight on our major project. Hopefully, one more frenetic day yet to go.

The next day, we reconvened and again things were very active. Sure enough, Sam called for Hungate. No deal. He demanded to talk to me. I excused myself from the meetings and apologized and explained our situation.

Sam then told me: "I understand. Listen up, since I can't get through, and you're an operating director and seem to be fairly perceptive, I'll deputize you to deliver the message. He must remember that about six weeks ago he was instrumental in laying off about 160 employees in your group. Tell him that this plan was not well conceived or executed, and the feeling now is that the company is at considerable risk and so it is imperative that he recall all 160 employees right away, explaining that there was one humongous misunderstanding between the several levels of the company."

I went back in the meeting. Hungate was on a long and very detailed call relating to our pricing activity. I noticed that there were phones going unanswered out in the office, but I was hunkered down.

Finally he hung up the phone, "Now we've got to get hold of —".

I slapped the desk.

"We'll have to find out if he will also agree to —"

I slapped the desk again, harder, to get his attention. I blurted out the message in about twenty seconds. He slumped. He then raised his hands over his head.

"They told me this needs to be done. I get on the helicopter, I go to St. Joseph. I go to Lorraine. I go all over so this can be done within eight days. What the hell is going on? Get me Sam on the phone," he suggested over his shoulder to the outer office.

Nothing.

"Please get me Sam on the phone."

I left the room to find an empty office. I found out that our service employees had all been invited to the corporate Christmas tea dance, a rare and well-deserved treat for them, but extremely unfortunate timing. After some effort, I was able to get Sam on the line and I left Hungate to talk to him in private.

The phones were lighting up! I did the best I could. My boss' secretary had been calling. She originally called on an unimportant matter but was shocked when she didn't get an answer as we usually stagger the lunch hour, and was determined to call every thirty seconds until she did, to find out what was going on.

"That isn't being helpful right now," I offered. "Everyone will be back in about an hour."

Finally, I got to have a late visit to the men's room as did everyone else. I got to make a few of my own business calls that had been neglected. On Hungate's return from the men's room, the unattended phone was ringing, so he answered it. It was one of the salesmen's golf-club pro shop, wanting him to return the call; how did we want that handled? This was becoming a nightmare!

Hungate called his boss, the corporate president, to talk about the new panic (and grouse a little bit, I suspect), but couldn't get through. Where was the boss? You've guessed it, at the tea dance. That seemed to undo the normally totally controlled Hungate. He stomped around for a few minutes, exuding a few uncharacteristic epithets while bemoaning the helicopter rides, the urgency of such, why and who thinks that that was a bad idea now when it was such a good idea then. What a mess! He suggested that we finish the pricing efforts while he went to the corporate office to undertake the new imbroglio. We did. Merry Christmas.

For obvious reasons, my sales guys didn't get hired back, but I understood they got their palms greased somewhat. A few months later, my boss said that the corporate office suggested that we hire a replacement salesman, on the condition that it be a minority employee. What an unusual sequence of personnel events, I thought, although I was happy that someone was thinking of our vast and important customer responsibilities.

As we undertook a search for the ideal minority employee, the flesh peddlers sent us several candidates generally known for their athletic abilities. Not a bad idea, except this employee couldn't be primarily a glad hander. Our products were rather complicated and he must be able to participate in meetings dealing with technical issues, understand them and relay them to the customer, subsequently bringing back the customer response in accurate technical terms. We finally found what we thought was a jewel in one Chris Northcross. He has an engineering degree and a calm, pleasing manner.

We went about rebalancing the sales responsibilities, and it was obvious we had an urgent need for help at our major customer, Ford. Perhaps not a real problem but, as a Detroiter one can't help but remember Dearborn mayor Orville Hubbard's exploits of the Forties and Fifties making sure all the potholes were filled, primarily at Ford's expense, and that there was no minority creep into the neighborhoods. As a delegate at the 1952 national Democratic convention in Chicago, he attended wearing a full head mask, as did two of his cohorts, because he was not permitted to leave home because of a pending trial on red lining or some such anti-minority housing activity. I feared there may have been vestigial elements of that in a Dearborn organization. Having hired Chris, I introduced him around the Ford circuit with my head held high and, in general, he was received and accepted by the Ford personnel in an exemplary manner. In fact, and it's of no relevance, but I was pleasantly surprised that several of his contacts gave him insider tidbits or warned of potential pitfalls beyond what a normal competent salesperson could normally glean

These Ford employees, as I was, were undoubtedly concerned that he might be given less than a fair shake while toddling around the vast Ford organization and were trying to make pre-emptive compensation. I will always be indebted to these classiest of Ford guys.

I think I've previously laid upon you the fact that many "big-three" customer lunches have a duration of about 16 3/4 minutes. Someone unrelated to the industry must have suggested to Chris, or he may have noticed himself that, while dining in "mixed" company, diners of his race generally get the short stick. I'm not qualified to comment on this, but I did notice that Chris had a propensity to send his meal back to the kitchen. I didn't have a problem with this in principle, but I did know that such requests extended the lunch period to an hour or so, and in the future might negatively impact the roster of those people who would accept a luncheon from him because of the unpredictability of timing. I talked to him about this and said that the sole purpose of the lunches was to give comfort and sustenance to the customers. If he had a problem with the food or the service, I suggested that he leave a note or meager tip or later write a letter to the restaurant, but try not to have our guests worry about a late return to their offices. Nibble around the edges, make pertinent conversation about business or any other subject. As for his own nourishment, both physical and spiritual, he was entitled, at our expense of money and time, to have a leisurely and exquisite lunch after he had dumped the customers. He took this quite well and adjusted accordingly.

After several years of Chris' successful dealings, I sensed an undercurrent of a can being attached to his tail. At Ford engineering, one of our-soon-to-be-dumped new general-factory managers and a colleague of his had agreed that Chris wasn't totally competent, and they took the trouble to imply such to Bendix management. They purported that although he was a wonderful guy and that both were delighted that people "like him" were being put in responsible positions, this particular guy just didn't have it. Right! When I asked how the "incompetence" became manifest, the Bendix guy said that, while discussing issues with customers, he revealed much more than a prudent representative should do. He blurted out all of our secrets and our sins. (When I heard this, I recalled my favorite Pogo quote, "We have met the enemy—"[53]) The Ford guy maintained that Chris was far, far too close to the vest. It was difficult to ascertain what Bendix had done or what their posture was on any issue. Hey guys, it's implausible that you agree to condemn him for mutually exclusive behavior. I was just starting to put together a case study, when the Bendix guy was reassigned for an inventory bust and, sadly, Chris had turned in his resignation to accept what he felt was his ideal job, a Ford engineer. I hope he has prospered and I feel somewhat guilty for not keeping in touch.

---

[53] "...and he is *us*."

CHAPTER SEVENTEEN
Campaigns I Have Known

Perhaps I have been wrong in suggesting that all of the government's "help" through NHTSA had been grandstanding or power grabbing. There had been safety issues since the beginning of the industry. After all, I myself have had two cars spontaneously catch fire, once when I was in the left-hand lane of the Southfield Expressway. The first early benefit of inculcation of a safety mentality was to cause all players to recognize that if components were identified by manufacturer and date of manufacture, when things went wrong it would be possible to ascertain how many vehicles were affected, where they were located, how to alert owners of potential danger, the most prudent way to fix them, and to measure with some degree of certainty and fairness who should bear the financial burden of the fix. Accordingly there grew a sense—that all participants knew and understood—that avoiding the manufacture of defective vehicles was crucial, but systematically fixing the problem was urgent and doling out blame or financial burdens could be left for a later day because the data was so specific and so incriminating.

When the engines started being "choked" (not in the old context of a car startup rich mix which involved a "choke" pull, but by having so many restrictions on the new ones for the purpose of clean air; "strangled" might have been a better word), Bendix feared it might have a big problem, as its pneumatic, power-brake units were "powered" by borrowing the vacuum generated by the motor. As this available vacuum started to dwindle from year to year just as the power brake units were approaching across the board application, they felt they had to find some other source on which to poach. Eureka! Power steering was also approaching 100 percent application. Perhaps we could devise something that was parasitic to that. We could. A hydraulic power-brake unit that used the fluid pressure of the power-steering pump.

Now, I'm a graduate mechanical engineer but even I envisioned that it must be harder to capture and manipulate air under pressure than it would be to do similar things with oil. Wrong! Our pneumatic brake units use several bladder-like membranes, a simple system of valves and a clever but inexpensive system that caused the air vacuum to assist in proportion and in addition to the force on the brake pedal. On the other hand, the hydraulic one needed a beefy housing with all sorts of alternative routes and cavities machined into it that let the fluid flow through alternative paths, which were controlled by a series of valves. At least the hydraulic one, even with its beefy construction, could potentially take up less valuable engine compartment space, as the basic unit was more the size of a hand grenade, whereas the pneumatic one was more like the size of a football or rugby ball.

As usual, things weren't as simple as they first appeared. A fortunate by-product of using air, as in the original units, is that air is very compressible. If there is some sort of failure mode while the vehicle is in motion, such as engine off or blown hose, although the first stop is harder than normal (I think most drivers have experienced that, or read about it in a John Irving novel), there is still some, albeit successively lessened, assist for the second and third stops even though the operator has long since sensed that there is a problem. Since oil is not at all compressible, the characteristic of the first braking after supply failure mode of the hydraulic brake is hard but thereafter the bottom falls out. Not only does one have to brake without any assist but, in addition, one must overcome the considerable friction of the unit. Now, it has been my feeling that a rational driver, having sensed a problem with braking, wouldn't put a gas pedal to the floor only to have to make an ensuing panic stop. He would tend to drive cautiously. Also, I also think that a ninety-year-old woman, knowing there is a brake problem, could push on the brake hard enough to almost break the seat back off. The government must have agreed with me, because they didn't publish any guidance on the issue.

Nonetheless, our customers and our own engineers took the posture that there should be no degradation in total brake performance with the new hydraulic unit. Accordingly, we had to devise a mechanism to provide temporary brake boost in the event of powering failure mode. We devised a mechanical spring accumulator. Because of the limited availability of space and the relatively high force requirement, such spring turned out to really be a sturdy little bugger. The "wire" used to make the coil spring was about the diameter of one's little finger and, after being coiled, the spring took up about as much space as a Rubik's Cube. It complicated the design and manufacture of the unit and, as it turned out, created many more than half of our problems.

One day, I'd just flown back into Detroit City Airport after a round trip to Cleveland or somewhere nearby. It was about 3:00 P.M. and I was delighted to be going home at an early hour, but knew I had better check in with the office. Mr. Treacy (Group VP and Notre Dame fanatic) had been desperately trying to get hold of me. I called him.

"Bob, we've detected an issue in securing the accumulator cover. There's a potential problem of this cover disengaging."

He filled me in on pertinent details.

"Our chief engineer and quality control guys are on a plane heading to Dearborn to meet with the Ford guys. Get over there and act as coordinator for us, the timing should be just about right. Finally, let me impress upon you that a field campaign must begin immediately. Do your best to convince Ford of that and impress upon them that we take full responsibility, financial and otherwise."

"Jim, I've been through a few of these previously. Ford will appreciate the efforts we are making by urgently sending our best guys to explain the problem and recommend a quick fix, which is undoubtedly the focus of their attention now. Thanks for giving me the authority to step up, but I don't think the issue of financial responsibility will come up, and there tend to be other people involved in that. Why don't we make them reasonably happy now that we're more than transparent and supportive on the current problem, and also make them happy later when we step up as they get to the financial aspects of the campaign. They might not even ask for the administrative costs (mailing, record keeping, reporting to the government) as they tend to think of these as normal cost of administration."

"Thanks for your input, Bob, but promise me you will make a highlight of the meeting, whoever is there, that we will take full financial responsibility and urge them to take immediate action."

That Treacy was a stand-up guy.

I got to the meeting where there was a technical discussion going on. What was the probability of the accumulator cover becoming disengaged? Very low, but our testing suggested that it may be possible. What were the implications if one did disengage? Remember, the contents are under quite a force. It's more than a pea shooter—more than a slingshot—more like a howitzer! The danger to humans was greatest to someone who may be probing under the hood.

The issue was resolved through a campaign and no one was injured, to the best of my knowledge.

A concurrent frustration relating to the hydraulic booster: The disc brake was just maturing into a highly reliable and safe product. Its characteristics were vastly superior to the conventional drum brake in that disc performance was directly proportional to the force input, whereas the drum brake tended to be "grabby" because of the wedging action of the shoes. At that time, most cars had disc fronts and drum rears, a situation that required an additional valve to proportion hydraulic line pressure between the dissimilar fronts and rears. The hydraulic booster enabled the absolutely best, simplest and cheapest brake system: four-wheel disc with hydraulic booster. Why were the cars still using disc/drum setups? Federal rules had very stringent standards for parking brakes. (I don't know about you, but I put it in "park.") Complying with such standards was incompatible with disc brakes, or should I more precisely say was not economically feasible with a four-wheel disc setup.

On the subject of campaigns, I seem to recall one other with American Motors, whose offices then were then about one mile from my former grade school. This was to be a routine meeting to outline procedures for correcting defects on regular power-brake units and negotiate our financial responsibilities. For this meeting, I was the spokesman and coordinator accompanied by the quality-control specialist and the director of engineering for the product line. Our Canadian plant had neglected to check some polyfoam filters, which slightly disrupted the action of the unit so that it didn't perform within specified parameters, but was not an immediate safety threat. Fair enough. The three of us were wedged shoulder to shoulder into the buyer's ten-by-ten office, waiting for other AMC participants, who would be specialists previously unknown to me. One guy stops by and our buyer told him that we'd be in conference room two; he nods at us and proceeds. Then comes a young woman (remember that it was now justifiably and appropriately a time for advancing capable women into management), with a young man apparently in tow. I begin to rise, only to realize that my left shoulder was at the frame of the open door. I sensed that if I were to continue to rise, I probably would bump into her and, even if not, she would be able to tell if it was Lavoris or Listorine. I aborted my rising motion and, instead, looked up and smiled as she took about a half step into the office. I again leaned back and adjusted to look, unable to avoid the angora sweater less than a foot directly in front of my face. She started speaking.

"I must alert you. I, myself, will not be able to attend our meeting. I have a meeting with—[some AMC big-shot], but I want everyone to understand that we at AMC have put an emphasis on safe and attractive vehicles, so I must insist that the issues to be discussed are not taken lightly."

I looked up periodically, but it was awkward and, even then, my face was only about 18 inches from hers.

"Accordingly, I am authorizing John here to be my delegate to the meeting, and I want to caution everyone that when John suggests something, it should have the same emphasis as if I, myself, were saying it. Let me re-emphasize that John has my full authority—"

We went to the meeting. We agreed to .2 hours (translates to about $15) for a mechanic to lift the hood and find the date stamp with a flashlight—we told him where he would find it. Four out of five would be outside the key dates and the mechanic will slam the hood closed. Of the 20 percent, the mechanic will do a simple brake evaluation to provided specifications, another .3 hours awarded. Of the 20 percent of the 20 percent that he found out of spec—the real problem ones—he would replace for another 1.5 hours. We would provide the power-brake units to AMC central distribution. Problem contained.

On our way out, debriefing with the other two guys and generally satisfied with the outcome, I mentioned the unusual vignette with the woman executive and my "parallel universe" take on the situation.

"How so?" asked one.

"I had the sense that I was seeing Jayne Mansfield but hearing Bella Abzug."

With considerable sniggers, they tended to agree.

Please bear with me for another "women getting ahead" story. My take on the whole situation was that although there were a few hard-nosed males that resented the whole idea of women doing work that was historically performed by men, most were fascinated by intrinsically assertive women with a knock-about (non-sanctimonious) and confident manner, combined with ever-present female attraction. Mike Blumenthal had just such an assistant: smart, poised, asked questions, listened to answers, commiserated with frustrations, shared her own, offered solutions, shared stories. He brought her to South Bend when he made a presentation. One of the guys was inordinately fascinated with the whole package, saying many of the things I've said above, but adding: "Terrific expressions, terrific legs and ankles."

"Wait a minute," challenged one of the other guys, "you never saw her ankles; you couldn't have seen her ankles."

"I can extrapolate from wrists," offered our critic.

I learned many things from the senior Bendix operatives, some of them counterintuitive. From one conversation with a former engineer, then inside marketing guy who doubled as an expert witness, I learned two unusual things. The first was that, in fatal automobile accidents, the brake pedal was untouched in more than half of the incidences. The second, and one in which he talked with great glee, was that he appeared at liability cases where our customers were being sued for designing brakes too small to actually stop the car properly. Could Ralph have incited action on civil cases of this type? Nah!

My guy would patiently explain that the laws of physics demonstrate that the coefficient of friction is not affected by the size of the contact area of the brake pad and the brake. One might conclude that the brake pad might wear out sooner because it is smaller, but that's not the basis for the suit. He was amazed at how many judges picked right up on this and how disgruntled and helpless were the plaintiff lawyers. Hey, this stuff is better than a pay raise.

CHAPTER EIGHTEEN
Into the Fire

During my first weeks at Bendix, there was an urgency to solve an industry problem created by an anomaly in new brake standards. These new standards had been issued by NHTSA a few years prior, obligating all manufacturers to provide brakes at the highest-existing performance level, which was considered satisfactory by all parties and to which all manufacturers generally conformed. Each company had to review their specific car lineups and conduct tests to ensure compliance. A few had to upgrade their brake systems to the next highest available brake line-up on specific cars, (brakes, power brakes and master cylinders) at the cost of a few dollars per car. Problems arose, however, when conformance testing was conducted on light trucks, at that time a growth product line for the domestics, and one that was not then in the import portfolio.

The problem arose because the standards outlined a conformance test procedure wherein the vehicle had to be tested in both a non-laden configuration, driver only, and a fully laden configuration. Now, obviously, the fully laden car can't add much weight in a context relative to the mass of the car, perhaps three pear shaped people, several suitcases, golf clubs and a couple of picnic baskets—about 800 to 1,000 pounds. The pickup, however, is a completely different situation. The weight to completely laden it is significant relative to the vehicle itself. Now, one can design a brake system for a car by using the mid-point of the weight range, and that system will permit the car to also easily conform to either no load or fully loaded conditions. One can select a conventional system for the non-laden truck that will include a considerable portion of the range, but not the fully laden, or similarly one for the fully laden condition, which won't conform to the non-laden. Though the problem seemed to be only that there would exist a technical breach of the standard, such breach didn't seem to be a compromise in safety. Nonetheless the problem was real for the manufacturers, and the solution was to add an entry-level adaptive braking system, consisting of a small computer, wheel sensors and means for pulsing the brakes.

Bendix had been working on such a system for several years, as had its competitors and the time had come to start tooling and putting in facilities so as to meet the introductory date one year away. We submitted our quotation and, as was relatively common in those years, Bendix had properly done its homework and swept all orders from the three manufacturers and undertook to manufacture the units, which was referred to as DotStop.

Unbeknownst to me at the time was the fact that the auto manufacturers had approached the government, seeking a waiver on the standard for light trucks and providing data to prove that the significant activity and cost required to ensure that light trucks literally conformed to the standards was a considerable waste of the nation's resources. Remarkably, this government/ industry dialogue was conducted under the radar, and the government granted the waiver only about three weeks before we were due to submit production samples, which coincided, in terms of time, to about six weeks before full production.

Although I had heard of the standards review several months before the waiver, I was surprised to learn that high level GM representatives had early on approached our top management to advise them of their activity and requested that we not seek to comment to the government on the issue, particularly if we were to couch an approval of the system in technical terms, when our real motives might reasonably be commercial ones. In commercial terms, I think our company was disappointed that the program might become inactive, not so much for the specific business but that this modest unit might be a precursor to more elaborate anti-skid systems to be applied to vehicles in the future and the experience could well be invaluable by assisting us along the learning curve which would certainly lower our unit costs.

I think that I correctly rationalized that the information was withheld from operating guys like me because it was thought that we might be inclined to lean on the oars if we sensed an impending cancellation. Remember, these were busy times and people were continually running on the ragged edge of missed sample-promise dates, rejected samples, start-up problems and other issues intrinsic to the business. I recall being dissuaded from approaching the customer when I initially heard the complete situation including the abortive attempts. The gist of my message would have been that I understood that we were obligated to continue the tooling program and I didn't have a problem spending GM money for potentially no purpose, but that I hiccuped if we were spending *Bendix* money for no purpose and no remuneration at GM direction. (Remember, for programs of this type, the vendor provided the equipment). My objective was to have them assure us that Bendix would be reasonably whole financially in all instances. Since decision day had to be imminent, I was persuaded that we continue to be a "no whining" team player for General Motors. Upon learning of the final governmental waiver, I asked my liaison engineers to canvas the customer base and attempt to learn of their proposed response.

"Good news," responded our guys, "other than GM, all of our customers assure us that the program is full speed ahead."

Having been around more than a few months, I understood that although the engineers ostensibly controlled specifications and design of the vehicle, the management controlled features of the vehicle, particularly where the customer doesn't perceive value. Accordingly, within a few days of our survey, we got a stop-work order from all customers. I suggested to them that since we were only three weeks from completion and submitting a production sample, why don't we do that and have it on the shelf. My selfish reason was that when one submits a sample that gets approved and certifies that it was made off of production tooling, the total quoted tooling bill is paid, no questions asked. For an aborted program, one must review lists of tooling, ascertain each tool's status and degree of completion and eventually escort a customer auditor to the locale where any particular chosen tool reposes.

Obviously, still in my craw was the fact that we appeared to be "stuck" with about $300,000 worth of specialized equipment, not a lot of money in the context of our business, but an expense incurred in extremely unusual circumstances. Naturally, I well understood the *usual* procedures, but this one I felt was unique. I composed a letter stating that we were delighted to receive the original order, that we diligently undertook the project totally committing to an ambitious delivery date, that we respected their request to remain silent during the government hearings and that we continued to expediently work on the project through the prolonged period of indecision. Consequently, it was my feeling that since Bendix persevered in having equipment built while GM was overtly pleading for its obsolescence, GM had an obligation to make Bendix almost whole by ponying up three big ones. In fact, even though I wasn't personally involved, I felt as though the GM request and our own acquiescence that we didn't speak up to protect our own contracted business in itself implied that GM would have protected us from financial loss. (Get a Kleenex to dry your tears. I'll wait.) Anyway, I composed the letter in one page, three spiffy paragraphs, got approval, sent it, and went about my business.

A few months later, I happened to run across one of the GM purchasing guys with whom I formerly did considerable business. We exchanged pleasantries and family news. He eventually said that he really got a hoot out of my letter about the DotStop equipment. Recalling how the generally perceptive purchasing guys used to get pleasure in "ragging" each other on "guy" things as well as job performance, I sensed that his statement about my letter had somehow let him create some satisfying mischief. He said that the lunchroom conversation often involved business, particularly regarding unusual deals and situations surrounding such deals.

He was listening to a cohort finishing a story of an unusual transaction and deliberately said, "That story isn't that unusual, I've run across a one page letter from a vendor offering a plausible case that we should pay for his equipment. He makes quite a strong and logical argument. I'm not involved but if it were me, I'd recommend payment."

"Ridiculous," said his pigeon of the day, "there's no set of circumstances that could possibly justify such payment, ethically, contractually, legally or anyway."

"You wouldn't happen to have two bucks if I could demonstrate that you'd be a schlock buyer if you didn't pay."

He claimed to have collected two bucks from three or four guys.

"Good story," I said, "are you (Chevrolet) going to pay for the equipment?'

"As I told you, I would, but it's none of my business."

Epilogue: Soon thereafter, there were personnel upheavals within Bendix to ensure that the businesses shored up their "analytical abilities." One of these successor bosses was trying to endear himself to some GM gathering and was somewhat uncomfortable because of his lack of acquaintance with the people or, for that matter, with face-to-face dealings. The notion of the "letter" and the awkwardness of it came up, along these lines:

"We don't normally pay for equipment," said one of the General Motors participants.

"Of course not," said this executive, "the guy that wrote the letter must not have understood the procedures. My apologies. Of course you're not responsible for our own equipment."

Now there's one hell of a negotiator. I'd like to see his "analysis" of that transaction.[54]

I bring up the Dot Stop story somewhat as a metaphor relating to the special interest or peripheral players that, ever increasingly, were creating distractions or demanding extraordinary efforts be placed on their notion of the year, thereby diluting the efforts to make product plans and improvements for the future, simultaneously introducing vehicles that the motoring public was willing to buy. A mentality of personal survival in Detroit was becoming endemic, rather than a mentality of optimizing the delight of the customers with exciting new products at reasonable prices.

Probably the worst examples of such "distractions" were from the state of California. When the federal government started formulating and issuing standards for limiting vehicle emissions in the late Sixties, California recognized its special air-quality problems in the Los Angeles area and, for the following years, issued their own more stringent standards. Historically, the industry had been quite successful in proliferating their models, with a minimum of cost inefficiency. In the Fifties, Chevrolet annually sold over a million Chevrolets (Impalas), 400,000 trucks and 30,000 Corvettes, by current standards a meager product array. By the mid-Sixties they had added Chevy II, Corvair and Chevelle with little decrease in efficiency. Nonetheless, the California rules required substantial modifications of the power train, creating considerable expense for the whole, now bifurcated, product line. Again, the preponderance of the development fell to the American manufacturers as the smaller imports generally conformed as they were already configured. I don't know if you've noticed, but they sometimes tend to get carried away at times in California; not surprisingly they did in 1990 by issuing standards requiring manufacturers that wanted to sell cars in California to be required to sell a certain minimum of cars (10 percent by 2003) with *zero emissions,* meaning (wink, wink) electric or battery cars.

---

[54] But wait! It got even better. Another of our new executives negotiated with our Japanese licensee a fee to use the Japanese brake features for several U.S. small-car applications. The accompanying fee approximated the cost of the Dotstop equipment. In his enthusiasm to become an internationalist by using hands-across-the-water technology, he figuratively ran off the end of the pier while still carrying the can of worms, as he already owned rights to use the Japanese designs. I loved the way new analytical guys are handling the negotiations.

Fifteen years later, I heard a panel of the chief engineers of the world's six largest automotive companies lamenting that activity, several years after it was terminated, because even the zealots in California realized that they couldn't rely on Yamaha, Club Car and EZ Go to exclusively provide the totality of personal motor vehicles for the state.

Correction! Not all of the zealots understood the impact of their actions. Several vehemently opposed the cancellation of the "zero emissions" standards with "over-my-dead-body" sounding rhetoric. Although they weren't killed, they were still carried out on their shields after the damage had been done.

The chief engineers discussed the California program. The Ford representative offered that she and her crew had diligently worked on a solution over the years, but couldn't come up with a vehicle that they felt would sell. Did anyone else? Universal head shaking. Such an aborted project might not be considered a failure if the industry learned something fundamental to use in the future. Ford said its review revealed that it learned nothing of any use, nor did any of the other companies offer that they had found any potentially useful nuggets. The conclusion was that the program was an abject failure, and an obscene distraction when considering decisions that had to be made in the intermediate future. Billions of dollars were spent and nothing to show for it when other configurations were screaming for development and evaluation. (Careful, Riley, you're coming perilously close to ranting). There were five or six seemingly viable new propulsion schemes to be considered (and several implausible ones—remember everybody's an automotive seer). There were five or six potential fuels on which to standardize, and almost as many politically popular shams.

CHAPTER NINETEEN
Café Absurdo

It was almost a foregone conclusion that the government would legislate to increase the gas mileage of automobiles. Accordingly, the U.S. Congress passed the Corporate Average Fuel Economy (cynically, "café") Act in 1975 to give domestic automakers dramatic economic incentives to design and build vehicles that conformed to these standards. A failure to comply with such standards wouldn't affect the consumer per se, but would be levied as a fine against those manufacturers who didn't accomplish the stated fuel-economy goals on an aggregate basis.

Obviously, the greatest impact would be on (1) the European luxury-car manufacturers, who gritted their teeth and were prepared to pay the fines for non-conformance, hoping to pass along these costs to their "cost-no-object" customers and (2) the native U.S. manufacturers who would have to race full out to introduce EFI (fuel injection) across the board along with other product disruptions. Policymakers adjudged that this would be attainable from hardware and financial standpoints, as the automobile companies seemed to have recovered after the first gas crunch.

A sports analogy now occurs to me. Obviously, one has to be a world-class performer to survive in the automotive business, as there are only about a dozen viable companies worldwide, where more than 100 times that have fallen by the wayside. To achieve such stature as an athlete is usually enabled by a combination of motor skills, physical attributes, attuned mental acuity that suits a certain environment, all conditioned by over 10,000 hours of repetitive practice. To earn and maintain world-class stature as an athlete probably requires that the game doesn't change after one matures.

Let's consider Michael Jordan, arguably one of the greatest athletes of our time. Having led the Chicago Bulls to three NBA basketball championships, he elected to try baseball.

Many thought he would soon be with the White Sox and lead them to higher levels. As it turned out, his attributes, particularly his hand speed, didn't quite match-up to the specific demands of baseball. Although he was a better baseball player than all but a few thousand in the world, he didn't even make the big leagues.

Let me further hypothesize that we consider two of the great hockey players, Gordie Howe and Wayne Gretzky. Let's assume that in their early twenties, they were forced to play soccer instead of hockey. Although the games have a certain similarity, I would surmise that both, although likely to be major leaguers and perhaps even all-stars, would not be considered as world-class or hall-of-fame soccer players. There is probably something in their twenty-year-old DNA that prevents them from playing at the same athletic level under somewhat new rules.

So, I maintain, had a similar phenomena befallen the U.S. automakers as they were forced to segue from a plentiful resource environment,[55] where their vehicles were expected to perform comfortably over America's vast spaces, to compete with others who were incubated in an environment of scarce physical resources and much shorter trip expectations. Their reflexive actions weren't quite optimal for the new environment.

A particular aspect of the law had seriously pernicious impact on the U.S. based industry, and was probably in second place in leading to the recent bankruptcies. During the difficult period of the early Eighties when Chrysler had to go hat-in-hand to the government, General Motors and Ford, particularly, had a successful line of small cars in Europe, South America and Australia. In fact, in Ford's case, their very popular Fiesta led them to compete for first place in the crowded European market and that success in Europe was all that kept the total earnings of the company in the black.

Those clever lawmakers in Washington just knew that if they established the universe of vehicles covered by the new café rules on the basis of *sales* in the United States, those slippery Detroit guys might tend to cheat. Knowing that their whole U.S. system wasn't very efficiently adapted to manufacturing small cars, with their "body-on-frame" construction, their UAW work rules and their conforming plant configurations, Motowners would probably import their already proven small cars and it was probable that the UAW would make quite a stink. With such a possibility in mind, the congress, in its wisdom, established the denominator in the rules to be cars *manufactured in the U.S. for companies based in the U.S.* Since other companies didn't manufacture in the U.S. to any extent, their conformance was based upon

---

[55] Particularly relating to oil

U.S. *sales*. Particularly in the case of the Asians, they simply had to select what lines of cars to emphasize in the U.S. as the matter of conformance itself would be a snap. Over time, it proved to be so easy that the Japanese, and subsequently the Koreans, decided that it would be a good idea to develop and introduce a line of luxury cars and heavier trucks solely for the U.S. because the U.S. government had so decimated the potential for exploitation of Detroit's most profitable vehicles as a result of café. (Note to author: Why do you subject yourself to *agita* by reviewing this stuff all over again?)

One of the up-and-coming "car guys" at Ford, Hal Sperlich, purportedly made an impassioned plea at a final-product meeting to cancel the new standard Ford Victoria (codename "panther") in favor of a more family friendly van in order to maximize the market for a "large-cube" vehicle. Mr. Ford let his personnel people know that he would probably be subject to the dry heaves if he ever had to encounter Mr. Sperlich in a future meeting.

Again, the standards were selected by using what the Environmental Protection Agency considered "reasonable," based on the best of the foreign imports. The impetus for such law was to lessen the economic impact of imported oil on the U.S. economy, with the added benefit of another assist with the minimization of exhaust emissions. An element regarding public policy never revealed or discussed was the conflicting goals between gas efficiency and safety. As the café standards took full effect in the early Nineties, about 2,400 fatalities per year could be ascribed to the less-sturdy vehicles required to conform to the new standards. Although such casualties have probably been lessened in ensuing years through design, I don't recall a public dialogue recognizing and rationalizing such demise—every two years —of human life equivalent to that of the total Iraq and Afghanistan wars as a trade-off for those material café benefits.

I do believe, however, that the most cognizant citizens, probably the most educated ones, that is, soccer moms, are aware of the rather large gradient of safety provided by a large, deliberately heavy vehicle over their fuel-efficient cousins. They're not fooled by the publicly revealed "best safety in Class IV" reports or advertisements. They also don't discuss this in polite company as (1) they would probably be considered a gas glutton, (2) they might be considered unpatriotic and, most importantly, (3) they recognize that if the unwashed start gravitating toward these types of vehicles embodying the ultimate automobile feature, crash survival, governed more by total mass than any other feature, it is likely that the social adjudicators in Washington will push back in some dramatic and perhaps not totally rational manner. Obviously, it's my feeling that the latter phenomenon supports the demand for Escalades, Navigators, Hummers and in a strange way, Volvos, cars that (certain enlightened) people want to buy.

There are several peripheral aspects to this activity that grate, perhaps not on a rational person, but certainly to one immersed in the industry. When the vehicles were produced in quantity and subject to government inspection, the U.S. manufacturers had their fingers crossed. Even though they felt they had made a reasonably diligent effort to conform, there were still several dilemmas of variability to be solved. The greatest variable was whether each U.S. company had an array of vehicles that would be purchased in a mix that would permit the company to conform as planned. Sometimes customers can be not only unpredictable but also unmanageable. Ford had a pretty spiffy full-sized sedan that was accounted for in their calculations, but at the outset the customers were leaning way, way too much in favor of the V-8 over the V-6, thereby putting their mix out of kilter on their mpg goal. Not to worry. Ford felt itself ingenious in adjusting customer behavior. As the customer was in the process of ordering, they quoted the Crown Victoria (or whatever) with the six cylinder at four weeks delivery and the Crown Victoria with the V-8 engine at eleven weeks delivery. *Voila.* A precise calculation and a pretense of availability would adjust the sales mix precisely back into equilibrium so as to conform to the standards and avoid any fines. Not so fast! Given that choice, the customer tended to order the Impala with the V-8 and the 3 1/2 weeks delivery.

One infuriating event was one that wasn't even considered much of a variable. As I've tried to explain, it was quite a complicated exercise to create a protocol that would account for any one company's total vehicle line and ascribe the proper weighting and equipping of any one vehicle line as part of the total. While I don't recall the minutiae of the variance, the testing agency interpreted and applied the testing procedures differently than the American companies had been led to believe. You can imagine how many nanoseconds it took the automakers to appeal to the principals of the congressional committee that wrote the rules.

I think the response was something like this: "You Detroit guys are right. The testing agency is not testing the vehicles in a manner that we told you would apply or, for that matter, we of the Congress intended [a collective sigh of relief went up from the Detroit contingent, somewhat prematurely]; however, we of the Congress have decided that now would not be a propitious time to intervene as it might appear to be kowtowing to Detroit's whining about the nuances of the testing procedures."

My last recollection relating to this *brouhaha* was when later reviewing features of cars manufactured over here and abroad, I was surprised to find out that the Japanese were manufacturing and selling cars in Japan with carbureted engines well into the Eighties, long after the U.S. was EFI across the board.

My conclusion was, after dealing with the Japanese in the ensuing years, they don't waste resources on matters of principle or on ritualistic changes or procedures intended to educate the public. They are constantly evaluating cost and value for rational decisions in the context of utilization of Japanese resources.

Although tightening the vise and leaving much less room for error or innovation on the part of U.S. manufacturers, the one public manifestation of the latest fuel-efficiency exercises was the dilemma for Chrysler. By this time, Mr. Iacocca himself had been fired by Ford[56] and hired by Chrysler, joining the quintessential car guy and recent Chrysler employee, Mr. Sperlich.

Common sense dictates that, in such a scenario of upheaval in power trains and vehicle sales and related expenses, each company would be affected in inverse relationship to its market share. Simply put, Chrysler had exhausted its resources just to get conforming cars on the road as its cost *per car sold* to develop new engines was about triple that of GM and half again as much as Ford. Accordingly, it successfully borrowed and repaid funds from the federal government to stay in business as a reasonably healthy competitor.

This was accomplished by creating a reasonably attractive new front-wheel drive intermediate-sized car with ample interior space, the "K-car" (named Reliant, Aries and LeBaron throughout the brands), and

---

[56] In his first book, Mr. Iacocca recognizes Mr. Ford's right to fire him for whatever reason, but expresses resentment that Mr. Ford's actions created anxieties for Mr. Iacocca's daughter. Upon his arrival at Chrysler, Mr. Iacocca promptly disposed of 35 of the then 37 vice-presidents. I wonder what impact those actions had on their daughters.

subsequently using the new platform, at Mr. Sperlich's direction, to present the aforementioned family van, the Plymouth Caravan and the Dodge Voyager, a profitable market niche that the remnants of the corporation leads to this day.

CHAPTER TWENTY
Who Speaks Motown?

It's perhaps suicidal to write a chapter title in the form of a question for which I don't have a specific answer, at least not at this moment. It's particularly risky when I purport to be an insightful observer of the business and its idiosyncrasies. Nonetheless, even much less insightful observers of the business or those have no interest in the business whatsoever must sense that there is a communications or philosophical disconnect between automotive employees of all rank and the general public. Something phenomenal seems to be happening over and above the notion that a wealthy Goliath didn't have a dialogue with David or his ilk.

Let's start by looking at the matter empirically. We've already described the indignities undergone by Mike Blumenthal during his approach to Hank the Deuce. Mike didn't aspire to speak Motown, he had high-priced help to do that, although it wouldn't have hurt him to shake hands and make small talk with customer chief engineers or purchasing agents that he happened to encounter on the Bendix nine-seat jet. No matter. After many denials, Mike was recruited to become Jimmy Carter's Secretary of the Treasury[57] in 1976. As I understand it, the Treasury job didn't work out very well as Mike had publicly let his frustrations be known that cabinet members had far less

---

[57] One of the "cutest" stories coming out of his stay there (as you can suspect, he wasn't very much into "cute" stories) was the occasion of him entertaining a table full of dignitaries in a prestigious Washington beanery only to find out that he had forgotten to put anything in his pocket (Mrs. Blumenthal remained in Ann Arbor). As he was explaining his dilemma to the maitre d'hotel, one of the dinner party asked the maître d' if he would accept Mr. Blumenthal's signature as identification if he could provide incontrovertible proof that Mr. Blumenthal was indeed who he purported himself to be. Of course. The guest provided a dollar bill, asked Mike to sign the chit, asked the restaurant representative to compare and verify signatures between that on the chit and that on the dollar bill as Secretary of the Treasury. Problem solved.

authority than their counterparts in the private sector. Politics rule! He left in about two years.

More pertinent to our story was the fact that the "analytical" member of the tri-partite office of the president, Bill Agee, a precocious 38-year-old Harvard MBA, was elevated to Chairman. The "automotive" member of the now defunct office of the president, the widely respected Bill Miron, left to do other things. Bill Agee wasn't particularly familiar with or interested in the automotive industry and, like his predecessor, exhibited a certain nervousness that so much of the company's assets and, particularly, its current profitability depended upon engagement with that industry. Although I can't make any concrete assertions that his public utterances had any effect on our businesses with our several customers, his constant assertions that automotive "was in the winter of its life cycle" or that "future deployment of assets will be dedicated to growth businesses rather than mature ones" made those of us who were trying to maximize auto-centric assets quite nervous. Was he trying to show how smart he was or was he tailoring these remarks to Wall Street? It certainly couldn't be giving comfort to our loyal customers that we would be there when they needed us. As you might imagine, we'll return to Mr. Agee's non-automotive exploits later.

Showing deference to one of the corporation's major sectors, Mr. Agee set about to find an automotive sector president, which he did, or fancied that he had done, with an MBA from one of the "Big 7" accounting firms. I had participated in several customer introductory meetings with him. He seemed very presentable and very smart, but one could early on sense that he didn't speak the language. As all of his direct-operating reports, the group heads, didn't reside in the Detroit area, he must have thought that he was the first line of higher-level customer contact, rather than a player to be inserted by the operating people as appropriate.

Shortly after he was on board and after the introductory meetings, I received a call from a long time senior buyer.

"What the hell has he done now? Who did he go to see?"

I didn't know.

"Let me read to you the policy memo I've just received. As you know, we periodically get memos that spell out guidelines as to what approvals are required for commitments to vendors relative to their size. For instance, my buyers were permitted on their own to commit to $5 million in purchases annually with any one company and they needed my approval for higher-level commitments. I could authorize up to $15 million annually, and so forth. These are welcomed as they spell out specifically the sign-offs required for all purchase orders. This one, however, came at a peculiar time in the annual cycle. I read this policy memo in detail and noticed an asterisk. The comment at the bottom connected to the asterisk stated that Bendix was a unique exception to the above authorization schedule. *All* Bendix purchase orders needed the authorization of the vice president of purchasing. What the hell happened? Who had he been talking to?"

I told him that I hadn't learned anything new in the last five minutes, but I would find out and let him know, but I would also instigate remediating actions to get us off of the crap list. I never did find out what created the blow-up in this particular instance, but the guy was gone within a year and we somehow lost the asterisk.

Mr. Agee then set out to hire "Mr. Automotive Guy" to head up his automobile and machine-tool businesses so he wouldn't have to suffer through the idiosyncrasies of those businesses and let it be known to his executive staff that he would think kindly of those staff members that nominated appropriate candidates. Shortly thereafter, he hired one Bill Panny, head of Rockwell International's automotive business and an extremely capable operating executive, that is if you indeed wanted a guy with Motown credentials.

The Bendix corporate "analytical" types were given the task of evaluating and introducing "modern" management techniques to the cretins in automotive. Instead of having the classic marketing/sales unit organized around customers, with the internal stuff being handled by staffs, they proposed an organization where all marketing/sales activities were oriented around product lines, much like those marketing organizations that handle the hand cream with the extra emollients. Several of our customers railed at this proposal. In fact, the Chrysler buyer took the trouble of enumerating twelve salesmen who he would have to contact to cover all of his purchases when one considered four from our group (up from one) and those of the heavy-truck group, electronics group and all of the Bendix separate aftermarket salesmen. Obviously, to a Seventies modern manager, the customer was the lowest on the automotive food chain and the proposal was put into effect. Rather than having a central guy, like me, running the sales office in Detroit, all the directors in South Bend would divvy up the Detroit sales guys by product line.

From a personal standpoint, there were good and bad effects. We would have to move from Bloomfield Hills to South Bend, but that didn't give anyone heartburn. Professionally, I considered it a lessening of responsibility, but it was technically a promotion, including a 25-30 percent salary raise (hush money?) and considerably much less stress. While not an immediately recognized benefit, the move also permitted me to sit in Notre Dame Stadium between the 40s, four or five times a year, while publicly sharing thoughts regarding the inadequacies of the ND coaches strategy, the superiority of the visiting team, both in philosophy and execution, and the questionable skills and quirks of some of the ND key players.

We moved to South Bend, renting a house while Susie and the architect built her dream home. Work consisted of relatively regular hours, with a trip to Detroit (four hours by car) about every two weeks. My relationship with the new marketing vice president was excellent, as the brake group had just traded positions with the electronics group. My product area, steering, had several profitable lines that were in some jeopardy but, as luck and a little diligence would have it, my potential competition self-immolated and new product start-ups were no more rigorous than usual. I was able to play in a golf invitational tournament with a Bendix associate in South Bend. He had a "heart episode" about an hour after we had finished the qualifying round. I played at my Detroit club with a customer and he had the courtesy of having his "heart episode" a week after the tournament. Apparently, I'd gained the ability to transfer stress to those around me. Either that, or my golf game is so atrocious that the bodies of those partners who depend upon it for sustenance during the tournament were telling them that life is so tenuous that it might not be worth living.

One thing regarding the shakeup occurred to me in the ensuing months. Of the four sales "bosses" in the brake group, only *moi* had much experience with automotive customers. I guess this didn't deal directly with "speaking Motown" other than if you include the rituals, with nuances, that recur during the earning of purchase orders and building the trust that leads up to it. Compounding the problem was the insistence of the corporate office that each customer quotation be preceded internally by an approval of a bids-and-proposal report. While I first shuddered upon hearing this requirement, in my usual wise-guy way I was able to isolate eleven distinct categories of "quotations," only two or three of which would ever lead to consequential business. One of these bids-and-proposal reports would justify a twenty-page treatment because of capital-investment requirements, risks in achieving costs as estimated, dilution of effort for more profitable or more promising product lines or any number of pertinent issues which would be known only to the writer of the reports. Knowing how difficult it was to submit timely quotations even on products where one was a world leader, internal procedural demands put one's professional life as constantly living in sin and attempting to assess the least sin to govern one's behavior.

I started getting calls from several of the guys who formally reported to me in Detroit and from loyal customers who kept telling me that the Detroit salesmen weren't getting proper support and information from South Bend. To both I responded that, as a courtesy, I will talk to the guy in charge, but I no longer had any direct responsibility. This started wearing thin on my peer directors who undoubtedly thought I was overly susceptible to being jerked around by the customer.

Let me give you a few examples. Our brake guy was really good at and really interested in proposing and evaluating new configurations of brakes that would perhaps get us a competitive advantage either through improved performance or cost savings. Accordingly, he would collaborate with our imposing engineering department to design, build, test and conduct cost estimates on new configurations of brakes. When something looked promising, he would gin up a presentation and go with his guys to a customer to make a pitch to engineering and, with our vice-president boss, to high-level purchasing. He felt this so important that he created a follow-up file to update potential customers on each project. One could sense that he felt that this is what marketing is all about and I will admit that the work to that point on such products was admirable.

On one specific project, the idea was to integrate the front disc brake with a redesigned front "corner" so that the four or five integrated pieces (some stamped rather than cast, as I recall), functioning as an integrated "corner" would save four of five dollars per "corner." A Ford buyer who would be responsible for this called me and asked me about it, as the salesman didn't know much about it and his boss hadn't briefed the buyer. This buyer kept hearing rumors about the program but didn't know what he was dealing with. I recalled talking to the marketing director and suggested that he stop and brief this seemingly loyal young buyer. He feigned that it was too early as he couldn't give out specific costs and he'd deal with that when he felt it was appropriate.

Fast forward six months. The buyer was obligated to buy a redesigned casting that would be rendered obsolete by introduction of the "corner." Simultaneously, he received a personal note from a purchasing biggie reminding him that the Bendix "corner" might save Ford big bucks and he shouldn't make any commitments regarding the casting that might preclude the savings generated by the Bendix proposal. He called me.

"I'm desperate," he maintained, "I've got to keep the line moving and I've got to make decisions or at least create a plan of attack that will integrate the 'corner.' Give me the guy's number. I've got to get moving!"

I otherwise went about my business. I heard luncheon conversation that there was not enough time to get the "corner" costed and the bid approved.

A week later, my buyer friend called to vent: "The jerk won't even return my calls! After making all these proposals and all of this blabbering in the halls of power, he doesn't even have the courtesy to send in a negative response or explanation that I can show my bosses. I had to ask for approvals for the casting without being able to explain why the Bendix proposal wasn't considered. I came off looking like an idiot!"

I commiserated as I best could and was somewhat relieved that no immediate damage appeared to have been done.

Fast forward another six months. At our once-a-month marketing/ engineering meeting, each of us made presentations of progress on all of the new programs. Interesting! The brake guy had the "corner" on his agenda. He got to the corner.

"I wanted to update you guys on the 'corner.' I've just recently found out that we missed the corner business by just a few pennies. I think this justifies our attempts to keep this program generically active."

As I recall, he got a general commendation for his performance on the program. Can you imagine the effort it took ole Riley to bite his tongue? It was maintained that we had almost gotten the business, in fact, only lost it by a few pennies. He hadn't ever talked to the buyer. He hadn't ever made a quotation. He had never submitted a design for the required approval. He never had a design to do a cost estimate. He had alienated the buyer and, worse, embarrassed him before his bosses. What the guy had done was a little study that showed that the equivalent current parts, as assembled, was about four or five dollars cheaper than his previous study. Reactivate the *Twilight Zone* intro.

Historically, there had been a somewhat unusual phenomenon when an automobile manufacturer decided which parts to make and which to buy. Many of the basic patterns had been established in the Twenties and Thirties, those patterns being established situationally by companies or when shortages or problems occurred in any product line. At any rate, companies bought anywhere from 30 to 50 percent of total product from vendors. It was the direst fear of most suppliers that their product line would be integrated into the automaker.

I came to believe an article from an academic economist who testified before congress that the company integrating a component would enjoy the efficiency equivalent to the least-efficient specialist. The phenomenon I refer to is that when things are normal, the status quo seems to make most participants comfortable. When things get particularly good, the automakers start thinking of expanding their component-making capabilities (integrating), the thought probably being that they are covetous of all the profits made by the vendors. The corollary is when things in the business are generally bad, companies tend to de-integrate or buy products instead of continuing to make them. To me, this has always seemed counterintuitive, as one would think that as plants reached capacity, marginal product lines would be pushed out to suppliers. Conversely, it would seem that companies would want to integrate products as plant capacity is underutilized. Only when a company is leaving an entire business would it seem to make sense to de-integrate components as the business is shrinking.

Back to the new Bendix marketing strategies. Brakes, being one of the components of the chassis, tend to be long lived relative to redesign or resourcing of any family of brakes. In the mid-Seventies, Chrysler was introducing a new car line that included a new disc brake. Although we had historically never made Chrysler disc brakes (one half Kelsey, one half internal), we of course had a proposal submission that we designed, built, tested and costed to the tune of about $500,000. The request for quotation embodied the whole Chrysler disc brake line, a "general inquiry," but we were easily able to submit a quote on the whole series as it embodied products similar to those sold to other manufacturers. As usual, there seemed to be hysteria on the part of Chrysler in getting the quotation in by the requested date. To "non-speakers" there was an implication that by emphasizing the urgency of a prompt response, the buying company would shortly be negotiating and letting out the business. Actually, there was usually considerable work required internally to ascertain that all quotations conformed to the inquiry and, if not, to rationalize all quotes so that the purchaser was comparing apples to apples. In addition, there were freight differences to be calculated and evaluated. When it became apparent that Chrysler wouldn't respond promptly to the quotation, its importance was lessened at non-speaking Bendix, as the players wanted to minimize executive inquiries into the status of the "urgent" Chrysler disc-brake quotes. One day six or eight weeks later, I got a call from the Chrysler senior buyer who had sought me out in South Bend.

"Who's responsible for the disc brakes? I want to talk about your quotation."

If I had been in my former spot, and he had called me, I would have responded, "Please tell your assistant to get me a room at the Kingsley. I'll drive over tonight and although it's too late to have dinner with you, I'll be in first thing in the morning with full authority to make a deal. By the way, have Janet make the reservation through Thursday night. Although you won't need me full-time, I don't want to leave town until you've made all of your decisions. I want to be at your beck and call."

I knew that perhaps we were a long shot for any business. I also knew that we'd ponied up about four big bits in getting where we were. I knew that he wanted to talk to us and the whole deal would be wrapped up in 48 hours. I suspected that another such window *would not occur for about seven years*. What internal issue could be more important than devoting a few days to see this through?

I talked to our brake guy.

"I know all about it," he said. "It's come at the worst time possible. I've promised our [post-analytical] boss that I'd have the two arrears bids and proposals in by Monday. I'll get back with Chrysler on Monday. He can't be in all that much of a hurry after all this time. Besides, their likelihood of standing pat and continuing their own partial manufacturing greatly reduces our likelihood of securing any business."

I went about my business. About three weeks later I heard the results of the Chrysler buy. Kelsey was out. Chrysler internal was out. German importer was in. English transplant here was in. Bendix, after all of its expenses, never got around the fourth turn. After all, it would have been inconvenient for the marketing guy.

Within a very few years, co-existent with the second gas crunch, Chrysler was pushed to the wall financially and made a general and very broad inquiry regarding the seven or so components of the braking systems to all suppliers that might be interested. I was only an observer because my product line was steering. Naturally, the proposal was discussed at the highest level of the company, and considerable current business was in jeopardy, yet opportunity for expanded business was possible, given that the whole thing was predicated on the fate of Chrysler with the perspective of 1979 prior to their soon-to-be-realized governmental assistance. Mr. Panny took an aggressive posture. He "knew" that Chrysler would survive and he wanted Bendix people to work around the clock in order to make an "all or nothing" proposal. Given that we didn't make rotors for disc brakes and that we didn't supply the calipers to Chrysler, there would be obligations to invest in capital equipment both for specialized machinery for businesses we were currently not in, and capacity expanding equipment for those that we were.

The quotation was submitted. Since this quotation was not for the purposes of keeping the production lines moving for Chrysler, but for the purpose of long-term sourcing feasibility, there was no pressure for the resolution to be made hurriedly. Chrysler was not at all happy that Bendix had taken such a unilateral stance on their quotation. Although they must have liked the symbolism that Bendix would step up with a broad gesture to support Chrysler over its current crisis, Chrysler understood that when they bought diverse product lines under a common purchase order, inevitably they were buying inefficiently made products as part of the package.

Several weeks later, Mr. Agee called all involved together. Apparently, he had done some homework on the future of his not-so-favorite industry.

"You automotive guys have talked me into something again. It's a mature industry and, with the Japanese coming here in both export and manufacturing, there are going to be some big companies falling by the wayside. Since Chrysler is currently one of the weakest, I don't see how we can stand by our recent quotation, with its inherent risks. Mike, will you see that our quotation is pulled off the table before the close of business today?"

Mike nodded his head and did so.

Now, this story isn't intended to critique Mr. Agee's judgment whether to persist with the blanket Chrysler quotation. My criticism has to do with the execution of the whole approach and how the activity almost seems to have been planned as a vehicle to absolutely enrage one of the major customers in its darkest hour. In the first place, it was very unlikely that Chrysler would accept, in toto, the Bendix proposal. They certainly wouldn't have done so without considerable discussion of the details and timing, which would have given Bendix an avenue to backpedal. It was customary throughout the industry when placing an order with a vendor who might not be sure he was getting a certain order to alert him and gave him forty-eighyt hours to "confirm" the quotation. In other words, there was no set of circumstances wherein Chrysler would accept and insist upon execution of the order without Bendix' further participation.

What a shame that Mike couldn't have said to Agee, "Bill I respect your decision and agree that it is a prudent one under the current circumstances. Yet Chrysler is a customer of long standing and it is conceivable that they may be in business for years to come. Why don't you take my guarantee that we won't have to perform under the quotation as submitted, as I think that an indication that they may indeed 'cherry pick' our quotation or one that we will shortly submit, will seem to them as a concession on our part, as it conforms to their initial inquiry. Certainly, it would be reasonable to assure them that we will continue to supply the considerable amount of stuff we currently sell to them. To simply yank the deal off the table might seem to them as a symbol of abandonment in their hour of need. Please accept my assurances that we won't have to accept business from Chrysler that we won't want to accept, and permit my automotive guys and me to handle this (by speaking Motown) for minimum fallout to the long standing relationship, for whatever that may be worth."

Mike, for whatever reason, wasn't able to make that proposal. He got in his car and dutifully went over to Chrysler.

Several months later, the Bendix vice president of automotive sales was attending the Society of Automotive Engineers annual banquet. Several tables over, a Chrysler vice president wanted to catch his eye. Sequentially, the message got passed along, "the guy with the yellow tie wants to get the attention of the guy in the stripped shirt over there," much as children will play "telephone." Finally, the attention was secured. Apparently, the Chrysler guy wanted to show the Bendix guy that he had a cuticle problem on his middle finger. Haven't I been preaching to you guys that Motown people are direct and above board?

And you were also wondering where Larry David got inspiration for his type of situational comedy. Maybe he spent some time in Motown, learning how to speak it.

Much later, I had a boss of middle-class New York breeding. Our licensing department, by a curious twist of fate, was reporting to the former Bendix automotive sector of the corporation. He was about to spend several days in Detroit at some sort of seminar or such where he would be immersed with non-Bendix automotive types. He seemed to be looking forward to it. He always had a few ideas that he felt should have been of interest to Detroit. In his weaker earlier moments, he expressed how lucky his mother was to have a blue-collar Ford pension and medical plan as a result of his father's career as an hourly worker at Mahwah, New Jersey. He went to the seminar. He came back.

"All those Detroit guys are complete idiots. The whole thing was such a drag with all those %/@#s around."

"I understand. Just remember that they were the 'arsenal of democracy' during World War II."

His reaction to my riposte? Berserk! *Absolutely Berserk!* I had to leave the room with epithets echoing about the offices. I never did figure out whether he didn't speak Motown or whether he understood it too well.

CHAPTER TWENTY-ONE
You Can't Go Home

The end of the Seventies were approaching and there were several developments occurring. The country was in Jimmy Carter's "malaise." Iran had defiantly taken American hostages and, most importantly, America was entering its second fuel-shortage hysteria. My product line was quite stable, rack-and-pinion steering configurations were increasing in direct proportion to front-wheel-drive vehicles, and it appeared that downsizing of vehicles was going to be a sure bet this time.

Although Bendix didn't participate in the rack-and-pinion steering business, we were interested in an invention by one of our Australian associates, who had devised a variable-ratio, manual, rack-and-pinion steering gear. This gear, through special configuration of the rack, enabled the gear to steer "hard" going straight ahead and "soft" near the stops when one was parking, exactly the characteristics one might want in order to avoid costly "power steering" options in the inevitably teeny fuel-saving cars of the future. After the first gasoline "crunch," automakers came to grips with conforming to the constraints for safety, emissions and mileage, and simultaneously were able to offer enough comfort and convenience features so that power brakes and power steering were approaching 100 percent installation rate.

Many in the industry thought that perhaps Motown would finally get religion regarding the new environment, leading to perhaps a new opportunity for our steering line. Most of the new cars embodied a front-wheel-drive configuration that had been used for years in Europe. This car configuration, in turn, required a rack-and-pinion rather than a conventional steering-gear setup. Accordingly, the domestic steering suppliers geared up for this configuration, but with a power assist so typical in U.S. specifications. We got the idea that if our "variable-ratio" manual gear could qualify for performance, we could offer a service to drivers and the industry by eliminating the need for the power-assist paraphernalia and permit us to be the leader in providing U.S. manufactured non-powered or manual-steering units.

Accordingly, I worked diligently to prepare a quotation for Ford that might get us in on the ground floor. I spent 21 consecutive days writing the 20-page bids-and-proposal for corporate perusal. I proudly got the quotation in on time and to the same guy that we had jerked around on the brake "corner."

I waited patiently for the first "leak." It wasn't long coming. We weren't even in the same ballpark. The British supplier of manual gears had decreased its prices to maintain and increase U.S. business for manual-steering units.

I happened to be at a corporate function when the VP international asked me how my rack-and-pinion efforts were coming along.

"I got the quotation in to Ford and even included a well researched forecast on foreign exchange and, although I haven't received an official response, I understand the U.K. incumbent has taken a dive to retain the business. I'm discouraged."

"Don't forget that some of our associates, particularly the Japanese, have long experience with this product line. So, instead of walking away, we may as a company want to introduce them to this opportunity."

This was a particularly interesting and pertinent idea, knee jerked by one known as a "brilliant butterfly," and one that I probably would never come up with because of my U.S. orientation and my recent sprint for the tape.

Upon confirming my status through official Ford channels as an also-ran on the subject quotation we, as a company, decided that a gesture of introducing an associate to a market where they have more chance than we of competing would have merit on several levels even if we don't generate any immediate new business. Toward that end, within weeks I was in Chicago at the Japanese consulate patiently awaiting approval of my visa application.

Tokyo, in the spring of 1980, left me with several impressions. First, there were *no* fat people. They must have the sumo wrestlers segregated on a ranch somewhere. In most public places such as restaurants and department stores, I encountered what we would call "elevator music," but that music consisted of "The Great American songbook" (1932-1954) that had long ago been supplanted by soft rock as elevator music at home. For some reason one was able to detect a Japanese sensibility that since more than 100 million people were subsisting on one small island, everyone must pull in the same direction, as internal friction could cause life to be as grim as it was immediately after WWII. Additionally, one was able to sense that it was difficult for an American to glean a sense of the culture as it wasn't customary for an American to be invited into a Japanese home, and there wasn't even a literal translation of a local newspaper, only newspapers written specifically for the nationalities of those reading a specific language.

Naturally, I had a few trepidations regarding the trip, its value to the company and, not least of all, my own daily situations. I knew that the factory where most of the technical meetings would occur was about 60 miles away from Tokyo, and I wondered if there would be anything to ingest there other than fish-heads or crawfish. I was reassured by discovering the "English" breakfast in the grandeur of the Hotel Okura before wandering out to the hinterlands. Such a sumptuous breakfast, I convinced myself, would prevent me from contracting deprivation-induced organ damage for the next 24 hours.

Secondly, I knew that most of the executives and managers of our associate company spoke reasonably fluent English, but what about the important technically oriented employees from the factories?

Both of these apprehensions were immediately dissipated. Of particular interest to me was the ease with which one could conduct necessarily detailed discussions on technical issues, as long as there were blueprints or lists of specifications to commonly point and gesture over, creating our own gesture/English discussion. Such successful interchanges reinforced my belief that learning a language while working is a distraction that causes even the most skilled executives to lose sight of the sparrow.

Several American institutions were clamoring for those negotiating with the skilled Japanese to think and speak Japanese. During negotiations in those days, discussions would proceed in English cautiously, but normally without the need for an interpreter, to a certain point. Then, the Japanese would request a caucus. *In situ*, they would conduct their discussion in Japanese, sometimes quite animatedly, while we sat with our thumbs in place, knowing that it would be a *serious breach of trust* if we had a Japanese-speaking sleeper. Thus was avoided the discontinuity that would inevitably occur if we had called a true "break." All of the top negotiators seemed to respect this negotiating procedure and those that didn't soon found themselves on the outside. Once you "know" something that you're not supposed to know, it's difficult to sort out what you really know and what

194

you don't "know" over, say, a negotiation of a week's duration. I hope you get the idea. A related phenomenon is why I don't have Caller ID to sort phone calls. Perhaps my boss is in his car at the curb watching me watch his ID number and not pick up.

A negotiating tactic I learned early on: If you respond truthfully to your Japanese compatriots' request for your departure plans (so they may accommodate you in scheduling), their real posture will be known to you about fifteen minutes before your limo is scheduled to take you to the airport. A better response might be to offer a smiling, "as long as it takes to firm up an equitable relationship," or, perhaps even better, would be to respond to their request, perhaps fudging on the side of nearness, and then ignoring the need for your departure as the time comes. That way, it could occur that later time pressure or imbalance might rather befall your hosts.

By the end of the week, the associate's management was enthusiastic about being introduced to Ford U.S. by the largest independent U.S. auto supplier and their visit was scheduled for two weeks hence. Ford was purportedly still "evaluating" the general inquiry so the door might not be totally closed, as there needn't be a great urgency to inform the current supplier that he was retaining business.

On the Friday night before I was scheduled to return home, there was, coincidentally, a celebratory dinner in a 13th Century teahouse commemorating 25 years of association and success by the two companies. With our assistance, the Japanese company was the sole supplier of power brakes to the Japanese auto industry and, in turn, the Japanese industry was approaching the same volume of production as the U.S., up from 55,000 annual vehicles during the year the joint venture was created. I was invited and was seated next to Mrs. Panny, the Bendix President's wife, amongst perhaps 30 other celebrants. I'd eaten while sitting on the floor before, but I wasn't very good company because I knew that the tingling in the legs would start in about 15 minutes, the pain would start in another 15, and both would subside in yet another 15, leaving me, on one hand, with a sense of relief and, on the other hand, with apprehension if I would ever be able to walk upright again.

The first course came, served by a kneeling geisha. It resembled a small ceramic building of some sort, like you would see in a fish tank, containing three vertical toothpicks, each offering what was probably some sort of delicacy.

"To not dishonor the hosts, I've got to eat at least one of these," I said to myself.

After considerable hesitation and visual evaluation, I grabbed one, gave it a few chomps and tried to get it down. It must have been an exotic Japanese delicacy known as a fleer, because its texture reminded me of bubble gum and I couldn't swallow it. By the time I had discretely disposed of the semi-eaten fleer, the third course was being served, lobster. This wasn't a Maine lobster as would be conjured up in an American's mind, but half of a South African lobster that resembles a humongous crawfish with a curled up tail, scorpion-like, split in half front-to-back. I'm not a shellfish fancier, but I could see some flesh meat that resembled "white meat" and undertook to devour some of this. As they were clearing the remnants of this course, I noticed that all the natives had picked their lobster pretty clean, except for the part that I ate, which they had all left untouched. I said a quiet prayer.

And so it went for about thirty courses, until I realized that nobody noticed or cared what I ate. Nearing the end, I was starting to again get anxious, as I was six or seven courses behind; but one of the serving ladies came up very close and whispered, "You finish? You want me to take away dishes? You want me to bring melon?"

I expressed an affirmative response in every language and gesture that I could conjure up, perhaps even in tongues, knowing that a *saint* had come to deliver me from my awkward situation.

As I was enjoying my melon, I noticed that Mrs. Panny was three or four courses behind.

"I understand it's hard to assimilate and eat all of this stuff when one isn't used to it," I comforted. "Would you like me to get someone to make you appear caught up?"

What a thoughtful and considerate guy, she must have thought.

Upon my return home, my knee-jerk reaction was to outline the presentation as I had a very good idea of what we wanted to say. I brought myself up short, however, reminding myself that the presentation was theirs to control and the conveyance of information to third parties by Japanese companies relating to current customers, competitive situations, costs and internal postures was very different and generally closer to the vest.[58] This was confirmed by our international executives and I awaited the Japanese executives' arrival to put the presentation together.

Two weeks later, I was pleased to pick up my new friend and very presentable director of sales, Tad, and his financially oriented associate as they arrived in Detroit on a Monday night. My intention was to put our heads together for a few hours on Tuesday morning to agree on what information belonged in the presentation. Then they could visit other Bendix people while I was doing the grunt work on the presentation prior to our Wednesday 3:00 P.M. show time. The VP international had other ideas. He immediately "invited" our guests (and me) and another few key players to share a few thoughts on the Pacific Rim which turned into a review of the litany of common issues or information. This lasted until about lunch. I was getting antsy. I was about to excuse us when the VP stated that he'd had several inquiries from other important Bendix people requesting that they be able to talk to representatives from this associated company on their next visit and he felt compelled to honor their requests. (Remember, this was a time where almost everyone was convinced that the 19th Century was Europe's, the 20th Century was America's and the 21st Century would be Japan's). These other executives were trying to line up their ducks. The duck-lining activity proceeded until 3:00 P.M.; 24 hours to go and not one pre-PowerPoint page outlined.

We finally got several productive hours to outline the presentation but I ran out of secretarial help by dinner time. We had gotten the presentation pretty much put together, but we still had some smoothing to do, and we were bumping up against copying, collating, compiling and binding time. We hosted an informal dinner with other Bendix executives.

When putting together the presentation, one couldn't help but be impressed with the Japanese company's success. Sales and profits were compounding geometrically and I thought that presenting the compounded growth rates of several of their businesses would be doubly impressive. How would I compute? I was not near an engineer's desk or my own desk at home in my South Bend office. I was in the corporate office with the suits in

---

[58] Except perhaps comparing and consulting on pricing with competitors, strictly illegal in the U.S. for which several Japanese/American companies have recently been flagged.

Southfield, Michigan. I went up and down the aisle, pleading if someone had a log-log-duplex decitrig slide rule with which I could compute such impressive growth rates in seconds. I found one. I computed.

The presentation was reasonably well received, after apologizing to the purchasing agent for saying that I understood that Bendix U.S. couldn't seem to get the business even if we had slave labor and stolen material. Nonetheless, the purchasing agent said that if our numbers were accurate, his opinion was that Ford itself should get into the business.

One sensed that the automotive business was entering another difficult period. I got a call from one of the VPs in the international department asking me to stop in the next time I was in Detroit. Easy enough. The caller was Les Larsen, a late-in-career, "father of the disc brake," engineering executive, who was also the loaner of the slide rule weeks previously, as well as being a highly respected and popular executive with a somewhat military bearing and the title of Vice President of International Licensing. He was interested in my take on the steering project and offered that he had received favorable comments about the activity from both sides of the pond. How nice of him to call me in to share that, I thought. With a smile, he recalled my frenetic behavior while trying to find a slide rule on which to compute. He first thought that unusual because, for the last six years in which we were acquainted, he assumed I had something other than an engineering background. My frantic plea for an arcane engineering tool caused him to look into my background. Would I be interested in becoming one of the three directors of worldwide licensing? Keep remembering that "tremendous trifles" graduation lecture.

The new licensing director servicing industrial and aftermarket operations would be a particularly interesting position at this juncture, Mr. Larsen continued, as Bendix had just expended $300 million to acquire the Warner Swasey machine-tool company, placing it on almost equal footing with Cincinnati Milacron. There would undoubtedly be a lot of action in integrating the technical activities of that company with that of those few, but prestigious, existing Bendix companies in the numerical control, precision-measurement and inline machining-systems fields. This activity would undoubtedly entail rationalization of the newly merged companies' entanglements throughout the world. When I found out fully what my promotion entailed and what I did, I had to explain to people who asked that "it's so important and wonderful and mysterious that even I don't understand it!" It really was strategizing and arranging for giving help and information to companies that wanted to make products like ours in countries where we elected not to manufacture or sell these products ourselves. A simple example perhaps would be the Fram (automotive filter) product line. We taught companies how to make automotive filters and, if they could maintain appropriate quality standards, permit them to actually make them look like our own under a trademark license. As I recall, royalty from twenty-plus worldwide Fram licenses amounted to about $20 million annually, with only administrative costs associated with the activity and favorable U.S. tax rules on earnings attributed to overseas royalties.

During our first discussions about me perhaps joining "Corporate International," Mr. Larsen offered several characteristics that he would look for in such a position.

"Since licenses tend to be so long in duration and the subject matter deals with the company's "crown jewels," that is its technology and intellectual property, one must be careful to absorb the minute details of the negotiations and fastidiously put them on paper."

He told several stories of businesses in which we were once leaders, carburetors for example, but were forced to leave the business as a result of injudicious licensing.

Secondly, because the complications and variables involved in international business were geometrically greater than those for related domestic ones, one had to use his best creative skills to ingeniously optimize these opportunities; one had to exhaust the various situations as to what associate in what region would be best, what the terms and conditions would be, how we would transfer technology to it, what were the unique legal and tax issues and would it be advisable for us to invest or invite a third party to invest with us?

Really big picture stuff!

I was generally nodding in assent during his rather long soliloquy. When he stopped, it occurred to me, "Hey, wait a minute. Those two characteristics you just described in some detail tend to be mutually exclusive in any one individual."

He winked! I was catching on.

Back to Detroit in about three months less than Susie's plea for three solid years in her dream house. I took a small apartment for the summer and we made arrangements to move before Labor Day. We'd leave the two oldest kids in Indiana, at Purdue and Butler, respectively. These moves tend to become more complicated as the family matures.

During my orientation period, which was quite short, I was led to understand that the VP international had high ambitions for his career. He wanted subordinates, particularly the licensing directors, to be at his beck and call at all times when he was in the office, in the event he needed information to respond to an inquiry on high. Unusual, I thought. In operations we tended to stagger our time in and out to cover the office in general. It also occurred to me that he expected to run the office like that of a senator. Here I thought I had rather specific responsibilities and a charter to use my time most efficiently.

In September, 1980, Mr. Agee rented out the auditorium of the Southfield, Michigan, town hall to present an expectedly routine "state of the corporation" to corporate office people. I was not yet totally immersed in the corporate culture, but there was embedded in this presentation quite a few things that even I understood might have enduring implications on the company and perhaps even on my own career.

First of all, Mr. Agee argued that the coming recession, rather than being a time to refine manufacturing operations, should be a time to refine the types of businesses in which the company participated. He admitted that discussions of this objective with President Panny, whom Mr. Agee agreed is a top-level operations guy, had not been successful. Consequently, Mr. Panny would pursue other interests. Mr. Agee will seek a new "President" whose profile is more oriented to "strategic" rather than "operating" perspectives.

Mr. Agee then ran down the several businesses and shared his take on each, what were likely to be our proposed "thrusts" and how he evaluated our prospects.

Then Mr. Agee heaped praise on his administrative assistant, one Miss Mary Cunningham, whom he maintained had given him several new insights as to how Bendix as a premier company should shape its values and its corporate mission. Miss Cunningham, yet shy of thirty, had come to us with a Harvard MBA and a series of apprenticeships.

"Let me tell you, if some of you guys would do your job as well as she does hers, we'd all be in a much better place," posited Mr. Agee. "But there's an aspect of this that I want to bring out in the open in order to put it in the proper perspective. I've heard there have been rumors of a personal relationship between Miss Cunningham and myself. Let me set the record straight once and for all: There is not and there never has been a relationship between the two of us, other than the one I've just described while planning our corporation's future and, coincidentally while performing her corporate tasks, becoming a friend of my family."

(In my mind was forming a scene to be enacted months in the future, Thanksgiving, at a impressive home in Vernor Estates: "Aunt Mary, would you please pass the gravy?")

Mr. Agee, barely forty, and chairman of a Fortune Top 75 corporation, already had embodied some of the characteristics of a corporate chairman. One in particular I'm referring to was the supposition that your employees only knew what you had told them. Here was a complete disconnect. Of the several hundred gathered employees, about 95 percent of them knew that the chairman had been divorced within the past year. This faux pas might have eventually passed as an increasingly cynical corporate staff found no incentive to publicly question the chairman's view of the situation. Unfortunately, Mr. Agee had invited the business press to attend the meeting, and also had invited the *Fortune Magazine* representatives to accompany him and Ms. Cunningham immediately afterward to San Francisco that evening where they were about to "spin off" the Forest Products Group as the first major purchase of Mr. Kravis and friends. Mr. Agee was very proud and publicly supportive of Ms. Cunningham, undoubtedly one of the reasons the business press had been invited to participate in one of her earliest "negotiating sessions." Probably the idea that he himself could be considered a leader in shattering the "glass ceiling" was also a part of the motivation for the public demonstrations. Another episode regarding this inclination would be part of his future undoing.

I walked the half-mile or so back to my office at headquarters and was somewhat surprised to find the Detroit based group VP for the industrial group in his darkening office looking absent-mindedly out the window. Giving me the high sign, he seemed anxious to converse.

"What happened?" he asked.

I told him as best I could.

"When Panny hired me for this job, he told me that although I would be working for the Warner Swasey guy in Cleveland, we would be the chocolate halves of the Oreo cookie. The Cleveland guy would be the icing in the middle. From my perspective, we just lost the wrong half of the cookie."

201

A Detroit sales office guy had used the Jetstar nine-seater that day to escort Ford plant visitors and returned more than an hour later than scheduled. He was surprised to be greeted by an impatient hubbub of caterers and travel department employees upon his return, only to piece together later that the plane was scheduled for that trip to San Francisco.

As would be expected, the takeaway story by the press from the meeting was Mr. Agee's disclaimer of a relationship with his corporate-planning protégé, the well turned out Miss Cunningham. The story, at least in Detroit, was building to a crescendo by the weekend, and somebody in the corporate office got the idea that perhaps someone ought to talk with Mr. Agee, still in San Francisco. They flipped coins, and the loser chose the unfortunate greeting, "What's going on out there?"

Obviously, there was nothing "going on" out there, at least outside of closed doors, other than the sale of the Wood Products Company. Mr. Agee told them not to worry in Detroit, he'd be back shortly and have a statement, or they'd have a joint statement to put everything to rest. Having recalled about ten years earlier when Ted Kennedy had his problem and the brainpower met in Hyannis to compile a "statement" which never was really forthcoming, one couldn't but help make the connection in anticipating the forthcoming "statement."

After almost a week, the company put out a somewhat plausible statement by one of the distinguished members of the Board of Directors. Although the detail escapes me, it had something to do with how fortunate it was that Bendix was blessed with two such brilliant young corporate visionaries and two such talented people would undoubtedly steer Bendix into areas in which it would flourish for years to come. Given that they would necessarily be flung together while recreating this steadfast company, it would be reasonable to cut them some slack regarding the privacy of their relationships.

The distinguished director issuing the statement was the noted founder of Kmart, and of mass merchandising in general, but unfortunately his name was Harry Cunningham, the coincidental surnames creating even more confusion.

The press was having a field day with all the speculation and hard news was joined by feature stories or new slants on the situation. The most memorable one for me was one of the slick newsweeklies that stated, "When one attempts to address and present facts regarding an issue that has heretofore been perceived as titillating by the teeming masses, *carnage ensues!* When one attempts to do one thing when individuals are otherwise expecting another thing, *carnage ensues!"*

I've kind of plagiarized that critique over the years. It's amazing how many events one encounters during a lifetime where someone or even oneself makes a small error in explanatory judgment and you'll never guess what ensues! (Or maybe you will.)[59]

Over the next several weeks, the dialogue became more intense as the participants became more insistent on their innocence. I believed them, at least on the carnal[60] aspects of the accusations but perhaps not on the smitten aspects, particularly on his part. I made a mental note that the relationship sounded similar to what I understood was that of the King and Mrs. Simpson.

I'll create a demonstrative dialogue:

"I'm not so sure that the board will like being called to a meeting in—"

"But you're the Chairman, you can call the meeting for anywhere you chose!"

"Although I agree with our plans for automotive reorganization, perhaps we should wait a few months until our business for 1982 has been secured."

"I thought we had agreed the sooner the better. If we wait for events to be undertaken by our automotive customers, we'll lose our momentum. After all, as Chief Executive, we're remaining in the automotive business only at your pleasure."

At any rate, unfairly or not, Miss Cunningham was soon to leave the company. The story seemed to be a self-perpetuating one, and for the good of the company and the individuals involved, her leaving would be the answer. Don't forget that she had friends of friends in high places, and within a month or so she was on the staff of Seagrams Company, New York City.

Our new house in North Bloomfield Township was a nifty Marcel Bruer knockoff and our friends were happy to see us return after three years. Nonetheless, Susan's friends had settled into their normal young matron Bloomfield Hills activities, whereas she was enjoying that the "caboose" baby was approaching school age and, even more lifestyle directing, had

---

[59] John Edwards does.

[60] Adjective, not to be confused with the noun of the previous paragraphs.

come to the conclusion that her immersion in photography during the South Bend years wasn't enough for a fulfilling business career. Accordingly, she enrolled at Center for Creative Studies in downtown Detroit, taking Stevie to their day-care service. The two teenage girls at home re-acclimated reasonably well, but three years is an eternity for kids of that age, and even my former golf foursome wasn't available. And the usually adaptable college kids experienced some downers related to the scarcity of reasonably paying summer jobs in the Detroit area.

We spent the holidays with family and friends and hoped to settle down in generally familiar and amenable surroundings. After the first of the year, the second gas crunch and a recession had settled in, and there were rumors floating around about corporate organization and staffing. On a Friday in mid-February, I happened to mention to Mr. Larsen that rumors were becoming more persistent, particularly about a corporate presence in Washington, D. C. He said that he would keep his ear to the ground and let me know if anything was cooking. That afternoon he called me back into his office.

Mr. Agee had decided that, as a preeminent company, "We need a New York presence! Why don't we position the international department as permanent representatives in a New York office?"

"I didn't know this when I hired you six months ago!" Larsen implored.

"I know. Calm down." I offered.

I learned that our VP department head was deliriously happy with the prospects. He'd already made deals for a Princeton condominium and an apartment near the office. He'd become the nominal administrative head of the New York office, in a city where the chairman himself might want to spend some corporate (and other) time. (You think?)

In fact, he was so happy with the prospect, that he was putting forth new rules to ensure that nothing could lower our departmental profile or prestige. While, you remember, the current rules were that we were to be in the office whenever he was, now it was also important that we be in the office when he was, but is even more important that we also be in the office when he was not, to cover, if you will. To follow those rules and to accommodate a committed 25 percent travel schedule, even giving up vacations didn't balance the account.

Although life was going to have a lot of interesting events and quite a few perks, the Rileys were approaching a few years of negative cash flow (college) and negative discretionary time.

At this juncture, perhaps it is appropriate that one contemplate his career and perhaps his disappointment that he hasn't approached a higher level of management. Although my education was *exactly* the same as the current Chairman of General Motors (even though he was soon to be defrocked), a level had not been reached wherein all college tuitions were ensured—nor a carefree retirement. Even the most skeptical reader will admit that I appeared to be on top of my position, had a problem-solving orientation, expressed enthusiasm for the firm's goals and objectives, gave unusually good service and assistance to our customers and consistently generated record or near-record profits.

Granted, I tended to be conservative about leaping into questionable ventures, and there was some oblique feedback about my issue orientation, rather than a political one, wherein my demeanor was that I tended to talk to, rather than *up to,* bosses and looked at, rather than *up to* those same cats. It was a situation that I found hard to finger.

Please fast forward thirty years to the present. I was watching a PBS Masterpiece Theater presentation of *Page 8,* wherein Bill Nighy plays a dedicated senior Home Office operative presenting a report to his superiors, the (female) Home Secretary and several others.

"Have you read page 8?" he inquires.

"Yes, of course"

"You obviously haven't read page 8 or you'd be tearing out your hair!"

It seems as though the Prime Minister knew that English citizens were in harm's way and did nothing to alleviate the particular situation. Further, the incident was about to be revealed to the press.

Later, that operative is seen in a casual setting with a sympathetic cohort and lamenting his lack of hierarchical rewards, despite his insightful and accurate assessments of difficult situations, loyalty, studiousness and so on.

"You know," she offers, "I sense that your superiors appreciate all of your insightful and diligent contributions, but I also think that they sense that you are having more fun than they are, and they tend to resent that. They tend to resent that a lot!"

Speaking of insightful.

CHAPTER TWENTY-TWO
Give My Regards

After sharing several weeks of speculation and rumors with my bride of more than twenty years, I let her know the final plans on the way to a Ford retirement party. As always, she looked at the bright side, responding that the proposal might be quite interesting and, besides, in the current economic situation, we probably didn't have any choice. (Little did I know that the plans weren't that final after all, as there were stutter steps along the way as the Board made Mr. Agee jump through a few hoops. I suspected something because several times that summer I was asked, "What is the amount of your transitional costs that you have irrevocably committed?" I'm confessing only now that I don't think I shared this with Susie, and the plan did eventually reach fruition.)

We were in our new home back in Detroit for about 5 1/2 months and already we were obligated to make new plans, with a difference. No longer would we be able to simply choose the town or city in which to live. Not only were we moving from a depressed housing market to a New York post-bankruptcy vibrant one, but Mr. Carter's malaise had pushed mortgage interest rates to a level of about 17 percent. Even before this had occurred, we knew that to live a reasonable lifestyle in Manhattan in 1980 with a few children would require a middling six-figure income, and by that we didn't mean $150,000.

Accordingly, we would have to find housing in one of the four states surrounding New York City. In their honest attempt to "help" or "expedite" our transitional endeavors, the corporate personnel department threw a dinner and seminar for the twelve or so of us that were making the move, where we were exposed to and lectured to by real-estate, financial, legal and mortgage specialists. I don't know about you, but I would rather have spent the time listening to the George Shearing quintet. (Ironically, that was exactly what we were doing at Michael's Pub six months hence.) Since our new eastern estate would be the seventh place where we had lived as a couple or family, my cynical take on the way home was that we really didn't need help regarding real-estate dealings or securing mortgages. What we really needed were tips on which areas were amenable and affordable for families with kids, yet commutable to New York City.

Now for the hurry-up planning and searching. In the early Seventies as mortgage rates were escalating, companies created mortgage-assistance programs to make relocation at least somewhat attractive and affordable for transferring employees. Under the Bendix program, employees were reimbursed for expenses incurred as a result of the increased interest rates, withdrawing such reimbursement gradually over five years. I viewed this as a mechanism for one to become insolvent at his leisure but, hey, their heart was in the right place and it was better than nothing. In a department-wide planning session, the bosses asked for ideas on additional benefits might they consider and perhaps provide that neither they nor the personnel department had contemplated. In one of those few lucid moments, I blurted out that it would seem reasonable that neither another recent recruit nor I, who were transferred into Detroit only six months prior, should take a beating on homes purchased at that time. The proposal was accepted within days. The house sold about eighteen months later for about $55,000 less (or 30 percent less) than we had originally paid for it. Whew!

During that disruptive time, one of my associates had been transferred from South Bend to Detroit. The offer by the company's vendor to buy his South Bend home was reasonably considered insufficient by him, so he took the company-offered, interest-free, six-month "bridge loan," offered for the purpose of temporarily substituting for the equity in his current home. Using that as down payment, he purchased his Detroit home. In the continuing down market, his South Bend home didn't sell over time, and after six months, the formerly interest-free "bridge loan" now demanded interest-bearing payments. In somewhat of a financial pinch in spite of the company benefits, one day he sat down and studied his disbursements, finally realizing that the house payment on his vacant South Bend home, the payment on the bridge loan and the payment on his Detroit home equaled more than his take-home pay. Now both he and the company had problems. Certainly my associate had a problem. Even problem-solving Bobby would have distress in such a situation as, unfortunately, the Rileys were addicted to a couple of substances: (1) food and (2) clothing. The company had a problem in that one of their best employees had to be fomenting about the pickle he had gotten into by actions instigated by the company. As I understand it, someone from personnel blew the whistle and suggested that everything be backed up. The offer on the South Bend home was re-activated and somewhat further subsidized by the company. When that new offer was accepted, the bridge loan was paid off and everyone went their several ways as the employee soon left for other employment and in general disgust for Bendix.

As we were preparing to make our first scouting trip, I had a meeting with the working-level personnel guy. We got to the mortgage-assistance part. My first experience with that was six months before when being transferred from South Bend to Detroit. South Bend interest rate, 7 percent ($750/month payment); new Detroit rate, 12 percent ($1,100/month payment) for an equivalent house; the company had been paying pretty much the difference. This procedure was new to the company also. Now, if we were able to find an equivalent house at the same price in the East (are you kidding?), the monthly payment would be about $2,000/month at 17 percent. I mentioned that even though the considerable assistance representing the 10 percent extra mortgage rate was appreciated, my move would still be quite a squeeze.

"You must have misinterpreted," the personnel guy offered, "that way you get no choice. The way the policy is written, you may choose between the 7 percent to 12 percent differential or the 12 percent to 17 percent differential. Make a few computations and let us know which you choose."

I let him know rather firmly that what he had just said didn't match what I had been told nor did it, by any stretch of the imagination, begin to make me whole in the context that six months ago I was sitting in South Bend paying $750/month, and less than six months from then I would be paying $2,000/month, with the company contributing about $600/month. He explained that he was sorry that I misunderstood, but that his hands were tied. He encouraged me to keep in touch as the company (including the Chairman) wanted this move to go smoothly and, by the way, I should probably purchase a more modest home.

The minute it was announced that we were moving, our international office got bounced out of the main office to the development labs at the back of the property. As I was walking the quarter-mile back to the restructured temporary offices, I was thinking to myself that I was catching on. I was the first one in the company to request a "double dip" on the assistance program and the numerically challenged personnel guys didn't understand the implications. Nonetheless, I'd just taken a haircut for about $650/month in real dollars (that was my whole salary seventeen years prior). What were my alternatives? We hadn't even started the process and already I was getting heartburn.

I got back to my office and started piecing together the deal as I understood it, when Mr. Larsen gave me the "come over here sign."

"As you were walking back here from your meeting with Mr. [Personnel], he called me and said that I should know that Mr. Riley was misrepresenting me on what I told you about the deal. I asked him to explain the details and I told him you had represented it *exactly* as I had put it to you. He maintained that I had no authority to represent the procedure in that manner, as it was contrary to policy. I told him if that was indeed the case, the policy would have to change. That's how it stands. Don't lose any sleep and I'll confirm when everything is officially copacetic."

Back to the physical and geographical planning for the move. I poured through the material given to us at the dinner seminar at the corporate office. Lo and behold, there was a letter-sized schematic map of the New York area, with isobars representing 30-minute, 45-minute and 60-minute commuting times to center city. Understanding that housing costs are approximately inversely proportional to the distance from the city, I studied the 60-minute isobar in quite a bit of detail.

Imagine an almost pure egg shape with the largest end up and canted upward to the NNE and about 20 degrees from vertical. The isobar indicated that remarkably few miles can be traveled in that hour in the north, east and west directions. This was because of having to go around water, general traffic conditions and bottlenecks getting in from Long Island, and density of traffic and local trains only from Jersey, respectively. The small end of the egg reposes SSW just past the borough of Princeton and the 55 or 60 miles is enabled by the main-line railroads. Although this information was not at that moment determining, it was certainly something to keep in mind during our search for housing.

We decided that the first of what we thought would be three or four trips would be a broad sweep of the areas in which we had an interest. We'd be able to get a much better general idea if we didn't have to make and keep appointments. We dressed up enough to handle any situation. We were cruising through Greenwich, Connecticut, on a Sunday afternoon and spied the open door on a realty storefront. It must have been fate. What could be more appropriate? We entered. A real-estate lady greeted us enthusiastically.

She sized up Susie in her matching gabardine dress/coat and decided that even the escort might be okay. We shared our price target. She got on the phone and told a compatriot that an "obviously Greenwich" couple had just stumbled into the office and what might be available in their price range? Hanging up without apparent satisfaction, she motioned for her supervisor to join. He listened, looked across the room and yelled, "Is that old lady with the little house down by the vacuum cleaner factory ever going to sell?"

We never looked at a house in Greenwich.

We visited a house in New York state. It was stone and somewhat resembles the Cotswold we lived in before we moved to South Bend. There was a tentative deal with another party, but, in the 17-percent mortgage environment, agents were writing subordinated offers because there were so many potential buyers who couldn't qualify for a mortgage. Overall, the house was quite impressive and quite reasonably priced, but we were unable to decide to make even a subordinated offer at the time. Why? Because we couldn't hear each other speak due to the fact that I-95 was at eye level about fifty yards away.

Remembering the isobars, we attacked Princeton. One of the few houses in our target price range was exactly the Techbilt house we busted out of nine years prior in Michigan. We started looking into obscure Princeton outliers and found several that might have been plausible, but the realtor insisted on showing new rural homes (where she knew the builder) rather than "in-town" situations that we had requested. The whole scene was absolutely exhausting and discouraging.

"Let's get out of here!" stated my dear Susan.

On the third trip we did "North Jersey." This was an absolute bummer. There was a "white elephant" in Pennington, New Jersey, one of the Princeton outliers, named by us as such because of its large area under roof and the related obligation to heat such a behemoth during the second and even more serious energy crunch. As the head of the household was convinced that no one would be happy if the family wasn't happy, we made a bid and successfully bought the house without ever learning the exact commuting time or, for that matter, the most efficient modes of transportation. After several weeks of experimentation, the answer was (1) drive to Princeton Junction train station, (2) walk a half mile to the train platform, (3) ride the train to NY Penn Station, (4) walk past Macy's to Herald Square, (5) take the subway to GM Building at 5th Avenue and 59th

Street. That was one hour and fifty minutes each way, thank you for asking. One of my cohorts who settled nearby called the commuting activity similar to that of the Olympic pentathlon, the shooting part most likely to occur in the subway. He did also point out a potential regional benefit of our housing choice: 25 percent of white-collar jobs in the U.S. are "commutable" from our chosen domiciles.

Within several months of us moving to New York and while we were still in our temporary office configuration, Mr. Agee made a public proposal for Bendix to acquire RCA. Generally, stocks were down, making it relatively cheap to purchase publicly traded companies and RCA was particularly troubled, its president having recently resigned for failing to file or pay income taxes for a period of several years.

The response from RCA was swift but effective, "Mr. Agee has demonstrated difficulty in managing his own affairs. How could the stockholders and other stakeholders of RCA trust him to manage their affairs."

Boy, was that a cheap escape for RCA. I made a mental note that our chairman was on the prowl, and bet he'd get his act together more precisely before his next foray.

The condition of the auto industry was grim. In spite of the interim commotion in my life and career it seemed that I had ostensibly made a good decision to broaden my professional scope by going international. The GM display of vehicles on the main floor of our office building, aptly named the GM Building where we occupied the twenty-first floor, showed that the quality and styling of American cars seemed to be coming back. Now that I was traveling more, I interfaced with more random, but generally upscale, business people. When they started a general conversation and asked of my business connections and responded upon hearing, they seemed somewhat interested in my lot, perhaps as they would be interested in a condemned man talking about his last meal.

During these conversations, I made it a point to ask my seat mate to give me his or her take on the auto business; what is the perception of current market shares, who's got the best cars, who's going up who's going down and so on. Only slightly atypical was this guy from Washington, D. C., who offered that in his suburban subdivision, fifteen of the sixteen homes had Volvos, but he knew that to be anecdotal, perhaps not truly representative, so he surmised that the market must be about 45 percent Japanese, 40 percent

Volvo, 15 percent American and European premium. At the time, U.S. makers still had about 60 percent of the domestic business, but his impressions and that of others clearly put Detroit makers on a slippery slope in their estimation.

Influential constituencies, notably the congress and the UAW, were starting to talk about the transitions and wondering aloud what the future would look like and whether there were insidious forces behind the unfolding phenomenon. It was my understanding that such U.S. discussions were making the Japanese "country fathers" very nervous. The government and the Japanese Automobile Manufacturers Association (JAMA) exerted a great deal of influence on the behavior of the Japanese manufacturers. During diplomatic discussions with Japanese government officials, the U.S. put on the agenda: Human rights in Japan and nearby North Korea, China, the sanctity of Taiwan and other similar issues. The Japanese listened politely and went along where reasonable. Their agenda reflected more pragmatic items, most of them having to do with protecting their U.S. automotive export business, which was starting to match the domestic Japanese in volume. It was important that there be no tariffs, no retaliation, no non-economic barriers for the Japanese in shipping to the U.S. At one point, they got so nervous about potential pushback from America that they voluntarily offered to place a volume ceiling on exports to the U.S. An unintended consequence of this policy, at least from the standpoint of America, was to create an artificial shortage, thereby causing many Americans to rush out and purchase these "rationed" vehicles so as not to be shut out of the market.

Previously, I have here commended Japanese companies for their rigorous and standup posture during negotiations and their history of living up to obligations. Note that I was speaking of company executives. The same cannot be said of those who made public policy. Detroit executives, on top of their problems generated by the shifting landscape, had been habitually criticized for not retaliating by exporting to or manufacturing in Japan. But at this time, the Japanese government did not permit non-Japanese companies to manufacture in Japan. Regarding export, the Japanese were consummate artists at creating non-economic barriers. One such was that foreigners could advertise only in their own language. Further, it was viewed as unpatriotic to purchase a foreign vehicle. Then, there were the severe restrictive controls on dealers. The steering wheel was on the wrong side and the expenses to convert to right-hand drive couldn't pay off for what could only be a niche business. In light of barriers like those, our "man in Tokyo" insisted on having a Buick as a company car and, when all was said and done, it was the financial equivalent to having a Rolls Royce in the U.S. Certainly, the younger generations of Japanese who were rapidly becoming Westernized would have loved to drive a Corvette, a Mustang or a GTO as "the first kid on the block to have one," if it weren't for the considerable expense, the negative social pressure and the extraordinary red tape required to procure and operate one.

I settled into a groove in my new situation and noticed the differences in making decisions about efficiently getting where I needed to go. My perfect day was seven-to-seven, portal-to-portal from home, but sometimes an hour each way on the train was semi-quality time where I could, for instance, read the *New York Times* in the morning and catch up on my business reading on the way home.

I had three or four internal clients in Cleveland and Detroit, but it took five hours to get home from there. Accordingly, I discovered that it took only two hours more to get from my Cleveland or Detroit hotel pillow to the office than it did from my home pillow. Sometimes then, I would stay in the Midwest after work, have an early dinner and commute to the office in the morning, thereby saving three hours of discretionary/sleeping time in the process.

One had to be quite organized, however. Sitting on the train one Friday evening and almost tasting the anticipatory gimlet as we were leaving Newark station, I had a spasm, realizing at that instant that I'm passing my commuter car, parked in the Newark Station, because I dropped off a college kid at the airport on Tuesday morning. Now I wouldn't have a way home when I got to Princeton, nor would we have a second car for the weekend!

My new work situation was quite stimulating. I traveled internationally four or five times a year and domestically many more times than that. Mr. Agee had purchased a minority position in perhaps half a dozen technology-related startup companies whose products and technology showed promise for being integrated to our product lines. My responsibility was to monitor the activity directed at the application of the technology to our products and equitably negotiate and establish rules for each party's rights and obligations under any application that might come to fruition. These rules would be embodied in a license that would govern transactions when the technology was incorporated in our commercial products. Not only was the work intellectually stimulating, but the participants on both sides offered opportunities to broaden horizons.

Mr. Agee married his intended and took a whirlwind honeymoon in Hawaii. A vestigial remnant of the honeymoon hung in Mr. Agee's spectacular corner office overlooking Central Park and the Plaza Hotel—a cozy little "home away from home," if you will. The Norman Rockwell painting was a familiar one, in which the past-middle-aged man has his back to us while he studies a Jackson Pollack-like painting, the disconnect being expressed by the man's posture and position of his arms. In addition, there was the homemade palette that Mr. Rockwell used, exhibiting the colors used in the painting. My free-spirited "pentathlon imagining" associate in mid-Jersey happened to be in Philadelphia on a weekend (it's closer to home than New York) and visited the Rockwell museum. The curator was on the floor and my associate related to the curator the story of the Rockwell, suspecting that his story would probably be of professional interest. When he mentioned the low six-figure purchase price paid by Mr. Agee, the curator became visibly agitated, maintaining that although Rockwell is revered, his paintings didn't command such prices. To this day, he doesn't understand what caused the discomfiture of the curator.

In August, 1982, I disembarked in California and heard on the radio that a mid-western company, Bendix, had made an offer to purchase Martin Marietta, a diversified but primarily aerospace/government manufacturer. At the moment, I was not qualified to adjudge whether this was a smart move, but I hoped he had a better advisor than when he made the weak pass at RCA. I found out that, at least in his own mind, Mr. Agee had a much better lead adviser——his wife Mary, who had taken a leave from Seagram's for the duration of the campaign. By this time he had appointed Alonzo McDonald, formerly CEO of McKinsey and Co., as Bendix President.

Incidentally, I happened to be in the audience when Mr. Agee introduced the new president to the corporate staff in Michigan. At the outset, Mr. Agee commented that he had instituted "casual Friday" as a cultural symbol of a young dynamic company several years prior. Because of the latest energy crunch and the related attempts to conserve, he more recently encouraged sweaters in the winter and cool clothes in the summer—for example, Casual Friday every day for those who are primarily internal employees.

"Why do I still see you guys always dressed in shirts and ties?"

Although the question was rhetorical, I did one of my all-time greatest tongue-bites, as the obvious response instantaneously came to me, *"Insecurity."*

The initial response from Martin Marietta extolled their preeminent situation as major supplier and developer of note for the U.S. Defense Department.

"These are real products. We must let the citizenry be reassured that this significant capability won't fall into the hands of accountants and consultants."

All of a sudden, our office of about twelve was inundated and surrounded with several dozen "task force" warriors. Martin Marietta made a counter proposal for it to buy Bendix and the skirmish began. Not only was the company carrying on a campaign to get Martin Marietta shareholders to tender their shares to the Bendix campaign, but it had to simultaneously try to convince its own shareholders not to tender Bendix shares to the Martin Marietta campaign. Bendix swagger, not only an attempt to intimidate the opposition, had some basis in that about 25 percent of Bendix was tied up in the 401k plans, owned by the employees, but inaccessible to them for purposes of tendering, because of built-in timing lags in gaining individual control. Mini-departments spring up in our New York offices as the public, through the financial and general press, had to be kept up to speed, particularly with the Bendix message. Board of Director meetings were held fairly frequently on an ad-hoc basis. One day my boss' assistant sidled in.

"I just participated in an unusual scene. As the board meeting was ending, I was called to escort one of the directors down and hail him a cab. The somewhat short swarthy guy. As he got into the cab, he looked at me and said *'good luck!'* Who was that and what did he mean?"

I said I didn't know, it probably was the Chairman of Mobil, Mr. Tavoulareas, but I didn't know what was going on. The "war" had heated up so much that a detailed story led the business section of every newspaper and the front page of every business paper. I found out that Mr. Tavoulareas had told Mr. Agee that he had supported him all along the way, but he couldn't run to a meeting every time that [very uncomplimentary reference to a woman, referring to Mrs. Agee] had a new idea; he's got his own company to run. Consequently, he said he was resigning, took several other directors with him, and walked out.

Here's another "one of a kind" episode. I was working late one evening, cleaning up routine business. The phone rang at about nine o'clock. I ignored it—a rare example of my good judgment. In the next day's *New York Times* I read that it was the independent trustee (for the Bendix shares embedded in the 401k plans) making a "courtesy call" to the local Bendix office to advise that they felt it was their fiduciary responsibility to tender those shares to the Martin Marietta offer. They had done so later that evening. As a result, instead of having to capture two-thirds of the open-market shares to secure a simple majority to succeed, now Martin Marietta had to secure only one-third of these shares. Such action by the trustee effectively marked the end of Bendix' hopes of remaining an independent company.

It turned out that the two companies bought each other's controlling shares, none being able to control the other's board because of chartering-states' rules, but neither had enough cash left to operate the businesses anyway. Allied Chemical stepped in as a white knight, permitting Martin Marietta to buy back its shares per an agreed schedule, but merging Bendix into Allied.

During this "sharks devouring each other" debacle, it became a habit in our office for we "working stiffs" to meet over coffee first thing in the morning and compare notes in a small conference room on what we could glean from the news and the rumors as, obviously, our own situations most likely would be affected. One morning I glumly relayed that the *New York Times* reported that the Bendix officers had approved the compromise deal and it appeared that, other than for peripheral details, the deal was done. The VP international (our boss) later entered, asked for my take and took umbrage at my assertion, as he knew for certain that there had been no such action taken by Bendix officers, of which he was one. I responded that I was just parroting what the *New York Times* had reported, not intending to make any conjectural or judgmental conclusions. What the boss knew was that any approval by the officers had to be unanimous in order to take effect and that he hadn't been approached. What he didn't know was that there were two classes of Bendix "officers," one group being the fifteen "voting officers" that unanimously approved the offer. He and the personnel VP didn't have a vote on issues involving restructuring of the company. The Bendix officers had approved the deal.

On a Friday, Mr. Agee was named Allied President by Allied Chairman Ed Hennessy. Whoops! A new press release was issued on Saturday to clarify that there would be no one reporting to Mr. Agee that didn't previously report to him. That, apparently, was to quiet the semi-hysterical Allied EVPs who, based on the Friday release, feared they were now reporting to Mr. Agee. (Doesn't there always seem to be a lot of sophomoric behavior occurring as a result of these macho deals?) At any rate, things settled down over the next several months.

There have been four books written on this ugly chapter of business, and I can't even recommend any one of them as something from which to glean helpful insight.

On June 1, Mr. Agee and Mr. McDonald were shown the door. It was not surprising about Mr. McDonald, but it was our understanding that Mr. Agee had a deal as part of the final settlement. I soon understood that was, in fact, the case, but events caused Mr. Hennessy to otherwise settle with Mr. Agee.

Mr. Hennessy was, as a young man, a former candidate for priesthood, who finally wound up in business. We were informed that there was no such thing as "casual Friday" at Allied and certainly not in the showcase New York office that Allied had inherited and had yet to rationalize.

The following story was only hearsay, but seems plausible, as I have heard it second- and third-hand from independent sources.

As previously discussed, it was hard to escape the news of the past nine months or so, and the people involved had become public figures. *People Magazine* did a feature on "Bill and Mary." It gushed on about how such an exemplary couple interacted, their value system and how they lived their lives. Early on in the piece was a brief discussion of the corporate wars recently completed, but most of the article featured current activity: several paragraphs and a picture of her instructing him as to how certain phenomena can be explained (this is the stuff that turns Bill on and probably causes them to agree to the feature), and how she negotiates at his side and as his equal, and depicts them playing some unisex sport, squash, as I recall.

In the interior of the story, however, was a rather large picture of the two of them, both in jeans and tennies. She was sitting on a the edge of a king-size bed, he was kneeling to face her and presenting her with a rubber ducky, symbolizing, they explained, their kindred spirits and the fact that ducks are "monogamous animals."

Now for the story—someone in our office showed Hennessy the *People* article. His first reaction was to be repulsed by further publicity on the corporate battles, but he went berserk when he saw the picture and the monogamous rubber ducky drivel. He started ranting about how he didn't listen to his better judgment and he was now going to have to bite the bullet and how he was going to have to regularize his executive staff and so on. Supposedly, this was the vignette that impelled him to dismiss Mr. Agee.

My prurient interest caused me to ask the question, "How could such a sophisticated and brilliant couple get sucked into such an only slightly less than tawdry PR situation?"

It was shortly explained to me in a newspaper feature article.

Look at it this way.

Assume you are a distinguished corporate titan and agree to be the subject of a feature article. No respectable newspaper or magazine will give you editorial rights; you understand and agree to that. Even though you are outside of your field, you understand that the article will be slanted toward what you tell them, how you answer their questions and what kind of pictures *you permit them to take.* They will take a picture of you conducting the annual meeting (four photographers, six lights and three umbrellas), they will show you lecturing at the economic club, they will show you working at your desk, all with a considerable amount of photographic stage management. Now they want to see the leisure you. They show the four in your family playing tennis and enjoying the boat. As one would expect, these are naturally less formal situations; consequently, the pictures are taken on a more candid basis. Finally they tell you that you are a terrific subject but the story perhaps should be footnoted with a really insider glimpse of your quiet moments. Well, you admit you do get dressed up as Daffy Duck on your son's birthday; it's a special thing you do for him. Could they see it for just a second? The interviewer himself snaps a reference on his portable phone.

If that represents the situation, then why were you surprised when a picture of you impersonating Daffy Duck with appropriate headline appeared on the cover of *Corp Magazine*? You had assumed that elements of the story will be featured in proportion to the amount of trouble taken to document that element photographically. Obviously, your assumption turned out not to be accurate.

There were three, brief, fall-out stories.

One of them, in the *New York Times* in its Tuesday science section, was a feature article about new behavioral patterns being discovered in certain animals through more thorough research. One of the featured animals, ducks, were assumed to be mated for life (and monogamous) because the male always came back to its own nest and its own partner and assisted in caring for the couple's young. Some wise-guy researcher wondered what the father duck did when he was away from the nest and, accordingly, set about to find out. The male would make some kind of communication with his mate, indicating that he would be temporarily away, foraging. He would fly to the next duck neighborhood that was not in communication with his own. Lo and behold, rather than spending his time foraging, he would spend it with female ducks in that neighborhood. Shocking! I've known a few guys and a few governors that are expert "foragers."

This doesn't amount to anything other than I had fun in sending the article to the remaining elements of the former Bendix corporate office, where Mr. Agee's esteem had been considerably diminished, and his valiant and symbolic presentation to his bride didn't seem to ring as true as it once did.

I don't know of any truth to this, but someone who was very close to corporate battles had apparently noticed and told me that when the corporate titans battle, certain New York females behaved as if they liked to consort with not just the winners, but those who have become known as "players." Certainly it couldn't have hurt Mr. Agee's ego with one more distraction to fend off.

Lastly, several years later, one of Mr. Hennessy's three group vice presidents was extolling the work of one of the "High Potential" (HiPo) women that worked for him and requested that he promote her to be the group's Vice President, Personnel.

"Her work has been outstanding, and I suppose you should know that we've recently become engaged."

"Have these guys been walking on a different planet?" offered the chairman after he hung up the phone.

CHAPTER TWENTY-THREE
Adrift in Manhattan

With Mr. Agee gone, ten or twelve of us remained in the New York office, led by our previously discussed VP international. We didn't have a permanent reporting situation, but our leader would negotiate on our behalf. We didn't know whether Allied would keep our particular New York office open; they already had one in the lower thirties—perhaps there was no need for two.

The cynics amongst us believed that we naturally would have the highest visibility because of proximity and cost of running the office, but we forgot that Allied must first digest the elephant formerly known as Bendix corporate offices located in Southfield, Michigan, after rationalizing the merged product lines and related organizations. Further, Mr. Hennessy and Allied thought they had put together a pretty nifty company worthy of a spiffy New York showplace where they could hold board meetings, press conferences, and discussions with financial and organizational professionals. As a result of all these distractions, our situation would be placed on a back burner.

Our leader, Mr. VP, called us together to assure us that the new corporate fathers appreciated the fine job we were doing and encouraged us to keep on truckin' while they solved other problems. Eventually, he said, they would evaluate our charter and responsibilities in detail, then each person would be interviewed and given a written proposal outlining his responsibilities in the new company. Several of us had been given "mini-parachutes" letting us collect a year's wages from an insurance company (Bendix bought this policy pre-merger) if shown the door. What an immediate relief this was, but we soon found out that living while waiting for the other shoe to drop was not all that great either. At any rate, Mr. VP would continue to negotiate for a comfortable reporting relationship.

Mr. VP went off on his three-week summer vacation. He phoned in occasionally to report that he was in touch with Southfield, and we read into it that he might be making at least a semi-permanent connection with the automotive sector, which didn't seem so bad. In the former Allied

Corporation, licensing was the responsibility of the patent lawyers who did this as a sideline. This was a very dangerous situation for us, as we probably were seen by them as a threat, not only to take over a portion of their responsibility, but also was a source of embarrassment as issues come up regarding the slapdash manner in which the Allied license portfolio had been put together.

Mr. VP came back from vacation and called us together. He revealed that he was unable to successfully negotiate a deal with automotive, and a corporate role was never in the cards. He would no longer be with the company. After what we intended to be a period of shock and polite lamentation, we asked about the likely fate of the rest of us. He offered that it hadn't been yet determined but they probably would be getting around to it soon.

By the way, we asked, what about the interviews?

"Interviews?"

What about the offer to be embodied in a letter?

"Offers? Letters?"

Apparently, our faithful and trustworthy mentor had pulled a Tonto on us. "Tough —, white man."

As I read the situation, the very capable head of automotive, Mason Reynolds, a survivor from the Bendix days whose justifiable survival was probably aided by Bill Panny who insulated him from Ms. Cunningham's barked orders. It seemed likely to me that Reynolds had waltzed Mr. International VP around by discussing, in general terms, the potential new role for him. Mr. Reynolds would ask him to consider a certain scenario and to discuss it at a later time. When Mr. VP indicated, "I can live with that," Mr. Reynolds, I surmised, must have responded that we must be very careful —as he then explained further constraints on Mr. VP's sphere of influence and power. He asked him to consider and get back. Each "I can live with that" probably caused Mr. Reynolds to further clarify the constraints until he heard, "I don't think I can live with that," causing Mr. Reynolds to remark that it was a shame that they won't be working together, but that's Mr. VP's decision.

So we wouldn't incur paralysis through analysis, we went about our business and the many issues that continually arrived.

When automotive sales goes into its periodic recession every three-to-seven years, volume usually shrinks by 15 to 40 percent. When the machine-tool business goes into a recession, however, the bottom falls out. Even as a novice in that, I knew there were about three reasons why a manufacturer buys a machine tool: (1) to increase capacity to support bigger customer orders—this segment was now zero sales, (2) to improve efficiency and reliability by replacing older, less-efficient tools—this was a discretionary decision and can be indefinitely deferred until the supporting numbers improve, and (3) to provide for new machining requirements for which your current tools aren't capable, a configuration requirement—this was the only segment of the business that continued to limp along.

Accordingly, the machine-tool business that we had proudly put together was in difficult straits. One machine-tool observer noted that total sales for this distinguished industrial segment, and one that was revered as an early economic indicator, equaled the Coca-Cola ad budget. That generated a lot of activity regarding the potential of manufacturing products jointly with other companies or entering into development programs with other manufacturers or technologically oriented companies. Those represented some real and some hard-to-imagine projects, but it demonstrated that the participants were "doing something!" We knew of about ten meetings held one week to advance these potential opportunities, when we found out the whole machine-tool sector was being "sold" the following Monday.

The early Eighties was the time of the "leveraged buyout," wherein opportunistic companies and investors feverishly sought out businesses to buy, quickly sold some of the pieces, raided the cash and set about to "fix" the rest. Upon hearing of the negotiations regarding our potential divestiture of the machine-tool business, it dawned on me that my particular business niche had some unusual aspects that were quite different than normal commercial transactions and, consequently, likely to be overlooked by our negotiators.

When a company ships a product, it's officially recorded as "sold" and the related dollars are recorded for payment, known as a "receivable." The seller of a business is normally credited for the assets of all "sales" made (including "receivables" booked) while he owned the company. Revenue from licenses is normally "earned" differently. As the licensee generally pays "royalty" based on some ratio related to sales activity, the amount of royalty "earned" is not known (or recorded) by the licensor until a time considerably later than the date of his sale; consequently, "earned royalty" doesn't appear as a seller asset on the spreadsheets as negotiated.

With regard to the machine-tool business, I was able to estimate the amount of royalty "earned," but not yet recorded, before we sold the company. It wasn't a tremendous amount of money as corporate accounts go, about $720,000, for which I made a handwritten chart and introduced it into the negotiations by faxing to the offsite location.

I later found out that my input was one of the last issues on the table, and was negotiated at 50¢ on the dollar seconds before the documents were signed. Initially I felt a little sheepish, as perhaps I was "nickel-and-diming" the buyer. However, I later learned that the $300 million investment of Warner Swasey three years *prior* and the five other machine-tool businesses that Bendix had previously owned were being sold for $53 million, more than a skosh less than 50¢ on the dollar. I coined a completely new title for such a sale—a "leveraged giveout." It didn't seem to be picked up by the business world, I suppose because that type of sale was a rare bird.

Although the insecurities and discussions of potential scenarios relating to the future of our cloistered little department persisted for years, the "international development" related participants one by one, spun off into various sector staff jobs, and our little licensing group of about eight wound up working for the automotive sector, helping particular divisions to properly position their technology and other intellectual property in overseas ventures.

CHAPTER TWENTY-FOUR
jesty the Queen

On my first visit to Hong Kong in the mid-Eighties, I was to join two or three others from Allied to explore potential joint activity with several Hong Kong based companies. I was a late addition to the team, otherwise being in Asia and having knowledge of several of our businesses that would be discussed. Being a latecomer, I couldn't get a hotel room on the mainland with my cohorts. No problem, I would stay in equally American-tolerant accommodations on Kowloon Island and take a cab to the first meeting. As Hong Kong wasn't on my original itinerary, I hadn't done my usual research on the local customs but wasn't terribly concerned as I generally understood then that if you could do business in London, you could probably do equally well in Hong Kong.

One approached Hong Kong from Kowloon via tunnel. From the back seat of my taxi, I was glancing at the briefing fax the team had sent me when I looked up and, in addition to seeing the fantastic profile of the city, noticed that we were entering the tunnel. Over our lane was a large sign, "jesty the Queen." Strange, I thought, what's that about? In my darkest of thoughts, I figured it might refer to a cross-dressing clown or some such thing, but very strange, particularly in such a prominent and government-controlled space. On the other hand, our own society had gone through some liberalization of life-styles in the recent past and we used to make a big deal about Soupy Sales in the 1950s when he was doing two network shows and a local nighttime on XYZ in Detroit.

At any rate, the meetings were businesslike but routine and, during a lull or a meal, I was able to question our guys and the locals about the strange sign. No help. The next day, same routine, meeting in Hong Kong with the parent of Cathay Pacific, no recognition of the existence of the sign or its subject. How can such an apparently permanent sign in a key artery of the city go unnoticed?

Third day, same routine, and I was planning to carefully notice any markings or references on the sign that might solve the mystery. No need, as they had finally put up the first half of the sign over the left lane, "Welcome Her Ma" [jesty the Queen]. Liz was coming to visit!

It was generally my traveling style to arrive in the afternoon or evening, have a quiet meal and maybe quiet entertainment, having made a business appointment for the morning and any business entertainment for later. One of my international department associates, a South American specialist, taught me this as a result of his experiences. South American politics were quite rough in the 1980s, as were the dissidents. If you recall there were quite a few businessman kidnappings and for a while the Ford executives were running the Brazilian plant from Argentina for safety reasons (or was it vice versa?). At any rate, my friend had accepted an invitation for dinner from the company he was set to visit; they would pick him up at his hotel. His sense was that everything was wonderful and secure until they dropped him later at his hotel. First the leading security car left, then the following security car left, then finally the limo left after effusive goodnights.

"Have we just signaled that a very prominent business person has just been left to fend for himself in a foreign environment?" he thought.

Although nothing bad happened, subsequently he ascribed to the quiet entry procedure and encouraged others to do the same.

I was traveling to meet a Fram licensee in New Zealand. In the modest *What's Happening in Aukland* magazine, there was a tombstone ad for a "modern jazz" big band Monday evening. As a nut for big bands, I thought it would be great fun and an opportunity to take in a bit of local color. It was—in ways I had never expected.

The "big band" consisted of about ten guys who were playing the same Johnny Warrington diatonic[61] dance charts that I was playing as a kid in the 1950s. On the other hand, the attendees tended to be families embodying three generations sitting at tables of eight-to-twelve and having a jolly old time passing around the dinner and intermittently dancing in a cross-generational manner. Remarkable! I hadn't seen American families behave that way since the 1950s, except perhaps at the occasional wedding or bar mitzvah. Apparently they did this weekly on Monday nights. During the second set, the band played some Latin arrangements, but they were no more exotic than Lawrence Welk playing "Besame Mucho." Never did the lights

---

[61] No modern chords or improvisational choruses.

dim or did there seem to be people scouting around for pick-ups. It just seemed to be families and neighbors socializing and having fun.

I was about ready to call a cab when the emcee exuberantly announced, "Stick around. Next set will be rock and roll!"

Much cheering! It took my best Motown biting of the tongue not to grab the microphone: "Give me that mike! New Zealanders, be careful. This might lead you to the same vacuous attractions[62] under which our culture suffers. Where 90 percent of the 'music' is but some noise and, of that, 98 percent of its fans say, 'I could do that! I could become a rock star if I could learn the same three guitar chords, lead a dissipated life and humiliate myself three nights a week—more if I make it big and am on tour.' "

Good going, Bobby, you wouldn't even think of doing something like that, attempting to inflict your values on another culture.

I attended a Thai religious ceremony in the presence of the jade Buddha, and unknowingly exposed the bottom of my feet to him. My friend and corporate Fram licensee of long standing, Lek, was introducing me to the wonders and customs of Bangkok. After I walked the streets on a scorching Saturday, seeing the burial grounds of the seven emperors (Shall we dance?) and visiting the museums (and encountering an elephant on the street), he insisted on meeting at a certain hotel in the mid-afternoon to have a ceremonial drink purportedly replicating and commemorating the exact thing he did fondly with several of my corporate predecessors. He confirmed that we would have a quiet dinner to include the quality-control inspector from his European propane-tank customers, as we had included his wife, Char, the night before.

"After walking around all day in the this heat, I need to shower and change [from my then spiffy Banana Republic khaki outfit], and I'm also low on cash."

"No hurry, relax," he offered, "we don't have a severe timetable."

Lek was a very highly regarded private businessman, educated at the University of Michigan, and son of the Admiral of the Thai navy who served during WWII. The family history is only slightly diminished when one understands that Thailand, formerly Siam, doesn't front any ocean; it only has a coffee-colored river that changes direction twice a day and is full of strangely shaped gourds floating in it. Only while writing this am I reminded

---

[62] With a capital "V."

that Lek had a secondary business, converting cabs and police cars to propane fuel, using his own manufactured high-pressure tanks, similar to what we use for gas barbecues. We chatted pleasantly about his lifestyle and his business. Suddenly it was time to meet for dinner.

"I haven't gotten cleaned up; I don't have much money!"

"No problem, it's just mainly us."

I later realized that he was successfully and purposefully negating my self-confidence on a temporary basis (for example, no money in pocket, sense of inappropriate attire) in the event that I had any American traits that might get me in trouble in Bangkok. I admit that he did show me the legendary fleshpots, but from a safe distance and with me ill-equipped to participate even if I wanted to. The experience was much like the U.S. "topless joints" of the 1970s, only the women were more attractive.

One of the most unusual Saturday evenings occurred in Taiwan, the independent Chinese island country. After dinner, we were escorted to "Snake Alley." What was this? A place where one can obtain fresh snake "blood and bile," a tonic purportedly held in high esteem in the far East for the purpose of improving male virility. It seemed that the Japanese had the idea of cross-breeding snakes for the purposes of warfare early in the Twentieth Century and figured that island—about 75 miles by 125 miles, oblong shape—would be the ideal location, particularly considering that such experimental activity "might get out of control." The Taiwanese mow the terrain surrounding Chang Kai-Sheck's former summer palace several times a year, but it seems that they are "cutting" more snakes than they are cutting foliage or grass. Certain rural areas, at least up into the 1980s, were infested with snakes.

At any rate, in the subject Taipai City Square there were large aquariums filled to the brim with snakes. As unsettling as this was to a typical American, even more unsettling was the hysterical animation of several cages of mongoose (mongeese?), legendary enemy of cobras and all snakes.

The routine was that the "operator" had a tabletop apparatus that resembled a yarn winder that permitted him to place and secure a snake behind the snake's jaw at the upper portion, and secure its tail 45° downward near the top of the table. He then slit the snake's entire underside with a deft slash of a razor blade and placed a beaker under the tail. Over about half an hour the blood, flowing down the underside of the snake, filled the small beaker, such liquid resembling Hawaiian punch. (Sorry, Dr. Pepper and 7-

Up!) The operator then sought out the liver bile duct inside the snake (green), ruptured it and drained it into the beaker, causing the liquid to now resemble V-8. (Sorry, Campbell's!) Although we saw people of Asian background expressing interest, there was no line-up to buy this stuff. Shortly, a guy kind of stumbles up, says something interpreted for us like, "I understand you've got some of that terrific snake juice," slaps down a single bill and downs the beaker, all in a period of about ten seconds. We were led to believe that the going rate was the equivalent of $20 U.S. We also thought that the guy was a shill.

Several years later, I ran across an article in an airline travel magazine that discussed the perceived dilemma of the Taiwanese promoters as to whether they should attempt to capitalize on such an unusual ritual as Snake Alley for the interest of tourists, or should they subordinate it, not wanting to highlight what might be considered a barbarian ceremony in an undeveloped country. I think they elected to err on the side of exposure. I wonder if the guy who demonstrated the benefits amongst the several booths finally got a good job in generally prosperous Taiwan? ("What! And leave show business?")

The next day's meeting involved the Taiwanese governmental technical evaluation and development department and laboratories, which we soon deduced was chartered to see what technology they could lift, rather than develop. (They had bought one of our aerospace-division's machines that grinds the super accurate curved mirror used in hand held CD players, undoubtedly for "evaluation.") The highlight of the day, however, occurred early in the meeting when our host suggested that we be served tea to enjoy during our meeting. Into the room came an *absolutely breathtakingly beautiful* young Chinese woman in a sailor motif dress, who poured about fifteen cups of tea in absolute silence. It occurred to me that the scene was exactly like the first glimpse of Liat in the 1958 movie, *South Pacific*.

In a later meeting at a highly placed mainline Chinese official's large office near Tiananmen Square in Beijing, we were wallowing in huge overstuffed chairs in the presence of the Remington sculpture that our Chairman had presented on an earlier visit. It was a quiet and mutually respectful meeting with the guy whose bureau oversaw the whole automotive and machineries industry of China. Though in those days the only industry of any size dealing with passenger cars was Beijing Jeep, a joint venture started by American Motors. Outside the door was a murmur of voices, then a louder voice.

Whoop, whoop, whoop—and a loud and prolonged breaking of glass—silence for fifteen seconds, and then a moan. Then a loud shout, with a response. Then many people shouting and eventually whistles blowing. We, of course, halted our meeting to see what was happening.

It turned out that the incident was created by our own driver, a very eager employee, who flitted constantly to see that everything was in proper order. As he was coming up the stairs to confirm that we didn't need him, he jumped over a washman's bucket, slipped on the terrazzo stairs and crashed into the large glass exterior window, breaking it. In itself, the falling and breaking would be a distraction enough, but in China, the proprietors of the government's buildings were absolutely responsible to see that the perpetrator was apprehended, as the one who does the "breaking" is totally responsible for repairs and, once the perpetrator "escapes" it is unlikely he could be found and arrested.

Even when the situation was settled and all the players identified, it took both the signatures of our cabinet-level host and our country executive, who guaranteed payment, before they would let our guy get bandaged. As we were reconvening our meeting, I asked *sotto voce* one of my traveling companions, "Do you have the feeling we are actually living *Chevy Chase Chinese Business Trip?*"

I didn't talk much at social gatherings about my international travels, as it was seen by some as elitist.

Shortly after an extended Far East trip, I slept in my own bed for one night, went into my New York office for the day and flew to Detroit that afternoon on a business trip. My flight schedule was tight because of my desire to attend, that evening, the retirement dinner of a former loyal associate in charge of the Ford account. Not yet being fully time-zoned, it was particularly annoying that the plane was going to be late, perhaps causing me to miss the dinner part but, hopefully, early enough to hear the speeches and punch my social/business time clock. As the plane was docking at Metro, I said to my seat mate, with whom I had been chatting, "In the last 72 hours I've been in Bangkok, Beijing, Tokyo and New York, and the only flight that hasn't been on time is the Laguardia/Detroit Metro leg."

I admit it sounded rather glib and blasé, but the woman in the seat in front of me stood up, turned around and glowered at me, and I hadn't even espoused a trip to Snake Alley for her.

What I'm getting at, dear reader, is that you may glower all you wish. You've already paid for this tome and have allowed me to collect my royalty. I'm thanking you as paying glowerer.

CHAPTER TWENTY-FIVE
The Airbag

It's your turn at bat! That's good, because your competitive juices encourage your love of participation in critical situations. Imagine that you're digging in at the plate. On the mound is "The Rocket" and he lets go of the first pitch that is two inches inside the plate, at the height of your uniform letters and is ripping through the air at a speed of about 100 miles per hour. Nothing is required of you other than to accept the "ball." But I'll bet you're at least on your heels. Nothing touches you but the breeze created by the ball passing, but the sound of the ball creating turbulence in the air and the "pop" into the catcher's mitt leads you to believe that you have been a participant in violent activity.

Now let's assume you're driving in Southern California when you encounter a drought-ending shower that causes the oil accumulation on the street to render your brakes useless or, more precisely, causes the co-efficient of friction between your tires and the road to asymptotically approach a number so low that you can't effectively stop. You're only going fifteen miles per hour (the approximate pace of a champion miler) so you sense the collision isn't going to be that violent, plus you have that airbag "cushion." The one thing no one ever told you was that the "cushion" was being pushed in your face at a speed of about 200 miles per hour, propelled by a hand-grenade equivalent explosive adapted to "blow up" your airbag.

The concept was first publicly discussed in the late Sixties, as automotive safety in general was becoming a real facet of the business and the proponents loved to talk of titillating concepts and hardware at their carefully planned press conferences.

Theretofore, the public rarely focused on the phenomenon that the danger in most crashes was that the car stopped, but the body inside kept proceeding at the same speed; consequently, the solution was more likely to involve controlling the deceleration of the body rather than beefing up the front end of the vehicle. The concept of the airbag seemed to resonate. At first, there was considerable dialogue as to whether such a concept was

231

feasible. Many people doubted that a physical device could act quickly enough during a crash to intercede between the body and what it was about to hit. The culture seemed to be implying that if such a concept could be proven to work, of course it should be included on all passenger cars and light trucks.

As a participating member of my first non-GM employer's product development committee, I was involved in other possible concepts to be used in controlling body deceleration. As a major seat and seat-track supplier having substantial development capabilities, someone was able to come up with the idea that maybe the inertia of the crash could be used to rotate the bottom of the seat 90° upwards, thereby presenting the driver or passenger's rump to the dashboard. Not too much more nutty than the airbag, what? We finally deduced that such g-force would undoubtedly fuse the entire spinal column. Such consequence would probably cause the usual motorist to prefer "selling the farm" instead. The logical solution for the front-passenger situation was to have the seat facing rearward, that position having been known as the "death seat" since at least the Thirties. The consequence of this configuration would be to induce customers to "not buy that car" or, even worse, publicly demean the intelligence of members of NHTSA or Congress passing legislation demanding such configuration.

Even in those early years, a continuous agitation of mine was that the question seemed to be "Will it work?" rather than "Even if it works, would the benefit be more than the payout?" To put such thoughts in perspective, let's again think of putting a parachute on all airline passengers. We could engineer it so that all the passenger would have to do would be to walk out the exit that would automatically open under certain conditions. If one were to think about that for more than a minute, one would undoubtedly come to the conclusion that probably fewer passengers could be accommodated using such a contraption and that the flying experience would certainly be a less pleasurable experience than it currently is. (Scratch that last phrase as absolutely implausible.) Probably the already fragile business model of using air travel as the mode of choice for the traveling public would completely unravel with this encumbrance. By now, you've gotten the gist that all the tear-up and the hardware doesn't make much sense, even though the product may work and a few lives may be saved. Such was my dilemma with the airbag.

GM, then still the major player, started a program to test the product and the market and by about 1972 introduced the availability of airbags on certain select upscale models. These first offerings of air bags covered from the lap to the forehead. As usual, a few people specified them immediately, but my recollection was that after a few months GM had to seriously discount those airbag-laden cars just to get rid of them. But they worked and, ironically, such activity enabled a business opportunity for my employer several decades later. Thus started what I consider the airbag dilemma—1969-present.

As a sideline to the initial airbag development, there was very little experience as to what was the maximum deceleration a human body, particularly the head, could endure without permanent damage. A GM development engineer and casual East Side poker acquaintance had been at the circus with his family where was presented the high-diving act, wherein one of the circus family members dived off a multi-story tower into something that resembled a damp sponge only to pop up and immediately acknowledge the crowd.

"Eureka," thought my friend, "if we could get or hire this guy to collaborate, we would have at least a starting point as to how deceleration affects the human body."

They got him to cooperate and instrumented him with accelerometers while he was doing his dives and quite quickly did learn about the behavior of the body in "accidents."

I'm going to have to apologize, but "accelerometers" lead me to one of my favorite stories. For those privileged enough not to be engineers, these devices measure how many "g"s or multiples of gravitational forces are incurred on whatever it is attached. The data needn't be instantaneously read; it retains the maximum force inflicted to it until it is reset. They are cheap, accurate and useful—something like a pedometer. The timing of my education was at the cusp of "science projects," wherein the student has to pick a subject for investigation and then perform and write up the results of such investigation. Let me remind you, the hard part is picking up something worthwhile to explore, otherwise you're going to look like a pin cushion from pinning a million bugs on pieces of cardboard.

A daughter of one of the plant managers came upon the idea of using accelerometers in packages to deduce what kind of abuse these packages got in the U.S. postal service. She went about it quite scientifically, mailing packages to collaborators in about twelve cities—who then mailed them back. For an extra fun wrinkle, I recall that she wrote "Fragile" on some of them to see if it made any a difference. I don't remember being exposed to the results, but I do recall concluding that you might as well save your ink rather than writing "Fragile." I also remember that the postal service not only wouldn't cooperate on analysis of the data ("Why was this box dropped the equivalent of six stories?") but were quite indignant that anyone would have the chutzpah to attempt to measure the quality of their package handling. If America's youth keep coming up with such ingenious "science projects," maybe we're going to survive after all.

Back to car safety and crash deceleration. Early on, the standards makers focused on seat belts, formalizing the lap belt in the front seats in the original rules, as I recall, then rears and finally all front- and rear-seating positions, lap and shoulder harnesses. Good! Data over forty years have demonstrated that these devices are the best and most cost-effective automotive-safety devices ever conceived. The problem? Particularly early on, not enough people took the trouble of "buckling up." Even I saw some danger in intimating to the aggressive driver that he might be "bulletproof" when securely fastened, to the further detriment of his driving behavior. Then came a series of various state laws requiring the use of seatbelts, the contention then becoming (and one which remains to this day) as to what guidelines should be used for enforcement.

NHTSA, the national rule maker, didn't, of course, have enforcement authority to ensure the belts were actually being used and were dismayed that the driver or passenger had to each take an "active" role to engage the current system. Finally, during the Eighties, the Department of Transportation (and Congress?) made a deal wherein standards for "passive" restraints wouldn't be compulsory if "X" percent (50 percent?) of states demonstrated that over "Y" percent (80 percent?) of passengers actually used the seat belts. This must have been intended as a compromise between the public, who were split on the issue but had a hardcore base of airbag haters, and the self-appointed consumer advocates, who demanded that their support for airbags be incorporated in the standards. This cockamamie scenario went on for years while the various sides jockeyed around for position and the lawyers were having a heyday trying to interpret the rules. At one point there was considered (and might have been briefly in effect for a short period) the idea that if the population wouldn't "buckle-up," the manufacturer would be forced to include airbags but, as a concession, they wouldn't have to install belts. This proved to be idiocy almost immediately as testing soon proved that the maiming, debilitating and fatal injuries incurred on the head and upper body at a certain speed for an unrestrained driver, had parallel but different maiming, debilitating and fatal injuries on the lower body for a driver in a vehicle with only an air bag. In other words, the air bag, as then configured, had *no practical effect* if the driver or passenger didn't have at least a lap belt. I don't ever remember hearing that publicly reported.

Recognizing that the recently created rules for states were so arbitrary and almost impossible to measure, NHTSA issued rules for "passive" restraint systems, for example, restraints that met a certain specification with no activity required on the part of the passenger, finally biting the bullet and being pleased, believing that they were to finally get their beloved air bags.

Not so fast! Regarding companies focused on safety-restraint systems, there was little correlation between the business of making airbags and that of making conventional seat belts, other than that one understood the standards and the testing procedures and had the required testing facilities. The gestation period of the airbag was so long, more than twenty years, and the future so uncertain that companies were in all different stages of preparedness. The original "airbag" company, the Autoceptor Division of Eaton Manufacturing Company, formed in the late Sixties, had folded the tent something like ten years before there were any requirements of any volume, and the few companies that had come later or hung in there had taken *gas* during the fitful stops and starts.

What was my company's situation? As one of the major suppliers, Allied, whose division was soon to be renamed Bendix Safety Restraint Systems (BSRS), was dead in the water regarding airbags. As usual, the introductory period for "passive" restraints was not far away, so we immediately took two actions. Our guys had heard of an efficient little European system about to be used by BMW and Mercedes, wherein a motor in the door pulled the lap and shoulder belt tight via a little mechanism moving over the side window. It seemed to meet the literal (if not spiritual) letter of the new "passive" specifications. They sent me over and, sure enough, they'd train us to use their patented system for a mark or so per side. A little testing and development later, it turned out that this system did satisfy the new "passive" directives. In addition to being a qualifier under the new specifications, this nifty little system had several other attributes which were attractive to our (also behind-the-eight-ball, airbag-wise) customers: (1) the applications engineering program could be easily contained within program time constraints and (2) the system was significantly less costly (thereby creating little downward cost pressure) than the equivalent airbag solution. As a result, we enjoyed several years of increased market share, at the same time quite profitable business. Hey! Those Washington &*^@#s weren't so bad after all.

Having now had more than twenty years of third-party (NHTSA) "help," however, we hedged our bets by securing gas-generator (hand-grenade equivalent exploder) technology from yet another German company. Even though we were enjoying a reasonable market share of quite profitable business under newly enforced directives that should remain in place over an extended period (given that it would literally require "an act of Congress" to modify or overturn), we had to be ready, at least to the extent of our competitors, if the airbag were to again rear its ugly head, or one of our customers wanted to strategically offer them on a specific vehicle. There continued to be dialogue about the attributes of the airbag, which I finally deduced was the totem of the consumer advocate movement. There were accusations that the industry deliberately and unethically introduced this mousy little system just as an end run to the governmental overseers and as a gyp to the "consumers" who would now be deprived of the purportedly far-superior performance of the revered airbag.

Earlier I had mentioned residual benefits for my company from the 1972 airbag introduction. In the early Nineties, when airbags were coming on as standard equipment, one of our guys remembered that we had made some prototype proposals of the gas generator that, instead of quickly generating gas to inflate the bag, contained air under extremely high pressure (3,000 psi) and the only requirement at impact was to puncture the extremely sturdy container and heat the air. One of the benefits of this system was to eliminate the sodium-azide chemical that was toxic, yet mandatory for airbag performance.

We approached several customers with this, and the response went something like this: "We won't have time to develop and test this speculative system. Besides, it seems unlikely that we could design a tank that would retain such high pressure under the ten-year requirement and it would take years to find out."

236

Our guys nonetheless thought they would try to find the prototypes from the 1970s to see if any information could be obtained from them. They found three. They tested them for retained pressure after the twenty years. All three retained 3,000 psi pressure. Immediate sales were made to several customers for specific applications.

You'll never guess what happened next! (Although having read this far, maybe you would.) "An act of Congress" mandated that airbags be installed on all light vehicles, starting with the mid-Nineties vehicles and extending to all such vehicles by the early 2000s. I was repulsed more by the governmental action than I was by my perceived skepticism of airbag performance. Initially, I was one of the guys who was told face-to-face in the Sixties that the government would never, *never* issue a directive that would specify the terms of hardware to be used. *All* of the coming directives would recognize only reasonably attainable safety goals that would be described only in terms of performance specifications. We were advised that it would be unwise for the industry to ever have public arguments over the government's judgment, as to do so would be to demean any new performance standard, which could be demonstrated to protect all Americans.

I recall being very angry and frustrated at this event, certainly about the government having lied to me, but probably more at my own naiveté, thinking that Washington would live up to its heartfelt-sounding commitment. In any event, partly out of belief and partly out of perniciousness, I created my own "squeaky balloon" theory to suggest how America might not embrace the airbag, and might even have the rule overturned through public dialogue, as they had done to the one about seat belts being fastened before the ignition would operate.

Let me share my soon-to-be-defunct "squeaky balloon" theory. Imagine you're sitting in your favorite chair reading the newspaper. A child enters the room with his balloon. The youngster seems to be enjoying himself by rubbing his hands on the toy, generating a squeaking sound. You (1) are quite agitated by the noises made by the balloon and (2) know that it will soon burst but that (3) no one is likely to be injured but (4) still it's going to be startling and (5) wish he'd take it somewhere else.

Knowing that the "bursting" of the airbag is equivalent to a hand grenade is bound to give Americans the willies, I thought. I'm astounded to perceive that they don't understand this. They've been fed a story of pillows and cushions and miracles. They don't even begin to perceive anything relating to violence.

By giving pretty good service to BSRS without a lot of corporate posturing, I was considered an insider at the division. One day while having lunch with the general manager and three or four of his lieutenants, I expounded on my "squeaky balloon" theory (there you go again, Rile). It was met with silence and an exchange of glances amongst the divisional people.

"Well, you're right about the hand grenade," offered the GM, "but apparently you haven't heard about the 'anecdotes.'"

"No I haven't," I responded, "please share them with me."

At that time there were several hundred thousand airbag-equipped vehicles on the road out of somewhat less than two hundred million total.

"The most egregious one seems to be about the young woman driving with her infant when she got her passenger-side wheels caught in a culvert in a suburban setting. Before she could get her wheels back on the road she hit the next driveway "fill-in" with her right front wheel while traveling at eleven miles per hour (a little less than twice the Boy Scout walking cadence). When the authorities got there, the woman: dead! The baby: dead!"

"What happened?"

"They don't know yet but it probably was a condition of 'out-of-position' riders. If you happen to be reaching to tune the radio or adjusting a mirror, the thing comes at you catawampus. They're studying the situation now. But let me tell you about more prevalent problems. This has to do with smaller people, predominantly older women. Do you recall when we added the tether inside the bag to restrict the motion of the air bag about a year ago? That was when we were finding out that when the air bag deploys, it doesn't necessarily stop when it contacts a human body. If that body is fairly near the steering wheel, the air bag pushes into the chest, dynamically breaks the ribs that, in turn, sever the aorta in most cases. There have been about six or eight cases to date and the tether won't entirely solve this problem because the specs call out that the bag has to blow out far and fast enough so that taller, huskier guys like you and me don't get moving forward after the crash. When you encounter friends and loved ones that have bag-equipped cars, tell them that they must be at least ten inches away from the steering wheel."

My God, I thought. That was really an upsetting story. How come I'd only heard about it from specialists in the business? Did Washington officials know about this? They must! With that many cases, there's bound to be a story or a leak pretty soon. How in the world is the government going to explain this to the public?

I always considered the feds to have a spotty record in making their case to the public. In this particular case, they were bound to be caught red handed in demonstrating their poor judgment regarding a mechanical contraption and its performance wherein emotional attachment to a symbol of their dedicated cause appears to have affected their knowledge regarding the product's unintended consequences.

By now you know that yours truly can occasionally be wrong. In this particular case, the government operatives were brilliant! You must remember the testy times in Washington when the Republicans won the off-year elections and presented the Clinton administration with a Republican House of Representatives. In the summer of 1996, the inability of the parties to agree on a budget and, subsequently, refusal by congress to again grant the authority to increase the deficit caused the government to dramatically "close down" for a few days, an act that created considerable attention and some disquiet throughout the land.

Who should step up and take the exceptional and dramatic action of temporarily "re-opening" the government during this period because of an urgent message for the American people? NHTSA! They had just learned of some distressing incidents regarding airbags, where young children were being injured *because their parents were improperly positioning them in an airbag equipped car.* They felt this urgent enough to take this extraordinary action so that parents would seek out proper methods to eliminate this type of incident and, simultaneously, the government would investigate other unexpected usages of cars so equipped so that these type of problems would not migrate to other groups using bag-equipped transportation. They even admitted that they may have to encourage the "manufacturers" to make the airbags less aggressive. (Most companies had been screaming for years that the government-created and enforced specifications were considerably too aggressive.)

Within the year, I happened to attend the annual SAE bash in Detroit and elected to sit in on an engineering/business session dealing with airbags that was in the middle of a series of weeklong related sessions. The moderator, a NHTSA official, started by saying that he had heard rumors that people were accusing him of being absent from the morning meeting because of a need to go back to Washington to get marching orders how to handle the situation after the brouhaha of the previous afternoon. (Gee! I'm sorry I missed that one.) He maintained that he had not gone back to Washington but had gotten a bad fish for dinner the previous evening. He then asserted that while he was on the subject, he would henceforth have no tolerance for further discussion on the aggressiveness of airbags, either with himself, the press or the public and, if he finds out violations of this edict, he will come down so fast on those culprits that they won't know what hit them. For forty years I understood that the relationship between NHTSA and the auto manufacturers was not cordial, but to me this seemed a little over the line.

This little performance exercised me enough to cause me to write a few "guest editorials" (which never got published) and correspond with a few sycophants, mostly from academia as I recall, who saw and cared about airbag edicts as much as I did. I found one of these "editorials" of a dozen years ago to see if my attitudes had changed.

I had created a quiz for the unanointed.

Q. What is the maximum speed that will enable survival in an airbag-equipped car when hitting a brick wall head on?

A. 40 mph.

I had calculated the costs of airbags as installed at $12 billion annually for hardware alone, not including all the new peripheral industries such as accident reconstruction, adjudication of degree of injuries, analysis of aggregate crash data and so on, all for the sake of some as yet theoretical benefit. I had forgotten this part of the editorial, but I also called for a forensic study of the system, integrating all aspects of the phenomena, including insurance, replacement and so on, as soon as relevant data had been secured. By now, all players were on board, as the manufacturers had all established capabilities and would in their new situation support the new status quo.

Sure enough, about ten years later, in a peripheral and poorly attended session, a PhD physicist from the U.K. had just completed and was presenting just such a study. He discussed his methodology and how much data had been collected and how much he had benefited from the mixture of such available data vis-à-vis many hundreds of thousands of identical vehicles, some with airbags and some without so that he could be ensured of accurate comparisons. He also had data from tens of thousands of accidents including data regarding survival rates and injuries in four or five categories of degree.

His conclusion? As I recall the data, some slight improvement on airbag vehicles on the passenger side, some lesser performance for the driver. Overall, the airbag created slightly more mischief than it averted. My worst fears were realized. Not only did the airbag not generate the desired benefit and subsequent payout, it provided *no* benefit.

My conclusion and recommendation today? Since the final argument supporting the introduction included the idea that they must be mandated otherwise there will never be enough usage to ascertain their benefits, that argument no longer holds. There must be beaucoup airbag data currently available, so why not permit companies to offer airbags as optional equipment, thereby saving customers some money and the country's resources in the process?

My favorite PhD's conclusion was even more terse, "We've got to be more careful about letting plaintiff lawyers participate in creating specifications for automotive hardware."

I could agree with that.

CHAPTER TWENTY-SIX
The *Rest* of the 20th Century

When I was last involved directly with the U.S. automotive companies, Chrysler had exonerated itself proudly by expediently paying back the federal government for its loan during the crisis of the early Eighties. The American manufacturers were segueing to smaller vehicles with front-wheel drive for the economies provided by these designs.

I sat down to create an outline of seminal events in the industry from the mid-Eighties through the end of the Nineties, to explain these events as I understood them and to further explain how they interacted and impacted the overall industry. I found that task to be very difficult. Although a lot was happening in the industry and with its players, no stand-alone events would I consider to be specific and isolated so as to lead, rather than just contribute, to the unremitting environment. Most of those main events occurred between the Sixties and the early Eighties. The overall drift was that the domestic industry, although demonstrating improvement in their products and services, were not forgiven for their sins of the Sixties and Seventies and apparently their corporate personas. Consequently, they suffered a continual erosion of market and continuing competition from foreign manufacturers as the latter have reaffirmed how avid are American consumers and how large is the fundamental market.

As for the City of Detroit itself, the one statistic that demonstrates its distress is that UAW jobs, having peaked at 300,000, now are approximated at 30,000. That would amount to about $1 billion per year loss in medical and pension benefits alone. An unremitting flight to the suburbs and to other jobs has left it bereft of the ability to support its infrastructure, or even make it worthwhile for citizens to maintain its once-impressive housing stock.

Let's assume that you are dying to get to the recommendations for a sustainable domestic automotive scenario, yet you wouldn't feel right by skipping the author's overview of the industry over the past 25 years. (I still feel guilty about skipping about 60 pages of Dagny Taggart's penultimate philosophical soliloquy in *Atlas Shrugged*.) Let's assume you are familiar with and not repulsed by the concept of *Classics Illustrated* comics. Accordingly, I am submitting an abbreviated outline of events and situations that you may review and then whiz right along to the concluding chapters.

Overview of American Automotive Industry, Mid-1990s-1999 (abbreviated):

- Product designs and other product-related decisions increasingly influenced by financial staffs rather than vehicle concept, engineering and marketing staffs.
- Second gas crunch of the early Eighties and its impact fades but gasoline prices remain volatile.
- California and a consortium of Eastern states conjure up their own emission standards, creating confusion in the industry and the federal government. Lots[63] of money and development effort wasted on wild-goose chases.
- Light trucks capture a larger market share, as do sport-utility vehicles.
- Japanese and Korean auto makers start building cars in the U.S., and locate factories in communities with anti-UAW sentiments.
- Government revokes on promise not to legislate hardware, and the airbag is introduced across the board. (You've heard this grouse before!)
- For a period, GM focuses on lowering purchase costs, tolerates the establishment of a cult-like purchasing staff that incorporates personal diets and rituals in their fervor to cut supplier costs, break existing contracts and insinuate themselves on heretofore loyal suppliers.
- Reciprocating internal-combustion engines remain the primary source of automotive locomotion to the frustration of many critics who feel they are within a spitting distance from dislodging it on a rational economic basis.
- GM tries a "clean sheet" approach to the small-car segment with an isolated division chartered to create a new car and a new culture to respond to "intrinsically green" younger buyers. GM gets a "B" for execution but never turns a dime on Saturn.

---

[63] 1 lot = $1 billion U.S.

- GM also tries a joint venture with Toyota at its California plant with no spillover benefit until many years later—too late.
- U.S. makers keep behaving as if market erosion is a temporary glitch, tend to be reluctant to structure companies and product mix to realistic expectations. UAW cooperates with this unrealistic scenario by negotiating for "worker job security" while moderating pay and fringe demands. Result is factories are kept running to meet UAW job-security agreements, despite low demand for a factory's output, resulting in deep discounting and therefore low to non-existent profitability on most vehicles.
- As a result of historical industry structure, the "Big Three" automakers incur costs of $2-3 thousand per car in medical and pension costs, a cost not borne by newcomer U.S. manufacturers or foreign importers.
- A reluctance by Americans to view personal transportation decisions on a rational basis,[64] and, probably even more importantly, or to correlate the benefits of a purchase of a vehicle manufactured by a domestic company with the general well-being of the country—as does almost every other country vis-à-vis durable consumer goods, often supported by public policy.
- Ford puts a namesake at the head of its company, to no apparent detriment to its operations and some benefit in its marketing plans. Eventually it puts the company back in professional hands; consequently, it weathers the financial crisis of 2008 better than its American competitors.
- As the turn-of-the-century approaches, David Cole, noted and serious industry observer at UM, suggests that any increase in current café standards would probably cause the "big three" to stop manufacturing vehicles, at least in the U.S. Shocking but not surprising.
- Oh, yeah. Chrysler is merged with Daimler Benz as "equals." (Author's note: we're entertaining nominations for whom you think the Germans consider as equals.) Former

---

[64] What comes around: the founders of the industry taught Americans to not be totally rational in their purchases of automobiles, with great success.

Chrysler chairman retires to Florida, wants to know where Kosinski got his shower curtain.

- And a big, "oh yeah"—by 1990 it is apparent that Japan will not be the superpower of the 21st century as previously anticipated and pretty much conceded. It turns out that its financial systems were much more rickety than had previously been acknowledged.

Now for the fleshing out of the above trends contributing to the diminuendo of the domestic automotive industry. Each bullet point would require 1,000 to 10,000 words. Wait a minute! Why would anyone want to wade through that stuff when the bullet items seem to be pretty much self-explanatory. The events described are pretty much factual, albeit presented in a manner to infer the author's bias. Let's take a vote! Who wants to read through a detailed description of the litany of trends outlined above?

The nays have it!

Let's look closer at the matter of corporate governance. As you recall, my own employer, Allied Corporation, was digesting Bendix under the tutelage of Chairman Ed Hennessy. I'll start with this example as it has most of the typical events and continues to have some of the extraordinary ones. Mr. Hennessy was a straight arrow, as I have noted in previous vignettes. He was a candidate for priesthood for a while before settling in with business and family. He wasn't inclined toward casual Fridays or frolics with the hired help. Now I don't know, but my guess would be that that the closest he ever got to Motown was Chicago, although he might have at some point visited Allied's Detroit coke plant. (That's the stuff like coal, used to make steel, not the beverage or the drug.)

My point is, in no way did he speak Motown.

My further point is, he knew that he didn't speak Motown, and freely admitted that he didn't. As Mark Twain observed: It's not what you know that will hurt you, but what you don't know that you don't know. I understand that he approached the major players at all of our American automotive customers, a move that surely caused some trepidation for the managers of our automotive sector.

His spiel reportedly went something like this:

"Hello, Mr. Motown chairman, I'm Ed Hennessy of Allied Corporation. As you know, we've just been through the imbroglio involving Bendix situation that turned out to be, to me at least, an embarrassment for corporate America. We've made some tough decisions but I wanted to call and let you know that as far as our automotive group goes, it's business as usual.

"I've got to admit that I don't have much experience in the automotive business myself, and it has was difficult to understand it and the Bendix position in it, given the frenzied nature of the recent negotiations that led to our involvement. Let me say this, however, after a cursory review with Bendix automotive guys and receiving from them understanding of their products and market position, I'm delighted with the business and the prospects. When having to negotiate with hour-to-hour deadlines, one tends to feel that he is bidding on a *very large boxful* of stuff of which he only sees the 10 percent spilling over the top, much like the TV series, *Storage Wars*."

He may have continued along these lines:

"I don't think the two of us will ever have to get into negotiations of substance, as we both have competent guys who are reputed to deal on top of the table. I do want to confess that I did have some misgivings as to what magnitude of capital projects would be required to support our [Allied's] new auto business only to understand now that they're not nearly as demanding as our chemical businesses. So my feeling now is that were ready and happy to support anything you throw at us.

"Are there any problems on the horizon? If not, I hope to see you sometime at the SAE banquet or when you're in the New York area, but of course I'm available in any emergency, understanding that the Southfield, Michigan, guys generally run the automotive business. Thanks for listening."

Where I give Mike Blumenthal a "C-" and former consultant hot shot a "D" in approaching Motown executives as a new participant, how would you grade Mr. Hennessy? Right! At least an "A-." (I'm a tough grader). Excellent approach and good vibes as far as I know throughout his tenure.

Next event, Allied earnings are internally forecasted to be not so good.

External announcement: "Good news! We've uncovered several organizational projects that we are undertaking that will deliver considerably more profit over the intermediate term. We're allocating $500 million to cover our costs for this activity."

Translation: We're taking a "pre-loss" of $500 million so that earnings will look okay for a year or so because the $500M won't show up as costs against earnings, it'll show up below the line as "projects." This will give us (me) some breathing room until things get better and by that time the "project" will hopefully be forgotten. Although there will always be money spent on "reorganization," this sleight-of-hand tends to be repeated and repeated without comprehension of otherwise savvy investors, business people or most of the business press. As it turns out, even $500 million wasn't enough to fully tide over the profit drought, but other events, as could be suspected, interceded.

In the late Eighties, the Hughes Medical Institute announced that it would sell Hughes Electronics to the highest close-sealed bidder. Although the deceased Mr. Hughes exhibited some unusual behavior over the years, his electronics business was a jewel in a high-tech and growing market. (Speaking of Mr. Hughes' behavior, I've had a few bad days myself.) About a dozen companies expressed interest in buying the company. Allied would have loved to be involved to supplement its substantial avionics and automotive business that came with Bendix but it didn't have the critical mass. *Voila*, it would team with Signal Companies, a conglomerate of eclectic companies, after preliminary negotiations with them on how to divide the potential spoils. The negotiations went on for months but GM became the winning bidder for Hughes.

Shortly thereafter, Allied and Signal proudly and surprisingly announced an agreement to merge. Not just an agreement in principal but a deal closed for all but the formality of signing the paperwork. The executives were ecstatic that the deal was pulled off with no prior press involvement (thereby no ability to critique) or, for that matter, no input or knowledge from all but a handful of executives from the respective companies.

Mr. Hennessy's message to the masses: "Wasn't it great that we executed this wonderful opportunity without the usual distractions, but admittedly we had to use some very sophisticated subterfuge to pull it off."

Many of us would have preferred to hear more about the "opportunity" and less about the "subterfuge."

The first action? To rid the company of some thirty operations that didn't "fit" in the new merged company. From where did these unwanted operations come? From Signal. Who procured these thirty-some operations then that didn't want them now? The same guys that we just vowed to spend the rest of our lives with. Not so fast! These were spun off to stockholders as the Henley Group under one of the Signal conglomerators. Speaking of eclectic conglomerates with unrelated companies.

Now was formed Allied-Signal. The remaining businesses were somewhat rationalized and their responsibilities rearranged. From the Allied perspective, sales increased appreciably. Also from the Allied perspective, profits stayed the same. The implication, of course, was that the part of the company that came from Signal (minus the thirty-some companies that no one had any interest in) performed somewhere between covering their own variable cost and break-even. This level of profitability stayed the same until Mr. Hennessy's departure.

"How did that merger make sense?" wonders one who is paid not to wonder but to perform specific responsibilities. My conclusion, and one that was soon to be replicated over and over, was that when a corporate titan is preparing to retire, not unlike U.S. presidents, he starts thinking about his own legacy. Since the retrospective performance of a corporate chairman is considerably more quantifiable than that of a U.S. President, the former must make extraordinary efforts to *prevent traceability*. In Mr. Hennessy's particular case, he had merged with a conglomerate, spun off 30-plus companies that had multiple dealings of their own and reorganized the two companies to the extent that only the most adept forensic accountant could possibly trace the value of his contributions. Accordingly, you will notice that with chairmen of long standing who have considerable influence with their board will conclude some unusual or only partly rational major transaction shortly before they retire, especially if they have used "special projects" and the like to prop up perceived earnings.

Mr. Hennessy encouraged the Board to search for and designate a new chairman so that he would have several years to provide "training." They did —Mr. Larry Bossidy from GE, who asserted that he had more than enough "training" at the knee of Jack Welch; consequently, Mr. Hennessy was provided an early retirement.

Mr. Bossidy came on board and publicly reveled in the extraordinary earnings that he espied. But first, of course, we needed approval for a "project" or two. Allied, subsequently Allied-Signal, then AlliedSignal (Larry laid out $250,000 to have someone advise him to drop the hyphen) were generally earners of reasonable profits. In that context, I fastidiously followed Mr. Bossidy's performance by making the adjustment of adding the cost of "projects" to "costs" and computed that he didn't make his first cent of "real" profit until seven quarters on the job, at the same time ostensibly demonstrating modest but consistently increasing profitability, the mantra of

Wall Street in adjudicating well managed companies. "Maybe he saved in taxes," you may argue. It doesn't matter. Through the benefit of international entanglements, AlliedSignal didn't pay American corporate tax. The eyes of my otherwise perceptive associates glazed over. The stock market didn't see anything fishy. In fact, it seemed to embrace his dynamic style and statements, and the market responded favorably. I had the queasy feeling that I was the innocent babe, espousing "no clothes" as the emperor passed by, only no one ever agreed or, for that matter, even seemed to recognize or understand the phenomenon to which I referred that, incidentally, benefited my own personal finances. Thank heavens I didn't have a say in the matter.

CHAPTER TWENTY-SEVEN
Alternative Fuels

As we turn to an evaluation of fuel alternatives that might help recreate a dynamic and sustainable U.S. automotive industry, perhaps I should outline those attributes that contribute or detract from the desirability of any particular fuel:

- Should be plentiful and available at reasonable cost to the motoring public.
- Should embody minimal carbon content and, therefore, the carbon compounds emitted that lead to global warming as well as other effluents, all as a result of normal combustion process.
- Production should not be seasonably cyclical as throughput of material is huge and all plausible fuels are expensive to store.
- The fuel-production or distribution process should not create environmental problems of its own, either through effluents or by requirements for prohibited land usage.
- Should be such fuel or energy that can be transported within the vehicle for an extended range.
- Ideally, production and pricing should be controlled by a global and competitive free market so that opportunity for international political leverage or intimidation is minimized.
- Preferable that production not be co-mingled or become a by-product of products for other large markets so as not to create price volatility in all involved markets; for example, corn.
- All of capital, energy and labor resources used in the conversion of "free" energy sources (such as wind, solar, nuclear) to usable energy must be considered for a rationally sustainable automotive system, or any sustainable systems for that matter, as viable systems are not built upon good intentions or ecologically related good feelings.
- Refueling or recharging should take no longer than "leg stretch" or "rest stop."

- Highly desirable would be a system that does not obsolete the current vehicle population. This implies a fuel that would directly replace gasoline, or one to which current vehicles could be easily converted.
- The ideal fuel should have almost inexhaustible reserves.

Now let's whiz through the litany of fuels and other energy sources with a brief description of each of these and how they conform with our list of attributes and, if applicable, the power converters with which they are paired.

Petroleum

Petroleum has been the fuel of choice for the past hundred years, a fact that supports its commercial viability. It's relatively cheap to produce and performs well when paired with internal-combustion or diesel engines. It's plentiful no matter what the president said in the Seventies, and improved techniques have moved the depletion of available reserves into the unforeseeable future. (Okay! I peeked between Chapter 14 and here).

One problem with petroleum is that much of it is controlled by a Middle East monopoly and its cohorts that have interests that are not convergent with the U.S. The cost has always been quite small to produce a barrel of oil,[65] a fact that allows the monopoly to adjust prices considerably downward from a former price of $80 per barrel as various alternatives appear to threaten its market share.

Further, petroleum fuels are carbon based, so that their usage is in opposition to the effort to halt global warming. Combustion of petroleum products creates the main problem, carbon dioxide (CO_2), but also creates carbon monoxide (CO), that does even worse things.

Until further notice, petroleum is the king of the commercial markets.

Agricultural Products

When the supply of gasoline was thought to be limited in the mid-Seventies, the use of a methanol (wood alcohol) additive was proposed as a sort of "Hamburger Helper" for gasoline. This was greatly helped by Washington regulators as they gave instructions to several Northern locales to use that additive in winter. Methanol has several properties that are useful,

---

[65] Less than $10 per barrel at the most efficient sites.

in that it absorbs moisture better than gas and increase miles-per-gallon. Purportedly, it wouldn't disrupt performance of gasoline emissions, but some unanticipated problems of its own have arisen in that area.

During the gasoline price spike of 2008, there was some conversion of corn to methanol, creating even more havoc than usual in the market for corn futures. Recently, there have been studies conducted to determine what other crops might lend themselves to methanol conversion, one of the most common nominees being whip grass, a low-maintenance crop developed mainly in China.

It is unlikely that these efforts will lead to any crop that will ever be more than an a small adjunct to the overall supply, as it has issues relating to non-cyclical massive availability and inherent cost competitiveness.

Electric/Battery
Electricity was the first form of energy to displace horses as a means of propelling carriages. (I recall reading about a New York open dialogue where one proponent espoused an urgent need for a horse replacement of any shape or color, along the lines I have talked about here of household refuse, bubble gum and rejected EFI systems.) When the internal-combustion engine was not yet developed enough to be suitable for commercial adoption, electricity seemed a logical power source for propelling automobiles, as it was available and had brought convenience and pleasure in homes of people in many cities. Unfortunately, electric energy in nature doesn't exist in a physical form that can easily be loaded and used for propulsion of a vehicle. It has to be generated and stored in ways developed by humans.

This has been the problem of electricity relative to propelling automobiles. The last "electric" automobile to be manufactured in volume was discontinued in the Twenties. The newer models, introduced by GM, Tesla and several Japanese companies, have been produced in modest volumes, even though being subsidized during purchase and refueling.

To this day, electric energy has a fascination that some can't resist. While riding in an electrically powered vehicle, one has the sensation of no vibration, no noise, no effluents and no gas purchased from guys dressed in white. Detracting somewhat from this seemingly "clean" immediate environment is that the "vibrations, noise and effluents," some of this generated by fuel purchased from guys dressed in white, are occurring just down the road at the power plant that generates the electricity. (I recall the very popular GM President, "Pete" Estes, being vilified for pointing this out when commenting on the design of an electric car. No matter, he had already been there by commenting on the government designed "safety" car that could be manufactured for $10,000 as proudly announced by its originator, NHTSA.)

"Our equivalent safety car could be sold for about $6,500," offered Estes to the absolute hysteria of the safety advocates and their sycophantic media followers.

Compounding this inconvenient truth is the reality that when generated, electricity must be stored to become portable enough to be loaded and carried on the vehicle. This leads us to batteries that in themselves create some problems in that they are made from heavy materials, such as lead, that are not only environmentally unfriendly but are also quite heavy. Although electricity has the advantage of relative efficiency in being converted to locomotive power, this advantage is diminished by the act of adding considerable dead weight to the vehicle.

Further compounding the problems with batteries are limited range and extended time requirements for recharging.

I have, I think justifiably, been critical of California in particular for requiring any carmaker to sell at least 10 percent of its product line as "zero emission" vehicles. This petulant action diverted the companies from seeking more-realistic alternatives. Nonetheless, General Motors has introduced a "production" battery car (called the "Volt"). Although such a vehicle has limited application because of its range, it is commendable to see such a company put enough cars on the road so that the technology can be observed in an other than prototype situation. That's the way General Motors tended to introduce unproven but perhaps viable technology in the "good old days," by finding an application on an existing niche vehicle, such as Corvette, or introducing a niche vehicle with the technology, for example, the front-wheel drive on Riviera/Toronado (the latter sometimes referred to as the "200-pound canary").

Wind, Solar

These "free" sources of energy cannot, of course, be considered as energy to be applied to the vehicle. They might be considered, however, as an "enabler" in the sense that these technologies might be the source of electricity that could be used to produce or extract other energy, such as hydrogen. In this case, they will be competing with those same sources of energy with which they otherwise compete, those discussed above in addition to hydroelectric and coal. It might be stated here that any contributor to a multiple conversion, by the phenomenon of conversion loss, must be able to provide massive amounts of economical energy.

Hydrogen

The very good news: hydrogen embodies several attributes that are ideal as a propulsion fuel: (1) zero ecological footprint after ignition and (2) the source of the raw material (water) is virtually unlimited and not controlled by any political influences, including guys in white clothes.

The very bad news: As hydrogen doesn't loll around in nature waiting to be harvested, it has to be extracted from higher-order material. As the logical material is water, there is some difficulty because each of those little pesky atoms of oxygen hold on very tightly to its two molecules of hydrogen; therefore, to produce enough hydrogen to run the U.S. automotive fleet would require really, really massive amounts of energy to extract enough to keep the pipeline full.

Some moderately bad news: Hydrogen is the lightest material on earth; consequently, to make it adaptable for a vehicle to carry, it would have to be highly compressed. Also, as you know, it is highly explosive (Oh, the humanity!) and would have to be handled under rigorous safety standards.

Comparisons and Recommendation

The above heading is fraudulent. Not only would we be comparing apples with bananas with kumquats, but to do so we would become a shill for some sort of material without even considering other parts of the *system*. As Charles Goren (bridge guru) used to say, "If you aren't in agreement with your partner on your rudimentary system, phone ahead to the poorhouse for a reservation."

CHAPTER TWENTY-EIGHT
Alternative Power Sources

Now that we've looked at fuel and other propellant energy sources, why don't we wade through a brief list of power converters that, together with the aforementioned "juice," will jointly constitute the locomotive power.

The attributes that support or detract from desirable light-vehicle power sources are as follows:

- Must efficiently use the energy that enables them.
- Should provide considerable acceleration upon demand.
- Would ideally be a low- or no-pollution contributor.
- Could use, or partially use, propellants that are not controlled by politically motivated cartels.
- Would minimize or eliminate the carbon-containing effluents.
- Should be competitive regarding use of incremental resources and creation of environmental damage for its own manufacture.
- Should be able to be refueled routinely by all reasonably healthy adults.

And the candidates are:

Internal-Combustion Engine (ICE)

We have previously discussed this and the ICE, at least in the U.S., is still king of the hill when paired with ordinary gasoline. Although it has been in use for more than one hundred years, it has been continually refined and is rarely the cause of a "lemon," runs for considerably more than 100,000 miles if reasonably maintained, and performs pretty well, even with all the claptrap that has been inflicted upon it.

Experts think that mileage for any given application can be improved by about 8 percent, but it is questionable whether the resources required to do this will provide a payout.

255

The major problem with the ICE is that is heretofore paired with petroleum and its intrinsic problems of price volatility, carbon footprint and political instability.

Diesel

To me it seems as though diesel engines, now called "clean diesel," have been under the radar in the U.S. regarding familiarity and attributes. Probably less than 20 percent of Americans could tell you that over 50 percent of new European light vehicles embody engines of this configuration. Probably this is a result of the GM offerings of the Seventies, where there were some problems, but Americans didn't seem to like the glow-plug starting system and availability of fuel was never prevalent in medium-sized cities and semi-rural areas.

I have heard proponents talk of the performance of diesel engines wherein they listed, without contradiction, the several areas where diesel engines out-perform the ICE. It has some of the same problems with its petroleum-derived fuel, although it is purported to be generally more efficient.

Things not impelling U.S. manufacturers to replace the ICE with diesels are probably: (1) not knowing if Americans would embrace this configuration in general and (2) the capital projects required to fully tool for diesel.

Fuel Cells

The fuel cell is a device that converts a chemical reaction into electricity. It has come into the automotive scene as a logical power source paired with hydrogen fuel. Although development programs persist, they tend to get hot and then cool, undoubtedly related to the feasibility of producing and handling hydrogen in an automotive environment.

The use of fuel cells would make the input to the rest of the power train as electricity and, although the high volume commercial applications of the cells have not been fully developed, when incorporated in a vehicle it would use an electric motor and a system that I imagine would not be that much different than those already developed for the current modest volume of electric cars.

Although the use of fuel cells is furthest down the road regarding development, a resulting vehicle would have those good attributes of quiet,

256

smooth operation with no environmental footprint. Again, the viability is paired to that of the possibility to provide hydrogen in a plausible commercial process.

Electric

This subject was pretty well covered when I discussed using electricity as a fuel source. We will soon be able to gather much more field experience with this kind of energy source. The industry has been flailing at this problem for some twenty years, some of that being frantic, as at one point it appeared that a company couldn't sell cars in California unless it also had a production battery-operated car that would be bought in quantity. One seems to think that by this time, all of the automotive developers throughout the world seem to be asymptotically approaching its optimum configuration. What is needed here is a breakthrough in chemistry or in pairing with another source within the same vehicle.

Hybrids

There has been so much discussion and background surrounding the hybrids that it will be handled in its own chapter—not coincidently, the next chapter.

CHAPTER TWENTY-NINE
Let's Talk Hybrids

Although this overall narrative is primarily chronological, I thought it best if the whole hybrid story was put in the same chapter, as it is unique onto itself.

I first heard about the hybrid vehicle in the mid-Nineties when I was attending automotive seminars for the purpose of keeping my consulting clients up on specific issues. The concept is interesting even if fuel savings aren't of urgent concern and so I spent perhaps an inordinate amount of time —say, two full days out of the week-long Society of Automotive Engineers Annual Meeting for a number of years—learning about various aspects and proposals for hybrid systems.

Way back in high-school physics someone asked our instructor, Mr. Belleville, about the plausibility of results for the then popular vehicle-mileage contest, the Mobil Economy Run. Professional drivers actually drove from Los Angeles to Kansas City with the sole criterion of maximizing gas mileage, using standard cars with standard engines. The winning mileage was in the area of 25 miles per gallon, wherein these same cars seemed to get about 12-15 mpg when we actually drove them around town. "They don't ever touch the brake," responded Mr. Belleville. "Imagine all the energy from a speeding car being simply dissipated into the brake pads as heat."

The enabling feature of the hybrid system is capturing just such dynamic energy from the braking process, converting it to electrical power (at approximately 35 percent efficiency), and subsequently using that power for locomotion. To do this, a substantial piece of equipment, much like a conventional electrical generator with an integral electrical motor, is mounted in or near the drive train to gather and store the braking power, then to propel the vehicle during startup. Nifty idea!

Typically, a hybrid vehicle features a small and efficient primary motor, the aforementioned generator/motor and an aerodynamic vehicle design. One turns the key, puts the vehicle in gear, pushes the "gas" pedal and the car proceeds on battery power from the new electric motor, all silently to this point in the manner of an electric golf cart. Soon the system will segue into the gasoline engine that propels the car until it again reverts to very low speed. When the car comes to a braking stop, neither motor is operating, a somewhat disquieting feeling for those used to a "throaty" muffler system.

On the early Toyota hybrids, imported from Japan, there was a "dimple" on the dashboard suggesting that a certain option was not elected by the buyer. What was the option that the buyer didn't get? For the same vehicle sold in Japan, there was a button that permitted the driver to elect to run the vehicle for the next mile on electricity alone, appropriate for use in areas congested with pedestrian traffic, in tunnels or any place where it would be desirable or more courteous to have zero emissions. Sounds to me like a good idea.

Why didn't American drivers opt for this? It wasn't offered. Why didn't Toyota offer this feature? They couldn't. It was *forbidden* under U.S. law as disruptive to applicable procedural edicts for official mileage testing.

During the Fifties, one recalls the conversion of the automobile electrical system from 6 volts to 12 volts without much hubbub. In retrospect, this undoubtedly was in anticipation of air conditioning and other features that might be added in the future. In order to provide the environment for a robust hybrid system, a new standard system of 41 volts was being proposed for all vehicles.

Why 41 volts? That sounds like an arbitrary number.

Not at all. (Incidentally, this paragraph will qualify this book as a sequel to those radical strategy books emanating from the Village in the Sixties.) A current of 41 volts is about the maximum amount of juice that the human body can endure without needing medical attention. If your car had a 41-volt system, your mechanic would get zapped once in a while, charge you the usual $80 per hour and go about his business. On the other hand, if you had for instance, a 60-volt system, it would be great for the hybrid system but your car would have all kinds of thick orange wires running through it, your mechanic would be wearing something that resembles a space suit, and he would charge you about $775 per hour. The practical information here is that if you really, really want to scare the bejesus out of somebody without lasting effects, jab him with 41 volts. On the other hand, if you want to maim, probably an upgrade to only 50 volts will do it, at the same time not wasting energy and simultaneously minimizing the contribution to global warming.

For several years, I tormented through the summaries that presented alternate-vehicle architecture to accommodate the new device in on-line and in parallel configurations. I watched alternative proposed wiring diagrams, as it seemed that a vestigial 12-volt supply might be desirable for lighting and several other components. Perhaps the use of two batteries was a good solution. The effects on other components was debated in considerable detail and the timing of the 41-volt introduction, which obviously had to be coordinated on an industry-wide basis, was as yet uncertain. Throughout all the deliberations, the German premium manufacturers (Mercedes, BMW) consistently urged introduction of the new electric cars at greatest haste, while the domestic industry continued to evaluate potential disruption to the overall system.

As the new century approached, the 41-volt system was off the table. The complications to introduce a new electrical specification created capital-equipment modifications that on an industry-wide basis ran into many billions of dollars. My understanding was that air conditioning created one of the larger dilemmas, but other component industries would have to undergo major upheavals wherein some would be untouched. In summary, the 41-volt system was off, but the hybrid system was still "on."

As the hybrids with the "puny" electrical motors were being introduced, I was nonetheless interested in finding out how they were received, culturally and functionally. I knew that the initial reaction would be considerable anticipation, as there is always a small portion of the driving public that will want to try something new, particularly if it supports and advertises their position on a particular issue, in this case on fuel savings and environmental conservation. In operation, the transition of the vehicle from electrical power to internal-combustion engine was surprisingly smooth, that segue earlier purported to being one of the engineering challenges presented. Although primarily only a bystander on this project, I was secure that I was on top of the issues as I attended a plenary summary on the status of the hybrid vehicles shortly after they were introduced in the early 2000s.

Question from the (obviously unwashed) audience to the distinguished panel: "Let me get this straight. These vehicles don't plug in to anything, right? They run around and every once in a while you pump some gas in them, right? Then just where does the efficiency come from?"

Obviously a question from a layman. There is a lot of eye contact and head turning amongst the expert panel. Who has a plausible answer? (A little eye contact and head turning of my own.)

Finally a response. "We start with a smaller and more efficient (and considerably more costly) primary engine [literally a "motor," these tend to be used interchangeably], such as an Atkinson engine. The biggest savings comes in the recapturing of forward momentum and converting that into electricity. There are also some savings while stopped, as there is no gasoline usage then. That's about it."

Second part of question: "Will the buyer overcome the extra cost of the vehicle by the savings in the cost of gas?" Not by the normal first owner.

Third part of question: "Will the savings in operating energy be more than the energy expended in manufacturing the extra equipment?" This was a gesture response. Note to reader—replicate answer yourself as follows: Using either arm, partially extend arm, palm down, fingers splayed. Wobble hand side to side. Comme si, comme sa. We don't know. At least not to any considerable extent.

Would the robust hybrid, as promised by the 41-volt system have been more promising? I think that is anyone's guess. Although a valiant effort at an interesting concept, the hybrid won't be selected as our "system" choice for the future.

CHAPTER THIRTY
America and the Big Palette

If you're reading this, you must recognize that America is a unique place. While I started this tome believing the idea that America and Americans sometimes worry about the wrong things and later criticize our lack of civility between people with diverging opinions and our lack of respect of anything and anyone that doesn't appear on *Hollywood Tonight*, I will submit that America is a place that keeps inventing itself.

Perhaps we will again be able to agree on or at least tolerate projects that benefit the vast amount of Americans by recalling recidivist thinking of a period where "what's good for America—" tended to bring together citizens whose own individual charters or goals were not necessarily congruent with the project at hand. When we set out to develop the West, we didn't augment the Pony Express with dodgem cars or permit the dodgem-car purveyors and their lobbyists to influence lawmakers to legislate on behalf of dodgem cars. We sought out and brought together institutions that sought out and supported, or at least didn't inhibit, whatever solution they believed was best for the country. We invented and enabled the railroads, the first transportation medium that permitted humans to travel at a speed of more than that of 35 mph (on the back of a horse), while simultaneously carrying vast amounts of goods and many people as it moved across the country. When the automobile itself was invented, civic and governmental observers saw the broad intrinsic benefits and established roads, rules and conduct for driving, signs and other paraphernalia that permitted the manufacturers to improve the vehicles themselves rather than be distracted by conditions of driving in mud, smashing into other cars, and the like. This was repeated in mid-century when the government led a huge program to develop a vast system of intercity and interstate roads,[66] recognizing that Americans liked to come and go as they wished in privacy, with the freedom to accompany whom they

---

[66] Incidentally paid for by auto drivers via their gas taxes paid into the Highway Trust Fund.

wished, talk about any issues they wished, listen to music they wished at any volume they wished and to stop and rest when they wished. There have been enough empirical examples to demonstrate that Americans, even when forced to pony up considerably increased individual funds, choose the auto for short and intermediate trips. This phenomenon occurs even though every other form of transportation that is not provided by their own feet or their own bicycle is subsidized by you and me, often to a considerable extent.

When polio was a constant concern, America enabled Dr. Salk to solve the root problem, rather than have other institutions invent, at probably great expense, means to isolate children from each other or other ways to prevent contagion. (The Rileys were quarantined for about a week in the late Forties.)

Back to business: In solving the problems associated with American automotive transportation, let's first attempt to identify these problems, perhaps even the order of their importance:

- The issuance of carbon-containing gasses is creating an imbalance in the earth's ecosystems, leading to rising oceans, revised shorelines, food shortages and political upheaval.

- The dependence of the world on Middle Eastern countries for stability of delivery and prices of petroleum seems to have created distortions in worldwide relationships and lends extraordinary influence to those who are blessed by situations of nature rather than by their own personal industry and diligence.

- The need to establish an efficient, reliable and non-politically influenced fuel supply so that the country, and others if they so desire, optimizes its automotive systems and stabilizes the transportation systems against a known energy availability and cost. Heretofore, alternative systems have been facing a moving target, thereby wasting resources in the stop/start nature of the process. At this juncture in our culture and lifestyles, I am presuming that personal automotive access is considered a given rather than a special situation or privilege. Accordingly, I am submitting that the lack of plentiful and inexpensive fuel from a human-behavior standpoint is a "taking out the garbage" issue in the context that one isn't consciously "happy" when gas is cheap and plentiful, but "extremely unhappy" when it is not. The "garbage" analogy is that garbage is presumed to be taken away and one only considers it when they become "unhappy" when it is not.

Let's stabilize the fuel supply and go about our real businesses.
- Fluctuating fuel cost and availability have also created distortions in the way Americans utilize their vacation and leisure time, making it difficult to plan for purveyors of leisure activities and other transportation systems.
- Instability in the fuel-delivery system makes it difficult for Americans to plan their day-to-day lives in the context of where to live, work, shop, see friends and plan leisure activity—and probably has some influence on the rural, suburban, city residential mix.

A few years ago,[67] I sat through a panel discussion of five or six chief engineers of the largest automobile companies, where there was a discussion of potential new power systems, much as I have provided you previously. When the discussions got around to predictions of which system they were going to recommend to their company, while unanimously lambasting the California exercise relating to batteries, they all seemed to waffle, until the lady from Ford explained that although there were perhaps three or four plausible alternatives to the conventional ICE, "—first of all, we're going to need some help on what type of fuel will be available and at what cost, but secondly, if we were to chose a system that seemed most logical for even a niche of our product offerings and, for any number of reasons, it didn't resonate with our customers, we'd be out of business."

At the time, it seemed a shocking statement. No longer.

Wouldn't it be nice if we could come up with one "Big Palette" scheme that would solve the majority of these problems and let the manufacturers attempt to optimize the drive-train system as they see fit, but get basically back to cars with size, features and capabilities that Americans want to buy. Let's start a national dialogue of how such a system might be set up, with all of the issues on the table, and together make a national decision on a direction prior to assigning tasks on how to bring it to fruition. During this

---

[67] By the way, what do you call this first decade of the 2,000s? The oughts? The zeros? The "no name" decade? Please let me know!

"dialogue," in an attempt to minimize the effect of political or "one issue" groups, the unwritten rules should be that discussions would stay as close to principles of fact and science as possible. It would be permissible, yes encouraged, that those tempting to distort known matters be discredited on the basis of scientific or economic fact.

Your modest and unassuming author will have the chutzpah to propose what he believes to be one superior such system that will push most of the above problems to the back burner, simultaneously providing a sustainable individual automotive culture with a minimum of transitional upheaval and obsolescence of current equipment. Sounds great, doesn't it? However, my system won't disappoint you from the standpoint of no one noticing. I didn't promise that this system won't create an uproar from those who will suffer dislocation.

Stay tuned or, better yet, get involved. Let's stop wringing our hands. Let's stop thinking up reasons why the automobile is not good for our health, our mental state, our interpersonal attitudes or our libidos. Let's stop whining and let's get going. Speak up! Let Detroit and Washington know what you think would be good for the industry. You, too, can make a judgment, as my boss did, about Motown guys as they graciously (or not) react to layman advice.

Let's start one helluva project to push automotive issues and problems to a back burner so that we can get on with more important things.

CHAPTER THIRTY-ONE
Proposal for Sustainability

As one reviews the litany of potential fuels, it's difficult not to be fascinated with hydrogen. After all, 70 percent of the earth is covered with molecules that contain it, and yet there are seemingly daunting problems to be overcome before it could be used:

- There's no generally accepted electrical source that is cheap enough to produce hydrogen gas from water.
- Even if a plausible source for hydrogen could be developed, its fuel-cell power converter isn't fully developed.
- Even if the fuel cell were fully developed, all the energy would be presented to the propulsion system in the form of electricity, creating a requirement for all new gears, transmissions and the like, plus the manufacturing tooling and equipment to produce them.
- Hydrogen is the world's lightest material; it would have to be highly compressed to be practical from the context of energy requirements between fill-ups; accordingly, that brings safety concerns, as does its combustibility.

Many years ago, I knew, but mentally laid aside, that my Thai friend, Lek, had in the Eighties started a side business wherein he converted taxis to propane for the purposes of ensuring clean air as the car usage in Thailand, particularly Bangkok, was projected to greatly increase. (It didn't and it did; the car population exploded, but the air quality was horrendously bad in the early Nineties. It takes only a few whiffs of Bangkok or Mexico City air to concede that our efforts in the Seventies weren't completely wasted.) At that time, he described such conversion as a relatively routine procedure, wherein one adjusted the carburetion system and the spark-plug gap to coincide with the energy intrinsic in the new fuel mixture, much as I had to do when I bought a "gas" kitchen range but had to use propane rather than natural gas. If various gasses can be substituted for a gasoline, could existing vehicles be converted to hydrogen? A few years ago I understood that they could. The fuel-cell hysteria was created by the fuel-cell guys. They perceived a *substantial* new market for their products, and naturally wanted to insert themselves into the dialogue and the process for a new automotive power system.

Let's assume that if we could provide hydrogen, both new cars and existing cars could run on it. All current production equipment to make cars could be salvaged and no existing cars would be obsolete.

But where could we get cheap energy to produce hydrogen? At an annual Society of Automotive Engineers convention there was a presentation by an MIT PhD representing a consortium committed to revisiting the usage of nuclear energy as a power source. At that point, the consortium had made a new design of a nuclear power plant and were scouring the country, encouraging dissenters and general citizens to propose potential "failure modes," such as plane crashes, bombs dropped, earthquakes, monsoons and so on. The idea was that such events would be accounted for and serious problems be averted by features designed into the power plant. The absolute worst tolerable condition after suffering any of these catastrophes would be something like quarantine within 200 yards of the plant for 100 years.

They would then build a prototype plant. Assuming that no unforeseen problems were encountered, their intention would to have fifty plants built. What would this do for America? It would provide power to completely fill the electrical grid *plus* power to produce enough hydrogen to run all U.S. passenger cars and light trucks.

Let's assume that we indeed have enough hydrogen. How will we accommodate it?

At the same convention there was a presentation by top executives of BMW, as you undoubtedly know, one of the most capable automotive engineering companies in the world (albeit its forbearers didn't always have America's wellbeing at heart). As a sideshow to their previously formal presentation on another subject, the chief engineer and others discussed the potential use of hydrogen.

The dialogue went something like this:

"What would be the difficulty in creating a procedure for converting existing ICE powered cars?"

"That wouldn't be too difficult. It would take little more than a weekend."

"What about a foolproof system for delivering and using hydrogen?"

"That would be much more difficult. Probably the hardest part would be to get the players around the world to agree on specifications for a common standard. [There are several auto-related safety and emission standards that are regionalized to this day.] But let's surmount that problem by assuming the U.S. settles on its own specs. Give us specific performance standards and it would probably take about six months to design systems and equipment and a little longer to do testing, certifications and the like."

At that point, the top U.S. BMW executive (and American by birth) took the microphone and laid out the following allegory:

"Suppose it's 1893 and you are Gottleib Daimler, German manufacturer of the finest carriages for transporting people. You are proud of your accomplishments and your products, but you properly sense that carriages will shortly become self-propelled, exchanging some sort of transporting contraption for the horse. You know that you will have to defend your market position by creating your own self-propelled vehicle, but how do you go about it? What form of propulsion system do you use?

"Let's consider his alternatives.

"Perhaps he should consider electricity. It has made remarkable improvements in city living. It easily lights our streets for safety and permits citizens to enjoy reading after dark, and has enabled many implements to supplant otherwise backbreaking chores.

"Undoubtedly, he should consider the steam engine. Its application to rail locomotives has made travel between cities much more expedient. Its application to boats has contributed greatly to shipping and transportation. In fact, in the United States, it has been the key factor in making accessible by rail its vast Western regions for development.

"But perhaps he should consider new systems.

"Perhaps he could develop a system using a series of controlled explosions."

As you have deduced, good old Gottleib was thinking "outside the box."

Let me share another helpful explanation that I stumbled across. As previously stated, it would take a significant amount of energy to create the hydrogen needed to operate vehicles. It has been suggested that we look at the process from another standpoint. Let's assume we make hydrogen by an electrolysis process, using an electrical charge in water to separate its hydrogen from its oxygen. We take a certain amount of electric energy and create hydrogen. The hydrogen atoms, in the form of their natural state, a gas, intrinsically contain an amount of potential energy, incidentally less than we started with. We then contain the hydrogen and load it on the vehicle for use as a fuel. The energy then can be recaptured through an ICE, as an explosive mixture, or a fuel cell, to generate electricity. Looking at it from this perspective, doesn't the hydrogen act in the same manner as a battery? The hydrogen is potentially superior because it can be replenished more easily and because it doesn't leave behind caustic chemicals or heavy metals.

Let's say that we also let our minds wander and assume that indeed a nuclear/hydrogen (N/H) supply system might not be a house of cards but a plausible source of automotive fuel. Might there be ancillary benefits? Let me enumerate the ways:

Environmental

I'm going to walk you down the garden path for just a moment. Do you recall my ranting about the emission rules that created the legendary air pump and the super expensive catalyst and the traveling-car fire starter? These rules were created to minimize six pollutants categorized as "criteria" pollutants: ozone, carbon monoxide, sulfur dioxide, nitrous oxide, particulates and lead. Of these, all but ozone and nitrous oxide would now be off the table as the hydrogen process does not involve any material that has common molecules with the offending materials. Could we ditch the catalyst and its expense? We don't know yet.

You'll notice that the above litany doesn't include any "greenhouse" gasses that are currently the greatest contributor to global warming. How does the hydrogen process relate to this? Do you recall the public discussions about carbon taxes or carbon credits or carbon trading? Since there would be no carbon involved, either in producing the hydrogen fuel (nuclear) or in the hydrogen itself, there are *no* such gasses produced. What comes out the tailpipe? Predominantly *Water!* (H_2O.) This is called a zero environmental footprint.

How does this affect us? Quite favorably I think:

- It lets us leapfrog any and all commitments relating to the environment like Kyoto, because of the removal of carbon-based emissions from light vehicles. This action alone would reduce the *national* total production of greenhouse gasses by about 25 percent when N/H is fully up and running.

- Also, there is an additional 40 percent reduction available relative to the electricity-generation business by using nuclear power.

It's admittedly almost too good to be true. Two thirds of our total U.S. carbon-based emissions could eventually be eliminated by adoption of N/H.

Thus far, a more than passing grade on environmental.

Oil Consumption

Heretofore, America has perhaps rightfully been criticized for its propensity to guzzle gasoline in spite of the needs of other developing countries and its contribution to our annual deficit. Obviously, the above adjustments to our energy mix would change the worldwide scene and, because of our current appetite, change that to a considerable extent.

America currently uses about 25 percent of the petroleum produced worldwide. A rough computation reveals that introduction of the full N/H system would eliminate about 35 percent of our needs or about 8.5 percent of world consumption, equivalent to the combined needs of Japan and India or about one-half the requirements of the European Union. Looked at from another standpoint, it seems as though the Western Hemisphere would change from a modest importer to a modest exporter. The U.S. itself would change from a huge net importer (11.8 million barrels per day) to a modest importer (4.4 million barrels per day).

Enough about the statistics. How will N/H affect various producers? Another bit of obscure information gleaned in MBA school was the nature of markets. In about one-and-a-half minutes, one learned that the cartel was not a naturally occurring phenomenon, not any more than naturally occurring pure hydrogen or aluminum. It was created by producers of similar products who conspire to keep prices abnormally high. They hope to form a quasi-monopoly so as to have enough leverage to control prices by agreeing to production quotas.[68] The theory is that, in time, they invariably will implode. Why? Because the personal aspirations of the parties don't coincide with those of the group (after all, they're natural competitors) and because the scheme only works when there is a near balance of supply and demand or, particularly when demand tends to exceed supply for the subject product.

---

[68] Theoretically, the available price increase created by a monopoly approaches that of the producer's fixed costs. Enough!

Will the N/H scheme, namely 7.8 million barrels a day removed from the market, affect those involved in an oil cartel? Let me remind you that with all of the price volatility of petroleum over the past 40 years, these guys would get together and collaborate to, in aggregate, increase or decrease output by only by 1 or 2 million barrels per day. That empirically suggests that the short-term price of petroleum is highly elastic relative to demand. Supporting that premise is the theory that competitors tend to match each other's price declines in profitable product lines. "Elasticity" means the relationship between price and volume of a product. "Highly elastic" means the price moves up and down faster than does the volume. "Inelastic" means the volume doesn't move even though the price does.

I want to express my predictions reflecting global implications in a manner that is calm—relative to the event. If the N/H program would be introduced instantaneously, in the Middle East there would be—brace yourselves—are you ready?—there would be—*Hysterical Panic!*

Remember, most of the Middle East countries plan their national budgets relative to the revenues from oil exports. Although the Middle-East cartel continues to embody the low-cost producers, the worldwide price will tumble until it matches the variable cost of the guy who is at the 8 percentile highest-cost producer.

Let me explain this in more detail. As the permanent demand for petroleum falls, the price will fall until the market again reaches equilibrium, that is when the same amount of petroleum is being sold as is being produced. This means the production of petroleum must fall until this point is reached. The most logical occurrence for decreasing production would be where those high-cost producers who will stop operating when the price drops lower than their cost to keep going. At what price point is that likely? Unknown. The current price of a barrel is now hovering around $80, but the recent volatility had shoved it down to the mid-$30s. At that time, I don't recall anyone limiting their short-term production of oil because of short-term cost problems. This would suggest that the price has a long way to fall before the players start pulling out because of day-to-day cost pressures. Imagine the effect on producers: Not only are their sales falling in number of barrels shipped, but the price received for a barrel is *significantly* decreasing, thereby compounding the falloff in revenue.

If, as expected, the system is introduced on an attritional basis, the Middle East reaction will only be *Panic!* Before I continue the technical stuff, let me further alert you that there will also be *Panic!* in Texas, Mexico, Halliburton and Hollywood, among other places. Don't worry, there will be enough havoc to go around.

Primary Energy Source

Remember, I'm the guy that keeps babbling that if you don't consider the whole system or the whole supply chain, you can't draw logical, only political (would you believe?) arguments or conclusions. What have we left out up to now? Let's see, we've made the car run on hydrogen made from electricity which, in turn, is made by the nuclear power plant. Right! (You're smarter than Mrs. Riley's kids.) We've left out of the system, as so far explained, the fuel that powers the nuclear plant that makes the electricity that—and so on and so on. When we explain this, I think we will have covered the whole system. And do you know what? Perhaps this is the best part of the whole story.

Do you remember the arguments about disposing of the partially spent fuel rods previously used in existing nuclear plants? The Department of Energy wanted to send them by train to Nevada where they would be buried in Yucca Mountain, creating one hell of a flap. Not only did the Nevadans want no part of that, but the towns with the tracks over which the stuff would travel went berserk. They must have thought that, at any instance, 25 percent of all trains are crashing and spewing out all sorts of nuclear, biological and disease-infested material, particularly in the middle of cities. What's the good news? The new plants can use this fuel to create the electricity. What's even more mind-boggling is that there happens to be enough of these rods lying around to power the 50 plants for 100 years into the future. (Try not to hear the *Twilight Zone* lead-in.)

Let me summarize. I'm making a proposal stating that appropriate institutions—auto manufacturers, government overseers, the power-generation industries and suppliers, research institutions and other parties with potential contributions—agree to collaborate to establish a new approach to the automotive industry wherein:
* Existing fuel rods be used to power—
* New nuclear-powered electrical generating plants that will—
* Completely fill the requirements of the whole U.S. grid with excess enough to—

- Manufacture enough hydrogen to fuel all light-transportation vehicles.

The first-order effects would be:

- The environmental footprint of the light-vehicle industry will approach zero.
- As a nation, greenhouse gasses will be reduced by two-thirds.
- U.S. demand for petroleum will be reduced by 35 percent.
- Annual balance of payments deficits will be reduced by about 250 billion dollars per year.

The second-order effects would be:

- The value of a barrel of oil will plummet.
- There will be serious regional disruptions in national and worldwide energy-supply industries, although there will be many employment opportunities in the construction and machinery-building industries.
- The politics relating to the middle East will undoubtedly be affected.

The third-order effects would be—? (Help me!)

The fourth order effects would be—? (Help me!)

"Hey, Rile, you've given us only half the story! What are our obligations? What are the risks? What other problems might we generate that we haven't considered?"

I will grant that your questions are pertinent but I will submit that I have given you 80 percent of the story. Although I'm not an expert, let me give you the downside or unknown stuff that I was about to give you before you accused me of flannel mouthing:

- The building of the electricity-producing plants, the hydrogen-producing plants and the proliferation of hydrogen stations throughout the country will be a series of tremendous and costly capital projects. How would these be financed and what would be the payoff on a systems-wide basis?
- There would have to be an environmental study to ascertain what impact the projects and their eventual operation would have, particularly the nuclear plants. I seem to recall that the old nuclear plants warmed the contiguous water, to what extent I don't know, but there was a lot of "bump in the night" blather associated with nuclear facilities. I now walk around thinking

273

that the Three Mile Island episode did less damage than did the flame retardant/cow feed debacle in Michigan. Chernobyl, poorly designed and operated, was a disaster waiting to happen just preceding the last days of the Soviet Union. Even so, a National Geographic special presented its 25-year later scenario, demonstrating a surprising resurgence of flora and fauna. One of my former bosses used to say that "nobody ever died with nuclear, where many have with conventional electricity-generating factories." Fear seemed to get a toehold because the potential modes of failure were not apparent to the normal citizen. What they mostly understood was that they were spooky, they often hummed, they glowed and they might go "boom" at any moment. (They've seen the actual movies.)

Many of the "talking head" commentators are proposing that nuclear power to generate electricity should be revisited, given all the acknowledged problems with our current systems. Some have even suggested that if one purports to be concerned about the planet and yet discourages the investigations involving nuclear energy, then one can't be sincere in one's planetary concerns. It would be my supposition that one is more concerned with using one's purported environmentalism to exert control over the ordinary people, suggesting that such bring in their used cooking oil to be used as automotive fuel and that they separate the insect wings from the mouse droppings in their trash, only to have both eventually tossed in the same landfill.

There may have to be some concessions made on the range between refueling of hydrogen-powered cars. Since I anticipate that the fuel will be inexpensive and, for practical purposes, inexhaustible, there will be freedoms for the car planners to make larger envelopes inside cars, but it will be their responsibility to allocate space among drive trains, passengers, luggage and fuel storage. My guess at a worst-case scenario would be that these cars would have a minimum range of 200 miles, as opposed to about twice that now.

Let me assume the following pushback:

"Last question, Rile. You have been bloviating for all these chapters of how all the events of the last forty years have occurred to the detriment of the domestic industry, yet your solution seems to be a generic one. We would have guessed that you would espouse some sort of system where the domestic industry would get some reworking of the rules to purportedly level the playing field, some tax holidays or some tariffs on the overseas manufacturers. Your proposal doesn't seem to solve the problems that you earlier address. How is your proposal going to help the domestic industry?"

My "answer" would be: "I don't think I suggested that the domestic guys were totally blameless, but I do think they were put in very difficult situations that were out of their control. I think I made that argument reasonably well. Let me turn the tables for a minute. If you take the approach that the fault all lies with the domestic guys, you're obviously assuming that the industry that prospered for its first sixty years stumbled only through its own arrogance and stupidity, and the outside influences occurring coincidental to the stumbling had little or no influence—then I will submit that you are stretching credulity. To take it one step further, you're accusing *all* of the domestics to be incompetent and *most* of all the other guys to be competent. I can't buy that! I don't buy that!"

This leads to the basis for my proposal. All I'm suggesting is that we put the industry back where it was. The café requirements will die a natural death because they're no longer relevant. We can get rid of a whole lot of governmental overseers and mini-departments of test analyzers. We can redirect NHTSA as we've probably exhausted hardware approaches to safety and redirect the personnel toward self-help planning for safety for automotive trips and driving-under-the-influence and inexperienced drivers who are involved in more than half of fatal collisions.

I will submit that the domestic industry would flourish—given the privilege of playing on a field unfettered by absurd rules with officials running around re-interpreting these rules and attempting to lower the hammer when they themselves make errors. We can put crash analysts out of business. We can make it futile for insurance companies and plaintiff lawyers to attempt to influence automotive designs.

If we can truly set up a lassiez-faire environment where providers can concentrate on their cars and its features and what Americans really want to drive, I like my domestic-guys' chances.

CHAPTER THIRTY-TWO
Epilogue One—If Only Hank the Deuce Were Here

I hope all of you had a beloved aunt or similar relative like my Aunt Gladys. In spite of the hand she was dealt, she was always cheerful and fun loving and yet seemed to have a calm, almost religious demeanor, usually empathizing with the person committing the faux pas and rationalizing the behavior with the hope of helping. Her husband, a member of a prominent but not particularly mentally well-arranged family, would stop on the way home from his clerical job and pick up a fifth of Corby's, 86 proof I think, and that evening would proceed to devour it undiluted at room temperature from a water glass. Similar to what I understand to be the curse of a considerable number of imbibers, he woke up in the morning fresh as a daisy to face yet another day. Uh, oh! For one of the few times in my life, I've digressed.

It was nearing Christmas of about 1922, and my aunt—Gladys Reichheld—was one of the favorite employees in the toy department of Hudson's, Detroit's flagship department store. She was in her early twenties, attractive, then single, and as I've mentioned above, she also embodied her other fine attributes. Her supervisor approached her one afternoon as to her availability to work overtime as there was a special customer to show through the department after normal store hours. She was always willing to accommodate the employer and she could always use the money, as her clothing, particularly the silk stockings required for her job in the then upscale department store, took an inordinate amount of her earnings.

It turns out that the "special customer" that evening was none other than Henry Ford ll, Henry Ford's first grandson, about five years old at the time, accompanied by his governess.

In the several times she told the story to me, she always described the encounter as a pleasant one, the little Ford boy seemingly very perceptive and analytical for his age. He would carefully survey the toys and pick up those that piqued his interest. He would then assess the toy quite carefully, see if there were moving parts and, if so, put it through its paces after figuring out how it operated.

After every assessment, he would hold the toy in front of him and say, "This is exactly—" [a pause—followed 90 percent of the time with] "what I don't want!" as he put it down.

Strangely enough, Gladys always made the case that the comment didn't seem to be delivered in a judgmental or wise-guy spoiled-kid mode, but rather as a child reciting facts, albeit with the presumption that what he thought about each toy was a fact to be noted.

Fast forward twenty years. Henry was in military service and the Ford Motor Company back in Detroit was performing admirably in providing military equipment; but the death of his father in 1943 at the height of WWII, and the fact that his grandfather, the original Henry Ford, again took over the company caused interested parties to become unsettled. This was due to the senior Ford's unpredictability and his tolerance for militant non-unionists that had taken senior positions within the company. Such interested parties, including the young Henry's mother and grandmother, convinced the senior Ford to hire his grandson as chief operating officer. The junior Ford was discharged from the service, installed as President of Ford Motor Company and, soon after, the highly respected Ernie Breech was hired as executive vice-president; then Robert McNamara, Ben Mills and the rest of the whiz kids from Harvard and the Army Air Force were hired to establish a company now grounded in modern-management techniques, including sophisticated cost controls—one of Henry Sr.'s Achilles heels.

The young Henry didn't have to take on this load. Running an automotive company may sound like fun, but the problems and the competition and the demands on one's time and the overall energy required are never ending. He could have elected to be a playboy or a dilettante, but he kept himself primarily to the grindstone for the next 35 years. For that, most of the people of Detroit origin, including me, give him a lot of credit. Just think, until 1955 the Ford family owned the whole company until a public stock offering was made. Certainly there must have been a temptation to lead a less stressful life.

On the other hand, owning and being the head of the second-largest automotive company in the world with your name on the building has some sort of panache. As I recall, at one point he was considered the most recognizable industrialist in the world, a situation that leads one to believe that he could have lunch with almost anyone he might choose. I seem to remember him being put forth as the "American poster boy" after the war, a symbol of a young and energetic American who would lead America back to prosperity during the postwar period, much like I sensed that the young Elizabeth held a similar standing in England. He mainly lived up to that, yet he was frequently seen around the town, at SAE meetings and participating in many "city father" developmental or charitable activities. I was one of the 4,000 who rose to cheer him as he was introduced at the SAE banquet shortly following his unfortunate episode of driving erratically in Beverly Hills with a woman other than his wife, the situation where the upstart officer requested he recite the alphabet backwards and subsequently made the episode public. His comment of "no complain, no explain," was enough, at least for the Detroit press, and seemed in sync with the Detroit mentality. (As admirer and self-imagined protégé of the basketball great Larry Bird, particularly with regard to his fastidious preparation, I have memorized a backward recitation of the alphabet in the event I am caught driving erratically in Beverly Hills).

I remember an article in one of the Detroit papers (what a luxury, multiple papers) wherein one of the respected writers was responsible for conducting a small meeting or seminar and was alone setting up perhaps an hour ahead of time. Who should walk in? Henry the Deuce.

"Doesn't the [whatever] event start at 6:30?" he asked.

"I'm sorry, Mr. Ford, it doesn't start until 7:30," responded the writer.

Henry was indecisive, he looked at his watch, apparently considering whether his driver was extant or whatever, but finally relaxed and asked "Do you mind if I wait here?"

The respected writer was apparently known to Henry, so after perfunctory introductions they started chatting. Henry asked for and got assurance that the conversation, wherever it went, would be off the record. The writer kept his word but did pass along in his article: how scintillating the conversation became, imagine what kind of opinions he has, imagine who he knows on a first-name basis, imagine any experience you could relate that he couldn't relate a similar experience—only involving household names.

He passed along how surprisingly knock-about Henry was when talking about ordinary and extraordinary things and situations that interested him. After almost an hour (it seemed to the writer about fifteen minutes) the first of the other participants arrived for the event. Henry stood and stretched, his chest naturally thrusting out as he hiked his trousers prior to putting on his suit coat, when the writer noticed the *HFII* in gold embroidery on the shirt.

"When I was reminded of the identity of my chat buddy, for about three seconds I thought I was going to faint," admitted the writer.

Henry thanked him for his hospitality and his conversation and joined the group.

Chapter Thirty-Three
Epilogue Two—Shake Down the Fun!

Now, it's unlikely that a situation will again arise where a scion of a U.S. automotive family will become chairman of an automotive company, eventually becoming the most recognizable businessman in the universe. Henry Ford, in about 1970, was reported to have ruminated that the car biz was no longer fun. To him it seemed that all the industry could afford to do was to downsize the car line and fend off unrealistic third-party inputs while incorporating those enforced ones into the products under unrealistic time frames. He was right and the country is poorer for it.

If one were to look at the industry and its products from the perspective of 1970, one would have thought that by now we would have stabilized the propulsion design of the standard car, not to mention that we should probably be "driving by wire" on "maglev" roads in commodious individually owned people movers in absolute comfort. In fact, if it had been known in 1970 that a small or personal computing device (enabled by space-exploration technology) could greatly enhance an individual's or a vehicle's ability to communicate, learn and control all sorts of devices, the aspirations probably would have been even higher.

Why didn't this happen?

Many businesses or governmental departments, that I refer to as "pilot fish" organizations, were created to fine tune the (wealthy Goliath's') existing products. Their sole purpose was to participate by generating and overseeing their ideas of appropriate tweaks to the status quo so as to accommodate environmental, political, and perceived safety issues. As a result, the companies were forced to allocate resources at accelerating rates just to be able to put *conforming* vehicles on the road.

The consequences to these activities have been immense:

- The costs of these incremental programs caused a severe strain on cash flow, almost bankrupting Chrysler in 1980.
- Funds for product planning and customer-pleasing features had to be constrained.
- Many of the most problematic edicts affected U.S. manufacturers only, opening opportunities for import market share.

- The necessarily slap-dashed early small cars were inferior to historic U.S. cars, creating disappointments in quality, design and features.
- The culture of the time became that cars were strictly utilitarian and only to be used for necessary tasks.
- There could be no attention to recruitment of extraordinarily gifted employees.
- As the general public's sense of the industry became gloomy, these gifted potential employees tended to go to California or the East Coast; besides, automotive wasn't hiring much anyway.
- And, oh yes, in effect the big three went bankrupt!

Isn't it ironic that the current (the fall of 2014) safety panic has to do with (mostly import brand) cars that have air bags that are actually *exploding*? (Duh!) It took even the most reliable reporting sources several weeks to realize that that's what airbags *are supposed to do*. They were expecting wisps, maybe? The irony is that we are now panicked by a very dangerous and unsafe *safety device*, a mess that will take many months and many millions of dollars to untangle. It's such a mess that people and the media have stopped talking about it, probably because nobody had anything intelligent to say or had information they didn't want to make public. The three or four involved parties are undoubtedly frantic to develop and agree upon a repair protocol in addition to convincing someone to make whatever millions of parts will be required for such repair. This expedited and frenzied activity (CFD) might lead to an *unsafe* fix for *an unsafe safety device*. (Enough, already!)

We, who "buy into" Chapter 25, have a quick and safer fix. Since the airbag has demonstrated, at best, only marginal value, our recommended fix is *turn 'em off!* Then go about a permanent solution at leisure.

Did someone just remind me that the word *fun* is in this chapter heading? How do we restore fun in the U. S. auto business?

First of all, why don't we "freeze" the rules on the industry. The current environment doesn't seem to require urgent mandates to solve problems (other than self-inflicted ones). That might give the industry enough breathing room so that it might again become creative. As a result, the industry might be able to generate enough momentum and discretionary income so that they may again focus the notion of elegant cars, great performance and advanced concepts so as to tempt voracious customers.

Perhaps they could build creative centers in the Detroit area (run by a John DeLorean disciple), California (run by a Harley Earle disciple) and Turin (run by an Argus-Duntov disciple)—all overseen by an Iacocca disciple for purposes of commercialization. Imagine the excitement created for next generation of creative automotive nuts regarding employment! Imagine the rekindled excitement for capable young people in all applicable professional disciplines.

Finally, here's where my native city may help.

I understand that there are many restorable homes available, at very reasonable prices, in some of those wonderful old Detroit neighborhoods. Sherwood Forest could become Cupertino Midwest, Palmer Woods could remain Palmer Woods (Detroit is yet 21st on the technology center list), and Indian Village could become Route 128 resurrected.

In a very recent visit, while researching cover material for this book, I sensed the new vibrancy of old familiar places. In Detroit's cultural center there were hundreds of people walking the streets. There was an open-air farmers market between the central library and Wayne State University. The assistance in both the library and the art museum was exceptional. The parking was difficult, in itself an indicator of prosperity.

As I was pleased to find a parking spot for my out-of-state rental car next to the library, I noticed an unusually dressed and bodily adorned (from my perspective) young man, who seemed to be hovering around the meter servicing six parking spots. He didn't look dangerous, but I just knew I would be "solicited" for something or other. Sucking it up while I approached the meter, the young man looked me in the eye and said, "I was waiting for you. You probably won't be able to get this meter to work. I just wanted you to know that the police aren't currently ticketing under that situation." Off he walked briskly while accepting my verbal thanks. I think I'm also going to like the new Detroiters.

"The fun is dead! Long live the fun!"

APPENDIX:
Assessment of Post WWII Events on the U. S. Auto Industry

Key:
★ — beneficial to the U.S. auto industry
↓ — detrimental to the U.S. auto industry

Event	Year	Assess-ment	Comments
Restart production after WWII.	1946	★ ★	General optimism. Pent-up demand. New options.
2-car family cultural origin.	1950s	★ ★	Suburbs enabled. U. S. mfr. 80% of world.
Interstate system initiated.	Late 1950s	★ ★ ★	Driving options perceived as expanded.
First Import, VW, takes hold.	Mid-1950s	↓	Introduces small car viability.
Federal excise tax on cars eliminated.	Mid-1960s	★ ★	Industry continues to economically self-support.
Safety law enacted.	1966	★	Regularize safety concepts.
Motor vehicle trade regularized.	1968	★	Rules for imports.
Seat belts compulsory.	1968	★	Memorializes best safety feature and other features.
Environmental Protection Agency est.	1970	↓	Ominous; apprehensive of participating bureaucracy.
NHTSA est.	1970	↓	Another bureaucracy partner. (?)

Nixon announces gas shortages.	1973	↓↓↓↓↓	Political and geographical issues commingled. Panic! Detroit forever plays "away" games.
No tariff imported cars.	Ongoing	↓↓	Reciprocity not quite reciprocal.
Car Average Fuel Economy laws (C.A.F.E. or café).	1975	↓↓↓↓	Detroit must totally redo car mix, imports need tweaks. Chrysler barely avoids bankruptcy while making attempts at conformance.
2nd gas crunch.	1980	↓↓↓	Recovery from #1 halted. Datsun cancels plans to exit U. S. Market.
Luxury-car foreign development.	1980	↓↓	Detroit distractions with EPA & café conformance enable breather for importers to develop profitable mid-sized luxury cars.
Japanese fear trade reprisals, consider quotas.	Early 1980s	↓	Ironically, U. S. buyers react to perceived shortage.
Union intransigence.	Ongoing	↓↓	Competitive market disrupts past equilibrium.
Foreign U. S. manufacture.	1980s	↓↓↓	Needn't conform to union pressure, minority considerations. Considerable cost advantage.
Perceived attitudes of U. S. manufacturers.	Ongoing	↓↓	Defensive, immoveable fat cats.
Effect of above activity on Detroit.	Ongoing	↓↓↓↓↓	Union jobs go from 330,000 to 33,000.

INDEX

Robert Riley was born in Detroit. He grew up in a happy and prosperous middle-class environment, and after graduating from college he started his long career in the automotive industry. He worked for GM, his GMI sponsor, only briefly. He mainly worked for companies like Bendix and Lear that sold automotive parts and systems. This gives him a unique perspective: He's an outsider and an insider at the same time.

Writing with a lively, albeit curmudgeon, style, he entertains readers with his wry wit and incisive comments on living and working.

A family man, Robert married Susan, the love of his life. They raised their children in Detroit and New York, trying their best to provide a piece of the American Dream.

Retired now, Robert lives in sunny San Diego, where he strives to continually fill his life with excitement and enjoyment, relishing in traveling, playing master-level bridge, musical gigs—and writing!

f

19827859R00184